Masterpieces of Short Fiction

Part I

Professor Michael Krasny

THE TEACHING COMPANY ®

PUBLISHED BY:

THE TEACHING COMPANY
4151 Lafayette Center Drive, Suite 100
Chantilly, Virginia 20151-1232
1-800-TEACH-12
Fax—703-378-3819
www.teach12.com

Printed in the United States of America

ISBN 1-59803-441-3

Michael Krasny, Ph.D.

Professor of English, San Francisco State University

Michael Krasny is Professor of English at San Francisco State University, where since 1970, he has taught courses on the short story, modern and contemporary American literature, ethnic American literature, transatlantic modern drama, and literary theory. He earned his B.A. (cum laude) and M.A. degrees from Ohio University, where he is a member of the Phi Beta Kappa Society. He earned his Ph.D. from the University of Wisconsin.

Dr. Krasny taught in the Fulbright Institutes for the National Fulbright Foundation, coordinated the Nexa Dissemination Program in Science and Humanities under the National Endowment for the Humanities and the Carnegie Foundation, and has been Visiting Professor at the University of San Francisco and Adjunct Professor at the University of California, San Francisco. In 2003, Dominican University awarded him a Doctor of Humane Letters at its annual convocation, and in 2007, he was honored with an Award of Excellence from the National Association of Humanities Educators.

Dr. Krasny has published a variety of fiction, literary criticism, and political commentary, including as a former regular contributor to *Mother Jones* magazine. He is the coauthor of *Sound Ideas* (McGraw-Hill) and author of *Off Mike: A Memoir of Talk Radio and Literary Life* (Stanford University Press), which was on both the *San Francisco Chronicle* and the *Marin Independent Journal* bestseller lists.

Dr. Krasny hosts KQED's award-winning *Forum*, a news and public affairs radio program that concentrates on current events, culture, health, business and technology, and arts and entertainment. He is a veteran interviewer for the nationally broadcast *City Arts and Lectures* and worked for many years as host of one of ABC's highest-rated radio programs. He has worked as host of KQED's television programs *This Week in Northern California* and *Civic Space* and as substitute host for National Public Radio's *Talk of the Nation.* Dr. Krasny provided live coverage for National Public Radio following the attacks on the World Trade Center and the Pentagon.

Throughout his distinguished career, Dr. Krasny has interviewed a wide range of preeminent scholars, politicians, and cultural figures.

The list includes Nobel laureates, such as Jimmy Carter, Francis Crick, Al Gore, V. S. Naipaul, Isaac Bashevis Singer, and Desmond Tutu; political figures, such as Patrick Buchanan, Hillary Rodham Clinton, Jesse Jackson, George McGovern, and Barack Obama; scientists and scholars, such as Noam Chomsky, Jacques Cousteau, Jane Goodall, Stephen Jay Gould, and E. O. Wilson; and authors, artists, actors, and musicians, such as Maya Angelou, Margaret Atwood, Ray Bradbury, Don DeLillo, E. L. Doctorow, Allen Ginsberg, Matt Groening, Annie Leibovitz, Maya Lin, Charles Schultz, Francis Ford Coppola, Dennis Hopper, Jon Voight, Joan Baez, Jerry Garcia, Yo-Yo Ma, and Wynton Marsalis.

Dr. Krasny has worked as a corporate facilitator for numerous businesses and has hosted or moderated meetings and conventions for a vast array of organizations, ranging from Businesses for Social Responsibility, the Society of Professional Journalists, and the technology publication *Red Herring* to the American Trial Lawyers Association, Harvard Divinity School, and the California Association of Public Hospitals.

Among his many honors, Dr. Krasny has received the S. Y. Agnon Gold Medal for Intellectual Distinction, the Eugene Block Award for Human Rights Journalism, the Media Alliance Award for Meritorious Achievement, the James Madison Freedom of Information Award from the Society of Professional Journalists, the Inclusiveness in Media Award from the National Conference for Community and Justice, the Award for Animal Rights Coverage from the National Humane Society, four Kudo Awards (including two for Best Talk Host) from American Women in Radio and Television, the John Swett Award for Media Excellence from the California Teachers Association, an award for best talk show host from the San Francisco Publicity Club, an award for professional journalism from the Peninsula Press Club, and the National Public Radio Award from the American Publishers Association. He was named a Fellow by the World Affairs Council and was awarded the Koret Foundation Fellowship. Dr. Krasny has also received two Emmy nominations for his television work.

In 1990, the California State Legislature—and again, in 2003, the California State Senate—passed resolutions honoring Dr. Krasny for public service. In 2004, he was made an honorary member of the

Golden Key International Honor Society at San Francisco State University.

Michael Krasny Day was declared in San Francisco in 1990 by Mayor Art Agnos, in 1994 by Mayor Frank Jordan, and in 2003 by Mayor Willie Brown.

Table of Contents

Masterpieces of Short Fiction
Part I

Masterpieces of Short Fiction

Scope:

This course takes you on an exciting ride through an itinerary that samples 23 of the world's greatest short stories. The form of the genre, as well as the various ways in which it has evolved, is highlighted along the way with a display of the essential nuts and bolts of storytelling—plot, character, setting, style, point of view, and theme. A mix of critical approaches will also be brought in to enhance analysis and interpretation and to explore some of the ways we judge and evaluate short fiction. We will key in throughout the lecture series on methods used by critics to discover meaning—the author, the reader, the language, and the world the story mirrors.

The great Roman poet and satirist Horace said that the purpose of literature is to delight and instruct. Each of the 23 stories we will work with do both in many ways. In addition, each story connects us to a broader vision of our lives and the lives of those around us, as well as to a specific cultural and historic context and to what Edgar Allan Poe, perhaps the earliest theorist on the short story, described as the unified aesthetic effect of reading a short story.

We begin with Poe, as well as five other storytellers who anchor us firmly in the narrative art of short fiction of the late 19th century. Poe is not only one of the earliest theorists on the form of the short story, but he is also one of the short story's pioneer practitioners. His mid-19th-century horror masterpiece "The Cask of Amontillado" serves as an introduction to the genre in its dawning form. With its murderous narrator Montresor confessing his carried-out vengeance and the carnivalesque world Poe plunges us into, we have a story strong in sensational effects, a harbinger of the modern psychological short story and a great deal of American and Western popular culture. From Poe, we travel to the more allegorical terrain of Hawthorne's "Young Goodman Brown" and Gogol's "The Overcoat." Both are hallucinatory tales with strong moral underpinnings. It was Dostoyevsky (or some say Turgenev or Tolstoy) who said that he and all other fiction writers came out from under Gogol's overcoat, and he and Hawthorne are both early seminal Fabulists. From this trio of mid-19th-century storytellers, we move to the end of the century, beginning with one of the earliest examples of a well-made tale built on irony and class division, Guy de Maupassant's classic

French set tale "The Necklace." After "The Necklace," we immerse ourselves in the Yalta set love story "The Lady with the Dog." In 1981, Vladimir Nabokov, the author of *Lolita*, described this Chekhov tale as "one of the greatest stories ever written." An important, ongoing question in this lecture series will be how and why we assign the label of greatness to a short story. What are our criteria, or what ought to be our criteria? We conclude this first quarter of our journey with "The Real Thing," one of the greatest stories by another of the world's great storytellers, Henry James, the only storyteller to have gained, and who still retains, the title of master storyteller.

As we move forward from one great storyteller to the next, we will see the connectedness, what critics call the intertextuality, that links great stories and reveals a linear progression in the genre as the years move us forward. Some connections are quite apparent; others, less so. As we travel into the early decades of the 20th century, we see both the more identifiable and the more subtle ties to storytelling of the previous century. We will also see a stunning array of new techniques and innovations through close readings and analysis of stories by James Joyce ("Araby"), Isaac Babel ("My First Goose"), Ernest Hemingway ("The Killers"), Franz Kafka ("A Hunger Artist"), D. H. Lawrence ("The Rocking-Horse Winner"), and Katherine Mansfield ("The Garden Party"). The stories are cumulative in their effect and each provides a portal to those that follow. These six stories bring us into the 20th century and what we will see is the emergence into Modernism, as well as the inauguration of major changes and innovations in the ways in which stories are told—the use of the epiphany in Joyce, the surreal in Kafka and Lawrence, the stylistic revolution heralded in the work of both Babel and Hemingway, and the emergence of Modernist women writers that begins with Mansfield. These six writers all begin to reflect more of the social and cultural upheavals associated with the first part of the 20th century, including the first of the two World Wars.

The last two clusters of great stories fall into the middle half and the later quarter of the 20th century. We look first at one of the mid-century's most provocative and disturbing stories, Shirley Jackson's "The Lottery," linked in many ways back to Hawthorne but also tied to the period immediately following World War II and all of the trauma associated with that colossal historic event. We follow Jackson with stories by two of America's greatest women writers, the Georgia native artist of the grotesque Flannery O'Connor ("A Good Man Is Hard to Find") and the New York–born author who introduced readers around the world to woman-centered feminist short fiction, Grace Paley ("An Interest in Life"). The other authors who round out this mid-century section of storytelling are the great Colombian Fabulist and Nobel laureate Gabriel García Márquez ("A Very Old Man with Enormous Wings"), the American Jewish Fabulist Bernard Malamud ("The Jewbird"), and one of America's finest African American writers, James Baldwin ("Sonny's Blues"). In this group of great authors, we see not only the continuing rising influence of women writers but the emergence of writers of ethnicity and color as identity politics begin to take hold in the world of short fiction and publishing and the acceptance of once non-canonical writers begins to open wide. We see as well in these six stories the rising overall effect of secularism—even in an Orthodox Catholic writer such as O'Connor—and the impact of Existential philosophy and all of the international cultural fallout associated with the aftermath of World War II.

These influences bring us to the last group of stories and the concluding lecture. The final five contemporary short story writers exemplify the greatness of storytelling as the last century ends and the present one begins; all of the works that we will look at here are anchored in the sense of manifold change that typifies the rapid social and cultural transformations of the era. We first focus our attention on a 1960s story all about change by John Updike ("A & P"), which reveals the quest for Existential identity of a boy becoming a man, themes that connect back to Joyce's "Araby" but also become inextricably associated with a decade that would become identified with change. The story "No Name Woman," by Maxine Hong Kingston, is also a post–World War II identity story that presents to us the tension of a girl becoming a woman and straddling the difficult Existential identity between her Chinese background and heritage embedded in this story of her erased aunt and her contemporary American life. The Canadian writer Margaret Atwood, who gives us the Postmodern, metafictional story "Happy Endings," exemplifies innovative and experimental storytelling and the kinds of new and unchartered territory many short fiction writers were claiming. "Happy Endings" also brings us into the world of a contemporary feminist sensibility with a work that has the definite stamp of sexual politics. We conclude with short fiction about racial identity in South Africa, "The Moment Before the Gun Went Off," by South African Nobel laureate Nadine Gordimer, a story about the change that resulted from the fall of apartheid, and a short story by one of America's best short fiction writers, Raymond Carver ("Cathedral"), which connects readers to a distinct proletarian or blue-collar, working-class identity with ultimate emphasis on positive individual transformation. Our final lecture provides concluding remarks about the nature of short fiction masterpieces and how they get written, where they get published, and how they have become democratized. We also conclude with a discussion of the future of the short story.

Lecture One
Excavations—Poe's "The Cask of Amontillado"

Scope:

This first lecture focuses on a working definition and historical outline of the short story and looks at the seminal work of Edgar Allan Poe: "The Cask of Amontillado," a 19th-century masterpiece of suspense and revenge. We also lay a foundation for critically assessing and evaluating what constitutes a short fiction masterpiece by bringing in Poe's theory of the short story and Aristotle's theory of tragedy and by focusing on the pedigree of the short story and its antecedents, including the German and American precursors to horror tales like Poe's and Hawthorne's. We consider elements of fiction, the historic background to the short story, and the ways in which Poe mines these aspects of the genre through the story's plot. We also consider Poe's biography, as well as some of the story's psychobiographic dimensions. We conclude by bringing into awareness some of the tale's weaknesses, an overall summation of its genius, and a consideration of the short story's initial path from the Realism of the 19th century to what ultimately will be a changing and more expansive global literary canon.

Outline

I. We begin with a brief look at the history of the short story.

- **A.** Edgar Allan Poe generally defined the short story in opposition to the novel or novella—in other words, a work of fiction short enough to read and absorb in a single sitting.
- **B.** Short fiction has a long pedigree, going back to oral history but also located in myths, biblical stories, and the anecdotes of ancient Rome.
- **C.** Short fiction has its origins also in the fable—folktales with moral exempla built in, like those of Aesop.
- **D.** The genre also derives from Western and European poetic forms of the 14th century, such as Chaucer's *The Canterbury Tales* and Boccaccio's *Decameron.*
- **E.** The modern short story bloomed in the 19th century with the market created by journals and magazines—often stories of

shock or horror, such as those published by the Grimm brothers.

II. In this course, we will see all of the techniques at work in the genre during both the 19th and 20th centuries, with historical changes occurring cumulatively.

A. We move chronologically from simple yet highly plotted and often poetically wrought tales to forms that are increasingly experimental, with a growing reliance on content related to psychology, ethnicity, sexuality, and identity.

B. We work from early examples of Realism (with elements of allegory, Fabulism, and the Surreal) to Modernist stories that are steeped in Realism or built on Fabulism and parable, folklore and myth, self-reflexivity, autobiography, or historicity.

III. Four major elements are essential to judging and evaluating short fiction, all of which are intimately connected to craft and impact: the text, the author, the reader, and mimetic reality.

A. We will learn how to read and savor short fiction that has been carefully selected from the pantheon of greatness.

B. Selections are based on historical and canonical considerations of critical acclaim and inclusion in a wide range of anthologies, as well as the professor's scholarly and personal choices.

C. The greatness of short fiction is attributable to authorial genius, impact on readers, universality, the emotionally evocative power of the tale, and its originality. Greatness is also inextricably linked to form, content, language (or stylistics), and craft.

IV. Poe's aesthetic theory contributes to his status as a master of short fiction, evidenced by several key elements.

A. The belief in the effect of reading a work in one sitting and the impact of a work neither too long nor too short was fundamental to the success of Poe's stories.

B. Washington Irving's legends and German tales of horror are precursors to Poe and Hawthorne in creating a sense of horror in fiction.

C. Poe's use of hubris and vanity in both characters in "The Cask of Amontillado" is a reflection of Aristotelian theory on the emotions of pity and terror.

D. The essential conflict of revenge, sustained from the story's beginning to its conclusion, contributes to the overall impact of the tale.

E. The voice of an unreliable and possibly insane, morally deficient, or evil narrator who has committed the perfect crime—and is recounting it a half century later with clearly mixed emotions—adds dramatically to the effect of the story.

F. Suspense is sustained through the use of a plot driven by a single incident with a decisive conclusion.

G. The story is propelled by character—Montresor's—which creates ambiguities for the reader, whom he may even call "my friend."

H. The relationship of the tale to the reader is complex. The reader might best be cast in the role of Fortunato, dressed as a fool, trying to guess the plot that is unfolding, and experiencing mounting irrational fear with the rising action of the story.

I. The psychological nature of the tale—its architecture of the mind and intimations of what lies below the surface of our actions—yields strong universal themes.

V. The origins of the tale supposedly lie in an anecdote Poe heard while serving in the army. The story also resonates with Poe's feelings of class difference and class envy, resulting in part from the impoverished and unhappy life he lived, as well as from the peculiarities of his upbringing.

VI. Despite its singular effect and its ascent to a climactic impact, "The Cask of Amontillado" has weaknesses.

A. The story is histrionic and has a style that could be described as puerile.

B. Henry James referred to Poe's work as "primitive," and T. S. Eliot called Poe "gifted" but "before puberty."

C. Poe's characters are not flat, but they are psychologically abstract.

D. There is a sense of gimmickry or manipulation used by Poe that some deem non-literary.

VII. The story remains a masterpiece because of its totality and its seminal role in storytelling.

A. Elements that may appear somewhat crude in Poe's work become more stylized and highly developed as the genre of short fiction evolves.

B. The voice in the story is masterfully sustained and compels us to stay right up to the end, embodying what Julio Cortázar called "the successful insistent race against the clock."

C. Poe provided much of the essential bricks and mortar for what we have come to see as the modern short story. His heirs include such popular writers as H. P. Lovecraft, Stephen King, and Shirley Jackson.

Suggested Readings:

Aristotle, *Poetics.*

Meyers, *Edgar Allan Poe: His Life and Legacy.*

Peeples, *The Afterlife of Edgar Allan Poe.*

Poe, "The Cask of Amontillado."

———, "The Fall of the House of Usher."

———, "The Impact of the Single Effect in a Prose Tale."

———, "The Tell-Tale Heart."

Reynolds, "The Art of Transformation in Poe's 'The Cask of Amontillado,'" in Silverman, *New Essays on Poe's Major Tales.*

Questions to Consider:

1. How mad is Montresor? Would you judge him guilty by reason of insanity despite the careful, premeditative method he uses to murder Fortunato?
2. The story was especially shocking, even mortifying, in its day. Would it be considered so by today's standards? To what degree were you shocked by it?
3. Does this story deserve a masterpiece mantle despite whatever deficiencies it may have?

Lecture One—Transcript

Excavations—Poe's "The Cask of Amontillado"

My name is Michael Krasny. I have a Ph.D. in Literature from the University of Wisconsin and have been a professor of English at San Francisco State University since 1970. I also host a weekday news, public affairs, culture and arts, and science talk program on the National Public Radio affiliate KQED Radio in San Francisco.

It will be my pleasurable task to take you on a conversation with great authors through a series of lectures on stories by some of the world's greatest writers, who will immerse you in their worlds and affect your minds and hearts as only great stories can. The value of studying stories like the ones we will be studying is in the simple fact that they transport our imaginations. They heighten our senses and consciousness and yield insight, knowledge, and—we hope—wisdom.

What discipline other than fiction combines nearly every other area of knowledge in its study and also provides a reality that many believe to be superior in its overall effects [to] what we normally believe reality to be? We read and interpret stories to enter into the exciting life of the mind and to see; as the poet Adrienne Rich said, "What we see, we see / and seeing is changing."

Let's have a brief look at the short story and its history, the arc of the stories we will be studying, and a consideration of how we interpret meaning and evaluate fiction. Edgar Allan Poe defined the short story generally as not being as long as a novel or novella—or what, at one time later on, would be called a novelette. In other words, short enough to read and absorbed in a single sitting. Short stories can be anywhere up to around 15,000 words if you're word counting, but defining a short story is a little bit like the idea of putting Jell-O on a tree.

A short story should grab you, engage you, and rivet you into what Gabriel Rossetti called "a moment's monument." You read stories—usually one at a time—and if they are great or even good, they keep you reading right up until the end. J. D. Salinger, the famed author of *The Catcher in the Rye*, once said he was a dash man and not a long-distance runner, though he did write one short novel during his career before turning to collections of short stories.

Short story writers run the dash, but novelists are the long-distance runners. Short fiction has a long pedigree: a history of the tale going back to oral narratives, oral storytelling, and oral history but also located in myths, biblical stories, and the anecdotes of ancient Rome. They have their origins also in fables—folktales—with moral exemplars built in, like Aesop, who gave us such famous fables as "The Tortoise and the Hare."

Western and European stories and tales have their origins in poetic forms of the 14th century, such as Chaucer's *The Canterbury Tales* and Boccaccio's the *Decameron*. We'll see, in a number of the short fiction writers that we'll be discussing, works of short fiction that—like the *Decameron* and *The Canterbury Tales*—fit into larger works. There are stories that are read and taught as stories that are, in fact, part of the much broader canvas of a novel but that can nevertheless stand alone as short stories.

The modern short story boomed in the 19th century with the market created by journals and magazines—often shocking or horror stories, like the Grimm fairy tales or German tales of shock and horror. In the United States, these were the stories of Washington Irving, the most famous being the ones about the legendary Headless Horseman of Sleepy Hollow and the tale of Rip Van Winkle, who falls asleep when King George is ruling the colonies and wakes up 20 years later to the visage of General George Washington.

Short fiction appeared and flourished nearly simultaneously in the United States and Russia. It flourished later in France, where Poe was greatly admired; and later still in the British Empire, where big novels, often serialized, held sway; in Ireland; and in German-speaking Europe, where medium-length novellas had been more the norm for short fiction.

The trajectory of storytelling, as we look at the masters of two centuries, moves from simple, highly plotted tales to increasing realism—putting the mirror up to nature—and then to forms of experimentation and an increased opening up in fiction to the complexities of modern life: psychological, racial, ethnic, sexual, and identity-based. That is, there's a movement from Realism to Modernism: from Realism, with some elements of the allegorical, or moral, tale; the Fabulist tale (based on myth and fable); and the Surreal tales (built from the unconscious mind), to more Modernist stories, both steeped in Realism or built on Fabulism, parable, myth, self-reflexivity, autobiography, or history. Voices change as writers open up to younger voices, ethnicity, and gender, and what we see in the evolution of short fiction masterpieces is a changing canon—the established body of what is deemed to be great literature—and a changing marketplace that is increasingly cross-cultural, cosmopolitan, and global.

The key to understanding stories is often vested in what we call intertextuality: stories building on other stories through the progression of time, and many of them continuing to possess within them related themes, ideas, and similar elements of expression, such as the use of allegory. We also see stories that draw us in by making us wonder what is coming next, stories that have more to do with characters being revealed or revealing themselves, that leave things out, that include pointed details and small observations, that are more like drama—as we'll see in the great storyteller Chekhov, who was also a dramatist—and stories that are more like poetry, even up to and including so-called confessional poetry, like that of Robert Lowell, Anne Sexton, or Sylvia Plath. [These are] American poets of the post–World War II era who explored personal terrain through the creation of characters who confessed the secret content of their hidden inner lives.

What we want is to discover what makes the stories we'll be discussing great, why and how they yield richness of meaning, and in addition to interpretation, how we evaluate their worth. This can sometimes be challenging—even vexing—but there are essentially four major ways of interpreting and evaluating short fiction, and each of the four is intimately connected to craft and to the tale's impact on readers. These are four good touchstones to assessing what a masterpiece is. First, there's the text: looking at the language in the story, its metaphors, symbolism, and meanings that we can attribute to the author's choice of words. We'll read texts between about 1,000 and 15,000 words.

Secondly, the author: his or her personal history and psychology, influences, and cultural background, all of which can—and often do—go beyond and outside the text. We're going to read 23 stories in depth by 6 authors born in the first half of the 19th century, 6 born in the second half, and 11 born in the first half of the 20th century. English is where the development of short fiction has been most firmly planted, and we'll read writers from Canada to South Africa to New Zealand, as well as 10 or 11 stories by U.S. authors and another 5 or 6 by authors from throughout the rest of the English-speaking world (depending on how you count Henry James, an American-born writer who was an expatriate in England). The remaining stories are by authors who were Russian, French, Czech (or German, depending on where you want to place Franz Kafka), and South American.

Third, the reader: How does the story affect you as a reader? We will also take into account how the role of the reader has changed through the course of the history of short fiction. As stories become more sophisticated and modern, the role of the reader becomes more collaborative.

Finally, mimetic reality: How does the story depict or otherwise represent—mime—what we distill as reality, with all the major changes brought in by world wars, industrialization, technology, and seismic shifts in mores.

Selections of stories that we're going to discuss are based on historic and canonical considerations of great critical acclaim and the inclusion of individual stories that have appeared in a wide range of anthologies and fiction volumes. The accepted taste of literary criticism and literary scholarship is a stock market, obviously in flux and up for debate. Somerset Maugham and Robert Louis Stevenson were once high on the stock exchange in short fiction writers, while William Faulkner and F. Scott Fitzgerald were not. Writers' reputations change and shift, but the greatness attributable to short fiction is directly tied to authorial genius; the effect and impact of the story on a wide range of readers; the universality of the story's themes and ideas; its emotional, empathic, and evocative power; its originality; and frankly, to this professor's scholarly and personal choices.

Greatness is also inextricably linked to form and content; language, or what's called stylistics; craft; the meaning that the individual story yields; how and to what degree it moves or stirs us; and how or to what extent it lasts or is likely to endure. When I was in graduate school, we used to have the notion that there would be a space capsule; it would go into the future. What works would we want to include in that space capsule? (As if we could decide somehow what would be the best works for ongoing generations.)

What better place to begin a course on masterpieces of short fiction than with the earliest American master of suspense, Edgar Allan Poe, who has given us such classic stories as “The Tell-Tale Heart,” “The Fall of the House of Usher,” and “The Cask of Amontillado,” which is the first story we will focus on. We begin with Poe in this course because of his emphasis on plot, and unity, and a credible-sounding—though quite possibly unreliable—narrator. We move through stories of greater realism and more open plots—sometimes no plots at all—as we venture also into some of the experimental fiction of the 20th century. Poe was also a seminal figure in the ushering in of detective stories, even years before those world-famous British detective Sherlock Holmes stories by Arthur Conan Doyle, who started writing detective fiction nearly a half century after Poe.

Poe was also an early contributor to science fiction stories with “Mellonta Tauta” in 1840 and other work of his, including the “The Thousand-and-Second Tale of Scheherazade.” In short, Poe pioneered three distinct genres of short fiction. Today, Poe might be classified as a commercial writer, despite his lack of commercial success—or woeful lack, I might add—and there still exists a Rubicon in the minds of many literary critics between popular or pulp fiction for the masses and more literary or aesthetically imbued fiction for the higher-brow reader. As we’ll discover, these are often indistinct lines that can be grossly exaggerated.

We begin with Poe also because Poe was a path-finding theorist of the short story who grounds us in a theory of short fiction and its effects. He wrote an early disputation, one of the earliest on record, about the singular effect of the short story. “The Importance of the Single Effect in a Prose Tale” was published in 1842, and in it, Poe used Nathaniel Hawthorne as an example of a storyteller who provides what only the short story can provide for a reader, unlike the novel. With a story like “The Cask of Amontillado,” Poe’s great tale of suspense and revenge, the effects on us as readers emerge from a single sitting.

Only a handful of pages, and Poe transports us to a world of masquerades and motley, a carnivalesque world of conical caps and bells, then into an underground world of catacombs and skeletons, and into what appears to be a perfect crime: a grotesque and calculated premeditated murder—a live burial, narrated by the murderer, from the perch of a half century later. The emphasis in this story is on plot, a compressed narrative that comes to us through the authentic and riveting voice of a murderer:

> The thousand injuries of Fortunato I had borne as best I could; but when he ventured upon insult I vowed revenge. You, who so well know the nature of my soul, will not suppose, however, that I gave utterance to a threat. At *length*, I would be avenged; this was a point definitely settled—but the very definitiveness with which it was resolved, precluded the idea of risk. I must not only punish but punish with impunity. A wrong is unredressed when retribution overtakes its redresser. It is equally unredressed when the avenger fails to make himself felt as such to him who has done the wrong.
>
> It must be understood, that neither by word nor deed had I given Fortunato cause to doubt my good-will. I continued, as was my wont, to smile in his face, and he did not perceive that my smile *now* was at the thought of his immolation.
>
> He had a weak point—this Fortunato—although in other regards he was a man to be respected and even feared. He prided himself on his connoisseurship in wine. Few Italians have the true virtuoso spirit. For the most part their enthusiasm is adopted to suit the time and opportunity—to practice imposture upon the British and Austrian *millionaires*. In painting and gemmary, Fortunato, like his countrymen, was a quack—but in the matter of old wines he was sincere. In this respect, I did not differ from him materially: I was skillful in the Italian vintages myself, and bought largely whenever I could.
>
> It was about dusk, one evening during the supreme madness of the carnival season, that I encountered my friend. He accosted me with excessive warmth for he had been drinking much. The man wore motley. He had on a tight-fitting parti-striped dress, and his head was surmounted by the conical cap and bells.
>
> I was so pleased to see him that I thought I should never have done wringing his hand.

> I said to him, “My dear Fortunato, you are luckily met. How remarkably well you are looking today! But I have received a pipe of what passes for Amontillado, and I have my doubts.”
>
> “How?” said he. “Amontillado? A pipe? Impossible! And in the middle of the carnival!”
>
> “I have my doubts,” I replied; “and I was silly enough to pay the full Amontillado price without consulting you in the matter. You were not to be found, and I was fearful of losing a bargain.”
>
> “Amontillado!”
>
> “I have my doubts.”
>
> “Amontillado!”
>
> “And I must satisfy them.”
>
> “Amontillado!”
>
> “As you are engaged, I am on my way to Luchesi. If anyone has a critical turn it is he. He will tell me—”
>
> “Luchesi cannot tell Amontillado from Sherry.”
>
> “And yet some fools will have it that his taste is a match for your own. Come, let us go.”

You see how he tells his story in terms of it being in the present—even though it is from that half century before—and you get a sense of a very distinctive voice here telling us how he ensnared this man, how he truly entrapped him, and got him to come with him into the catacombs, which is where they go, essentially, with Montresor deciding that he’s going to seal him up in there and bury him alive. But it’s all very friendly at first: He says he shakes his hand and is so delighted to see him. You think, “This guy’s going to murder him! Why is he so pleased?” He’s so pleased because he’s getting his revenge, but outwardly, of course, is the appearance of being warm, friendly, and wanting his advice. But—I’ll go to Luchesi instead; maybe he knows—ensnaring him with that sense that Luchesi is a better wine taster than you might be, Fortunato.

As is elemental in fiction, Montresor—the voice of the story—is our protagonist, main character. Fortunato is his antagonist, the man he wants to murder, and murder—as he says—with impunity. That's the source of all the action in the story. This is what many consider a perfect short story and Poe's best—a psychological journey into the mind of a murderer, original and carefully crafted, with readers experiencing the horror as the murderer entraps his prey and literally seals him up in a niche, tier by tier, with stones and mortar.

Montresor may indeed be mad, but he's credible, and from the outset, we're swept up into a story of shock and horror that is relentless, the ultimate terrifying campfire story. It appeared, by the way, a year after Poe's famous poem "The Raven" and just after the last of the three detective stories.

Poe is seminal, as I said. He's a poet, as well as an editor, a novelist, a short story writer, and an essayist. Let's talk about his background a little. He was actually expelled from West Point, and he lived a life afflicted by poverty, poor health, depression, and addiction. His wife, Virginia Clemm—who was also his 13-year-old first cousin—died young. Though his stories sold well all over the world and he published some 70 tales, his literary income as a short story writer never exceeded hundreds of dollars.

Let's look at what makes Poe's horror story great by starting with the fact that the story is a perfect example of what Poe's aesthetic theory of a single sitting was based on: the belief in the overall effect of reading a work in one sitting. Poe also believed that truth is the aim of the tale, and he was doubtless influenced by the classic thinking we see in the *Poetics* by Aristotle: the notion that great literary art—specifically, tragedy—creates a cathartic or purging effect of pity and terror and reveals the hubris, or pride, of characters.

"The Cask of Amontillado" reflects the Aristotelian notion of catharsis of pity and fear, and the two main characters, in different ways, are suffused with hubris, or pride—one in his wine connoisseurship and the other in what he relates as his perfect murder. The essential conflict of revenge is sustained from the story's beginning to its conclusion and manages to move through time in accordance with another Aristotelian precept: the unity of time, the fact that all of the action in the story takes place within a set unity of time, even though it's told from the perspective of a half century later.

The plot is driven by a single incident, with a startling and decisive conclusion that involves a man being buried alive in a story propelled by Montresor's character. Montresor, the murderer, creates ambiguities for his readers, whom he appears to be directly confiding in 50 years from the murderous act. The passage I just read where he says, "You, who know my soul so well"—who is he addressing that to, if not us as readers?

Why is he telling this story now and to whom? To us? Maybe to someone else? What are his real motives, and just how reliable is his version of what occurred in the nitre-filled underground where he lures—with the wonderful sherry Amontillado—a man who thinks he is a friend? Montresor may be unreliable, possibly insane, morally deficient, or evil. He tells the story with clearly mixed emotions that he quite possibly doesn't understand himself.

The setting and the atmosphere of the story in Europe during the madness and festive, masquerade-filled carnival season above ground shifts with dramatic intensity as we move into the underground world of the catacombs. This is part of the psychological nature of the tale and its architecture of the mind, as if we're entering the unconscious or taking the lid off id, moving to a realm below the surface of our outward actions to strong universal themes that embrace our unconscious motives.

There's a woman named Princess Maria Bonaparte—who was a patient of Freud's and a psychoanalytic critic—who said in her analysis of "The Cask of Amontillado" that we see all these wine bottles, and they are obviously phallic symbols. Freud also was at one point given to reminding us that sometimes a cigar is just a cigar. But this story does get us into deep psychological levels—psychoanalytical levels, if you will.

The relationship of the tale to the reader is complex and really quite artful. Montresor even seems to be directly addressing us, and we can all be cast a bit like Fortunato, dressed up as fools in a similar role. Because you—the reader of the story—like Fortunato, are being left to try and guess what plot is unfolding. You're experiencing a mounting irrational fear, emotion, and disbelief with the rising action of the story, and you're ensnared into the story.

I want to talk about the origins of this story. It goes back to Poe supposedly hearing an anecdote while serving in the army in 1827 about a lieutenant who was killed in a duel by a young bully of a captain. The lieutenant, while intoxicated, was allegedly sealed up alive. Poe, we should also remember, was poor and very sick, and the story resonates with class difference and class envy. Montresor seems to have fallen. He says of Fortunato, "You were happy as I once was. Rich, respected, admired, beloved as I once was."

Fortunato, as in the word *fortune*, is noble, and Luchesi, the other wine connoisseur who's mentioned in the story, has a name which suggests lucre, or money. Poe had neither fortune nor money. His stepfather, John Allan—who adopted Poe after Poe's father died when Poe was only three—was, like Fortunato, a Mason, as well as a man who considered himself a wine connoisseur. Fortunato explains to Montresor—not without contempt—"You? Impossible! A Mason?" and Montresor becomes a different kind of Mason as he uses a trowel to build tiers that will suffocate Fortunato.

Perhaps psychobiographers who look for meaning in the life of the author might argue that Poe was wreaking a kind of vengeance on his stepfather, as well as for the impoverished and unhappy life he lived. The great Argentinean fiction writer Jorge Luis Borges pithily once said of Poe, "He lived a short and unhappy life if unhappiness can be short."

The story was published in 1846 in *Godey's Lady's Book*, a popular mid-19th-century venue for short fiction—which also published Hawthorne—and reflects the popular interest in stories that carry sensation, horror, and revenge. This popular interest in stories that convey both horror and sensation continues to the present day and, interestingly enough, is reflected in an episode of the television series *Homicide* based on "The Cask of Amontillado," in which, as a kind of tribute to Poe and the show's setting in Baltimore—where Poe once lived—a character seals another character up alive. Poe continues to the present day to have many imitators and admirers in both the literary and the popular cultures.

I want to do some analysis now of the "The Cask of Amontillado." D. H. Lawrence saw it as a tale of hatred and murderousness, but envy is a strong motif, and we never know what any of the "thousand injuries" Montresor has suffered are or the insult that precipitated his lust for revenge. An insult to family honor appears to be tied in, and the reader is immersed into a world of coats of arms and family mottos, traditions that carry on for centuries as the dead linger in their repose.

Punishing with impunity is the course set upon by Montresor to bring his revenge to fruition, and the story engages us in questions of justice, both here on Earth and the theological variety. Fortunato explains and Montresor repeats, "For the love of God!" The story, we should always remember, is built on irony. Montresor, for example, early on gives explicit orders, he tells us, to his attendants not to leave the house, knowing that it will ensure that they will—psychologically astute of him, to be sure.

Fortunato says early on to Montresor that his—Fortunato's—cough will not kill him. "My cough won't kill me," he says, and Montresor replies, "True—true." Montresor offers a toast to Fortunato's "long life," and the supreme irony may be in the lack of understanding on Montresor's part of the effect of the murder on his own conscience: from his smiling at the thought of Fortunato's "immolation" to his admission—later on in the story—that his heart grows sick, and he blames it "on the dampness of the catacombs." That's where we get into even a deeper psychology. If his heart is growing sick and he says it must be because of the dampness of the catacombs, are we to believe him? Or is he perhaps unreliable? Is his conscience or his unconscious playing a role in perhaps precipitating some guilt?

There are weaknesses in the story, despite its singular effect and the building up to its climactic impact. It's histrionic; it has what can be described as—I suppose—a puerile style. Henry James called it primitive, and T. S. Elliot called Poe "gifted" but "before puberty." The characters are not flat, but they are somewhat psychologically abstract, and there's a sense of gimmickry or manipulation that Poe uses that some deem non-literary. Montresor, after all, does pull us in through Poe's ventriloquist manipulation of him manipulating us as readers, and it can seem a bit heavy-handed on Poe's part. But that, we realize, is just what a good, or great, story—especially a suspense story—is supposed to do. You could almost say it's the suspense or horror storyteller's mandate.

The story remains a masterpiece because of its totality and its seminal role in masterful storytelling. What may appear somewhat crude in Poe becomes more stylized and highly developed as the genre of short fiction develops. Julio Cortázar, a short story writer who wrote a book on the beginnings of the modern short story, viewed "The Cask of Amontillado" as a perfect story and wrote about its "successful insistent race against the clock." Poe sets us up for precisely what Cortázar describes:

> I took from their sconces two flambeaux, and giving one to Fortunato, bowed him through several suites of rooms to the archway that led into the vaults. I passed down a long and winding staircase, requesting him to be cautious as he followed. We came at length to the foot of the descent, and stood together upon the damp ground of the catacombs of the Montresors.
>
> The gait of my friend was unsteady, and the bells upon his cap jingled as he strode.
>
> "The pipe," said he.
>
> "It's farther on," said I, "but observe the white webwork which gleams from these cavern walls."
>
> He turned toward me, and looked into my eyes with two filmy orbs that distilled the rheum of intoxication.
>
> "Nitre?" he asked at length.
>
> "Nitre," I replied. "How long have you had that cough?" [Here we have Fortunato coughing.]
>
> My poor friend found it impossible to reply for many minutes.
>
> "It is nothing," he said at last.
>
> "Come," I said, with decision. "We will go back, your health is precious."

We know, of course, that he's ensnaring him—he's bringing him in—and it moves us forward in a relentless way. He's playing with him: It's like a spider and a fly, saying, "Oh, you're coughing. We'll go back," and so forth. But we know we're moving on, and indeed, we do march on. Revenge is, let's face it, a powerful and universal human emotion. It's what pulls us in, even though we don't know why this man—our narrator—is seeking revenge against Fortunato.

The man is buried alive for reasons that we can't discern, and the very lawlessness of that act—done by someone who has managed to conceal his true lethal motives—is terrifying; it affects us. Plus there are so many skeletons down there in that subterranean vault. You may remember, in fact, those of you who remember Hamlet, [the scene] when the gravedigger holds up the skull and says, "[Alas] poor Yorick, I knew him well." That's what we call in literature a *memento mori*, a remembrance to us of our own mortality. When you have a lot of skeletons in a subterranean vault, it's hard not to think of your own mortality.

The story's first three paragraphs really serve as a perfect setting-up—or exposition—of all that follows in rising and falling action, and the voice in the story is masterfully sustained. It keeps us compelled to stay with the story right up to the end. I want to just read an excerpt from the end of the story:

> It was now midnight, and my task was drawing to a close. I had completed the eighth, the ninth, and the tenth tier. I had finished a portion of the last and the eleventh; there remained but a single stone to be fitted and plastered in. I struggled with its weight; I placed it partially in its destined position. But now there came from out the niche a low laugh that erected the hairs upon my head. It was succeeded by a sad voice, which I had difficulty in recognizing, as that of the noble Fortunato. The voice said—
>
> "Ha! ha! ha!—he! he!—a very good joke indeed—an excellent jest. We will have many a rich laugh about it at the palazzo—He! he! he!—over our wine—he! he! he!
>
> "The Amontillado!" I said.
>
> "He! he! he!—he! he! he!—yes, the Amontillado. But is it not getting late? Will not they be awaiting us at the palazzo, the Lady Fortunato and the rest? Let us be gone."
>
> "Yes," I said, "let us be gone."
>
> "*For the love of God, Montresor*!"
>
> "Yes," I said, "for the love of God!"
>
> But to these words I hearkened in vain for a reply. I grew impatient. I called aloud:
>
> "Fortunato!"
>
> No answer. I called again:

> "Fortunato!"
>
> No answer still, I thrust a torch through the remaining aperture and let it fall within. Then came forth in return only a jingling of the bells. My heart grew sick—on account of the dampness of the catacombs. I hastened to make an end of my labor. I forced the last stone into its position; I plastered it up. Against the new masonry I re-erected the old rampart of bones. For the half of a century no mortal has disturbed them. *In pace requiescat!*

I had a mentor and professor named Walter Tevis who gained some fame by writing a novel called *The Hustler*, all about pool shooting, that was made into a famous movie; he also is the author of *The Color of Money* and *The Man Who Fell to the Earth*. He used to say, "Edgar Allan Poe, the father of American junk, all that tintinnabulation that you hear in some of his poetry." But it really has little to do with Poe as a short story writer. Even the American novelist and short story writer E. L. Doctorow—whose father named him Edgar after Poe and who also said that Poe was one of our junky writers—is really talking more about Poe the poet—"Once upon a midnight dreary" and all that scary, creepy stuff about dead young women by the sea. Beautiful young women to Poe were the most aesthetically moving things of all, and he was married to his 13-year-old cousin, who died young. But Poe was a master storyteller, and it should make you want to read more Poe—both poetry and short fiction—because his poetry is well worth reading, too, even if you think it's junky. Read more fiction, like "The Tell-Tale Heart," if you haven't, or "The Fall of the House of Usher." You also might want to read Washington Irving to see how Poe avoided the meandering quality in Irving's tales, which helped establish him, by many accounts, as the seminal figure in the modern short story.

Poe's heirs are popular writers, like H. P. Lovecraft, Stephen King, and Shirley Jackson—whom we'll be talking about—masters of the horror story. Next for us [are] two other great horror storytellers who shift the boundaries of the natural world into encounters with the world of the supernatural. We see in the next pair of authors we're going to study—Nathaniel Hawthorne and Nikolai Gogol—more didacticism than we see in Poe. Remember that Horace, one of the earliest literary critics of ancient Rome, said that the purpose of literature is to teach, as well as to please or entertain. With Poe, it's mostly about the pleasing or entertaining. Horror can be entertaining, as we see in all too many scary movies and TV shows. Writers like Hawthorne and Gogol entertain us, and they scare us with horror, but they also stretch realism and credibility and become more moralizing than Poe. You might ask the question: Why is early fiction so fixated on horror? Because magazines were where stories appeared, and horror was what magazine readers craved.

Could a writer make readers quake in fear with the notion that one could actually murder with impunity and escape moral or eternal judgment as secularism and loss of faith continued to rise? "The Cask of Amontillado" was a realistic, true-to-life story, a well-made tale driven by plot and a realism, or what we call verisimilitude—being true to life—that will dominate the 19th century, even though, with Hawthorne and Gogol, we see stories that veer off into the supernatural.

"The Cask of Amontillado" is Gothic, gloomy, grotesque, and violent, an arabesque, intricate in its design, but it cleaves to standards of realism, as do the other masters of the well-made tale of the 19th century, like Guy de Maupassant, Anton Chekhov, and Henry James, who wrote a famous supernatural, haunting ghost story called *The Turn of the Screw*. Despite the ventures into the supernatural in Hawthorne, and Gogol and a seminal writer like Washington Irving, we remain largely tethered, in 19th-century storytelling, to a strong sense of realism and credibility. Stories, as we shall see, become more complicated in craft, technique, and character. Great stories are connected to other great stories and build on their predecessors in a tapestry of intertextuality; Poe and Hawthorne admired and wrote about each other's work.

Our next lecture will be on Hawthorne, another of the great 19th-century American storytellers and author of a tale that is generally regarded as his most compelling. The sense of fiendishness, the frightful, horrific, and demonic—as you'll see—resonates in this other American master, as well, but we owe a lion's share of credit to Poe for masterfully bringing us into the world we recognize as that of the genre of the short story and providing much of—forgive me for the apt metaphor—the brick and masonry that created for us a whole new way of envisioning fiction.

Lecture Two

Hawthorne's "Goodman Brown" and Lost Faith

Scope:

This lecture anchors us in allegory and its use in Nathaniel Hawthorne's "Young Goodman Brown." The lecture connects Hawthorne to his Calvinist and witch-burning heritage, which we discuss, along with the essential plot of the story. We explore the significance of Calvinist belief, witchcraft, the wilderness, and the role of the Native American population in Puritan society. We then move into interpretation and meaning as we consider the connection between evil and human nature, the richness of the story's ambiguity, and some of the psychological dimensions of the tale. Finally, we examine a combination of other central themes: the story's sustained mood and tone, its language, its use of different means of expression, and its effect on readers.

Outline

I. Often regarded as a moral allegory—in which abstract meaning emerges through fictional characters serving as symbols for higher moral truths—"Young Goodman Brown" is a particularly successful example of Hawthorne at work in territory for which he is famous.

- **A.** This allegory is of an archetypal journey, an initiation story of an everyman character moving from innocence to experience, from faith to loss of faith.
- **B.** The name Goodman was common but in this story is also indicative of a good man who encounters evil.

II. Hawthorne was born in the infamous Salem, Massachusetts, and descended from ancestors who participated in the Salem witch trials and believed in a stern form of Puritanism tied to the teachings of John Calvin.

- **A.** Calvinist heritage and thought permeate this tale, as does Hawthorne's awareness of his own lineage.
- **B.** Calvinism, the religion of the Puritans, is a belief in the doctrine of original sin tied to predestination.

C. The Puritans' belief in witches is seen in the allusion to Goody Cloyse's broomstick being lost or stolen, perhaps by "an unhanged witch," and talk of magic potions of cinquefoil, wolf's bane, and "the fine wheat and fat of a new-born babe."

III. The Puritans feared and persecuted Native Americans, whom they viewed as godless, wild pagans residing in the woods—the central allegorical setting for paganism.

A. Preindustrial America often associated forests with lawlessness and with Native Americans, who were seen as part of that lawlessness.

B. In Hawthorne's *The Scarlet Letter*, the act of sexual union between Hester Prynne and Reverend Arthur Dimmesdale likely occurs in the forest. Later on in the novel, Hester removes her scarlet letter in the forest—in part because that setting was perceived as free and lawless and existing under a kind of natural rule.

C. In "Young Goodman Brown," we find talk of powwows in the forest and the fact that no church exists there.

IV. "Young Goodman Brown" can be seen as another horror story but with a New England setting, as opposed to Poe's southern-nurtured Gothicism.

A. The depravity of human nature is implicit in the story.

B. A sense of horror is inherent in seeing people beneath their masks and everyday appearances, including those of piety and religiosity.

C. Perhaps the most profound horror is in Goodman Brown himself—his loss of faith and the realization of the demonic force within him.

D. What happens to Brown is what Shakespeare in *Hamlet* called the "pale cast of thought," a descent into darkness that results from intellect.

V. The ambiguity in "Young Goodman Brown" contributes to the story's richness, and one wonders if Hawthorne's attitude toward the Puritans is one of indictment or affirmation.

A. It is unclear whether Brown sees members of the church in the forest or is bedazzled by gleams of light flashing.

B. It is unclear (though "some affirm") whether the lady of the Governor is present in the forest scene.

C. It is also unclear whether Brown's experience was a dream or, indeed, why he needed to set out on his winter solstice journey in the first place.

D. The dreamlike quality of the story is a precursor to the Surreal and brings the reader's unconscious into play.

E. The story creates a psychological division between the id-like woods and the world of Salem, which represents the outer, conscious self.

VI. Other elements also make "Young Goodman Brown" a masterpiece.

A. A central theme in this work is what Hawthorne saw as the unpardonable sin of divorcing the intellect from the heart, leaving his characters lacking in love and reverence for the human soul, as we saw in Roger Chillingsworth in *The Scarlet Letter* and as we ultimately see in Goodman Brown.

B. The opening paragraph sets both mood and tone, and both are masterfully sustained.

C. The language of the story is rich yet represents Puritan vernacular speech.

D. Elements of Realism, Surrealism (tied to the evocation of the unconscious), and Fabulism (fable-like in its effect) are combined within the allegorical frame of the story; these elements move us from outside the forest, to inside, then outside again.

E. The effect on readers is mesmerizing as they are drawn into a world of fear, horror, loss of faith, the palpable evil of humanity, and the evil communion of the human race.

F. With Brown left hopeless and gloomy, the story ultimately compels us to reckon with larger questions of how we choose to live our lives.

Suggested Readings:

Freud, *Civilizations and Its Discontents.*

Hawthorne, "The Birthmark."

———, *The Blithedale Romance.*

———, "The Minister's Black Veil."

———, *The Scarlet Letter.*

———, "Young Goodman Brown."

Melville, "Benito Cereno."

———, "Billy Budd."

———, "Blackness in Hawthorne's Young Goodman Brown."

Questions to Consider:

1. Is Hawthorne representing Puritan belief or criticizing it?
2. Why does Brown set out on his journey? Can we guess or presuppose his reasons or motives?
3. What is Hawthorne rendering in the story about the nature of faith and the human experience?

Lecture Two—Transcript

Hawthorne's "Goodman Brown" and Lost Faith

We now want to look at one of the most indelible and famous of all American short stories: "Young Goodman Brown" by Nathaniel Hawthorne. It is a story that is often characterized as a moral allegory, meaning that abstract meaning comes through the story and emerges through the fictional characters, who serve as symbols for higher moral truths. This is the territory Hawthorne is so famous for, works so well with, and succeeds with in this tale particularly.

The allegory in "Young Goodman Brown" is one based on an archetypal journey. It's an initiation story of an everyman character who goes from innocence to experience, from faith to loss of faith. The name Goodman was common and nearly universal—comparable to mister today—but it's also indicative in this allegory of a good man who encounters evil. The roots of Hawthorne's story go back to allegorical morality plays, such as the 15th-century English *Everyman* or John Bunyan's *The Pilgrim's Progress*, which appeared in 1678. Goodman Brown's wife, Faith, is left behind after keeping Goodman back awhile and leaving him thinking after this one night that he will cling to her skirts and follow her to heaven.

The story then plunges Goodman Brown into a primeval forest on an errand or mission—a journey—the purpose of which is never made clear. Brown meets a man with a staff which bears a likeness to a great black snake, and the man turns out to be the devil, who tells Brown—contrary to Brown's belief in his lineage, which he believes is from honest men who are good Christians—that Brown's ancestors were complicitous in the lashing of a Quaker woman through the streets of Salem and the setting of fire to an Indian village.

Hawthorne was born in the infamous Salem, Massachusetts, and descended from ancestors who actually participated in the Salem witch trials and who believed in a stern form of Puritanism tied to the teachings of John Calvin. Hawthorne's ancestor was William Hathorne, a colonial magistrate who persecuted Quakers, and William Hathorne's son John was a Puritan investigator of those accused of witchcraft. "Young Goodman Brown" is often read as a personal story of Hawthorne's rendering of his own ancestral heritage and the sense of guilt he felt about it. But before we venture further into Hawthorne's life or to a greater understanding of

Calvinism, let us go back into the forest and discuss the essence of what occurs in this strangely mesmerizing and powerful horror story of moral guilt and good and evil. The devil informs Brown that he, Satan, has had close connections with some of the most outwardly moral, exemplary, and upstanding citizens. This is soon borne out by the appearance of the woman who taught Brown his catechisms as a youth, as well as by the presence in the forest of the town deacon and minister. What can these religious figures be doing in the woods in the darkness of night? Having, it turns out, a black Sabbath, a communion with the devil, whom Goodman Brown believes he can resist and stand firm against "with Heaven above and Faith below." But it turns out that Faith, like all the townspeople of Salem—both religious and irreligious, the powerful and the pariah—is of one assembly with the devil.

See if we can get used to Hawthorne's prose style here; it goes back to the proverbial Puritan:

> "My Faith is gone," cried he after one stupefied moment. "There is no good on earth; and sin is but a name. Come devil; for to thee is this world given."
>
> And, maddened with despair, so that he laughed loud and long, did Goodman Brown grasp his staff and set forth again, at such a rate that he seemed to fly along the forest path rather than to walk or run. The road grew wilder and drearier and more faintly traced, and vanished at length, leaving him in the heart of the dark wilderness, still rushing onward with the instinct that guides mortal man to evil.

Let me stop there, because that really sums up much of the theology of Hawthorne and the Puritans. There's an instinctual nature, an innate nature, that drives man—men and women—to evil.

> The whole forest was peopled with frightful sounds—the creaking of the trees, the howling of wild beasts, and the yell of Indians; while sometimes the wind tolled like a distant church bell, and sometimes gave a broad roar around the traveler; as if all Nature were laughing him to scorn. But he was himself the chief horror of the scene, and shrank not from its other horrors.

In other words, what's in the mortal heart—this evil that we carry around in us in a demonic way—is even far more evil, perhaps (as

Hawthorne saw things and as he portrays things here) than the devil and what the devil can wreak.

> "Ha! ha! ha!" roared Goodman Brown when the wind laughed at him. "Let us hear which will laugh loudest. Think not to frighten me with your deviltry. Come witch, come wizard, come Indian powwow, come devil himself, and here comes Goodman Brown. You may as well fear him as he fear you."
>
> In truth, all through the haunted forest there could be nothing more frightful than the figure of Goodman Brown. On he flew among the black pines, brandishing his staff with frenzied gestures, now giving vent to an inspiration of horrid blasphemy, and now shouting forth such laughter as set all the echoes of the forest laughing like demons around him. The fiend in his own shape is less hideous than when he rages in the breast of man. [There it is, explicitly delivered to us by Hawthorne.]
>
> Thus sped the demoniac on his course, until, quivering among the trees, he saw a red light before him, as when the felled trunks and branches of a clearing have been set on fire, and throw up their lurid blaze against the sky, at the hour of midnight. [We're at the witches' hour here, literally.] He paused, in a lull of the tempest that had driven him onward, and heard the swell of what seemed a hymn, rolling solemnly from a distance with the weight of many voices. He knew the tune; it was a familiar one in the choir of the village meeting house. The verse died heavily away, and was lengthened by a chorus, not of human voices, but of all the sounds of the benighted wilderness pealing in awful harmony together. Goodman Brown cried out, and his cry was lost to his own ear by its unison with the cry of the desert.
>
> In the interval of silence he stole forward until the light glared full upon his eyes. At one extremity of an open space, hemmed in by the dark wall of the forest, arose a rock bearing some rude natural resemblance either to an altar or a pulpit, and surrounded by four blazing pines, their tops aflame, their stems untouched like candles at an evening meeting. The mass of foliage that had overgrown the summit

> of the rock was all on fire blazing high into the night and fitfully illuminating the whole field. Each pendent twig and leafy festoon was in a blaze. As the red light arose and fell, a numerous congregation alternately shone forth, then disappeared in the shadow, and again grew, as it were out of the darkness, peopling the heart of the solitary woods at once.

As the story moves us once again out of the forest and back into the town of Salem, Goodman Brown is a changed, a marked, man for life. A mysterious transformation has occurred as a result of his nighttime journey, what's often called—attributed originally to St. John of the Cross but really more aligned with the French philosopher Blaise Pascal nearly two centuries before—the dark night of the soul. This is indeed exactly that for Goodman Brown. Goodman Brown, as a result, becomes a man of gloom, cast for the rest of his life into the dark by an encounter with evil that could well have been nothing more than a vivid and disturbing dream. Hawthorne leaves the answer to whether Brown indeed was dreaming or not ambiguous.

Now that we have, essentially, the outline of the story and a feel for Hawthorne's prose, let's talk once more of Calvinism and Puritanism. Calvinism, the religion of the Puritans, is a belief in the doctrine of original sin tied to predestination and is associated with such stern figures as famed Puritan writer Jonathan Edwards, whose notion was [that of] all of mankind being sinners in the hands of an angry God. Puritanism is often associated with harshness and the punitive, with sexual repression, hard work, and draconic codes of conduct placed on men and women before they leave this "vale of tears," as Shelley called it. But the cornerstone of belief is in God's omnipotence, and his knowing who is to be saved and who is to be damned, and of all humankind being marked with the original sin of Adam that led to the Fall.

Hawthorne was consumed with obsessiveness about Puritanism and about his own Puritan ancestors. He wrote of them in a work of his called *The Custom House*, which is often considered an introduction to *The Scarlet Letter*. It seems clear that his guilt about the sins of the fathers, and his own need to exorcise that guilt, is part of the genius behind "Young Goodman Brown." Is Hawthorne being too allegorical, as both Poe and Henry James suggested? When you call a character Faith and make her the wife of a good man who goes out on a journey to confront evil and you move your reader into a world of deviltry that mirrors humanity, perhaps one can say Hawthorne has gone to a bit too much trouble to spell out his moral terrain. But the story, whether too allegorical or not, compels us into what Melville aptly described in an admiring essay he wrote about Hawthorne as "the great power of blackness." Hawthorne transports us into the dark part of the human mind, the part that wrestles with notions of human depravity and original sin.

Goodman Brown and Faith have been married for three months—one trimester—when the story begins, and the newness of their marital union suggests the ties between original sin and human sexuality. The Puritan belief in witches is seen in the story in the mention by one of its characters, Goody Cloyse—that's Brown's catechism teacher—of her broomstick being lost or stolen, perhaps by an "unhanged witch," and talk of magic potions of cinquefoil, wolf's bane, and "the fine wheat and fat of a new-born babe."

The Puritans feared and actually persecuted the Indians, whom they viewed as godless and wild pagans who were residing in the woods. That's, of course, the central allegorical setting for paganism: It's a place where Hawthorne tells us there is no church. There's talk of powwows in the woods, and preindustrial America often associated woods or forests with lawlessness, as well as with Indians, who were viewed as being part of that pagan lawlessness.

In Hawthorne's great classic novel *The Scarlet Letter*, the act of sexual union between Hester Prynne and Reverend Arthur Dimmesdale was likely to have occurred in the forest, where later on in the novel, we see Hester take off her scarlet letter—the mark of her adulterous sin—in part because the forest is free and lawless. Of course, D. H. Lawrence had a point worth considering when he suggested that imagining sexual intercourse of any kind involving the Reverend Arthur Dimmesdale is not an easy task. The important point here is that in "Young Goodman Brown" and in *The Scarlet Letter*, the forest is a place apart from the rules of faith and moral conduct, a place of anarchic freedom and the transparency of sin.

Before we discuss the story "Young Goodman Brown" and its effect, meaning, and value, let's find out a bit more about Hawthorne's life and who he was. Hawthorne's father died in 1808 when the author was only four years old, and his mother became a recluse.

Hawthorne would also live a life of seclusion and isolation, which would shape both his character and his vision, though all of that would change, and he would wind up a famous and prosperous man. He was an editor and a novelist, as well as a short story writer, and he also wrote children's stories, travel sketches, Gothic tales, and a children's history of the world that sold over a million copies but made him all of $100, the fee paid to him for the book.

Later on, success would eventually come to Hawthorne, and he wound up in a relatively high diplomatic position. He was a college classmate and close friend of America's 14th president, Franklin Pierce. In fact, Hawthorne wrote a presidential campaign biography for Pierce, and was appointed by Pierce to Liverpool as U.S. consul.

Hawthorne published his first tale in 1830, and five years later, he published "Young Goodman Brown" in an issue of *New England Magazine*. The story later appeared in a short story collection of Hawthorne's called *Mosses from an Old Manse*.

Let's talk about the story in terms of its meaning—interpret it, to some extent—and its effect. It's really another horror story with the New England or Boston setting, steeped in Puritan folklore and theology; by contrast, oppose southern-nurtured Gothicism and European-set tales. A horror in this story is, of course, in the meeting with the devil; it's also in seeing people beneath their masks and everyday appearances, including those of piety and religiosity. But perhaps the most profound horror—as I've indicated—is in Goodman Brown himself: his loss of faith, his realization of the demonic force that is within himself.

Implicit in the story is the moral suasion of the depravity of human nature and the evil that resides in the human heart. The fact of Brown's conversion after he witnesses the black mass in the forest is a chilling one, and one which Hawthorne saw as baleful; [it] really comes upon us in reading this story. I use the word "chilling" because we think of Hawthorne's Roger Chillingsworth, the cuckolded husband in *The Scarlet Letter*, who allowed his intellect to encase his heart and a desire for revenge against the adulterer, the cuckolder, the Revered Arthur Dimmesdale. Goodman Brown's heart becomes increasingly encased by his sense of gloom from having seen this black Sabbath communion that involved all of the righteous and highbred folk of Salem, as well as his wife, Faith. The loss of Faith, for Hawthorne, was a great horror:

> "Faith, Faith!" cried the husband. "Look up to heaven, and resist the wicked one." [This is Goodman Brown seeing his wife with this black mask and telling her to resist the devil.]
>
> Whether Faith obeyed, he knew not. Hardly had he spoken when he found himself amid calm night and solitude, listening to a roar of the wind, which died heavily away through the forest. He staggered against the rock, and felt a chill and damp while a hanging twig, that had been all on fire, besprinkled his cheek with the coldest dew.
>
> The next morning young Goodman Brown came slowly into the street of Salem village, staring around him like a bewildered man. The good old minister was taking a walk along the graveyard to get an appetite for breakfast and meditate his sermon, and bestowed a blessing, as he passed, on Goodman Brown. He shrank from the venerable saint as if to avoid an anathema: Old Deacon Gookin was at domestic worship; and the holy words of his prayer were heard through the open window. "What God doth the wizard pray to?" quoth Goodman Brown. Goody Cloyse, that excellent old Christian, stood in the early sunshine at her own lattice, catechizing a little girl who had brought her a pint of morning's milk. Goodman Brown snatched away the child as from the grasp of the fiend himself. Turning the corner by the meeting-house, he spied the head of Faith, with the pink ribbons, gazing anxiously forth, and bursting into such joy at sight of him that she skipped along the street and almost kissed her husband before the whole village. But Goodman Brown looked sternly and sadly into her face, and passed on without a greeting.

You can see the effect that this night in the forest—this covenant with the devil—had on him. When he left, he left his wife behind, and now he has gone and sees his wife greeting him with joy, and he can't even really abide her.

> Had Goodman Brown fallen asleep in the forest and only dreamed a wild dream of a witch-meeting? Be it so if you will; but alas! it was a dream of evil omen for young Goodman Brown. A stern, a sad, a darkly meditative, a distrustful, if not a desperate man did he become from the night of that fearful dream. On a Sabbath day, when the

> congregation were singing a holy psalm, he could not listen because an anthem of sin rushed loudly upon his ear and drowned all the blessed strain. When the minister spoke from the pulpit with power and fervid eloquence, and, with his hand on the open Bible, of the sacred truths of our religion, and of saint-like lives and triumphant deaths, and of future bliss or misery unutterable, then did Goodman Brown turn pale, dreading lest the roof should thunder down upon the gray blasphemer and his hearers. Often awakening suddenly at midnight, he shrank from the bosom of Faith; and at morning or eventide, when the family knelt down at prayer, he scowled and muttered to himself, and gazed sternly at his wife, and turned away. And when he had lived long, and was born to his grave a hoary corpse, followed by Faith, an aged woman, and children and grandchildren, a goodly procession, besides neighbors not a few, they carved no hopeful verse upon his tombstone, for his dying hour was gloom.

You're certainly left with a sense of the onerousness—the heavy burden—that this man carries with him from his own experience. Life can be like that, by the way; people do have those kinds of experiences that turn them around and turn them into gloom or—just the opposite, certainly, one could argue—into euphoria, as well. For Goodman Brown, we don't know why he went into the forest, but when he comes out—and we experience what he experienced in the forest—he's a changed man, and as a changed man, his life is gloom. This doesn't stop him from procreating—having children and grandchildren—as we find out, but nevertheless, it's a sense of, not desperation exactly, but—what Hawthorne called it—gloom that he carries with him for the rest of his life.

What happens to Brown is what Shakespeare in *Hamlet* called the "pale cast of thought," a descent into darkness that results from intellect. Brown really can't be relieved of the effects of what he believed he saw in the forest scene: a black mass and communion featuring the once-angelic, sable form of the devil and the panoply of humankind, both good and bad. What is significant is that the story is spun to us in a realistic way, despite its supernatural elements, and is made to include a strong didactic element, that is, a sense of teaching us about sin. You can see where Hawthorne was, perhaps, confused. The great Nobel laureate William Faulkner said [that] great literature is created when the heart is against itself. [Hawthorne] had this Puritan heritage—he felt it intensely—yet at the same time, in many ways, he wanted to relieve himself of it; he wanted to, perhaps, point out just how onerous and burdensome and how much of—I'll call it a curse—it could be.

The story is fraught with ambiguity, and that contributes, I think, to its richness, maybe to its greatness. It's unclear, at one point, if Brown is seeing church members or being bedazzled by gleams of light flashing. It's unclear—though Hawthorne tells us "some affirm"—if the lady of the governor was there in the forest scene. It's also unclear—like with J. R. in the TV show *Dallas*, if you remember that—if all was a dream or why Brown needed to set out on his winter solstice journey in the first place. It has become almost trite to think of stories that are built on the pattern of a dream and [the idea] that we don't know whether in ending the story it was supposed to be a dream or not. But Hawthorne was creating that ambiguity intentionally, I think, trying to give us a sense of just a dreamscape and the ambiguity of what can be imagined as opposed to what indeed may have been real. (There are other—by the way—popular culture ties to "Young Goodman Brown" besides *Dallas*. There's the film *The Blair Witch Project*, which makes us think—I think—of the story "Young Goodman Brown," and there's *Rosemary's Baby*. Of course, stories about human encounters of the devil go back to the Bible and from Faust up through *The Exorcist* and many modern tales.)

Brown had this covenant with the devil. That's what he discovered in the communion of his race, and that communion really represents an inability of humans—to borrow a bit from Jesus in the New Testament—to put Satan behind them. Not only couldn't he put Satan behind him, but Satan became ubiquitous in his life after he had been in the forest. As we saw in the passage I read, he couldn't even look at those people who were giving blessings—who are trying to do God's work—with any kind of a serious countenance anymore. He took them to be doing the work of the devil because they were tainted in his mind by their association and communion with the devil.

This dreamlike quality in the story is really a precursor to the Surreal, because it brings a reader's unconscious directly into play. We have all these Freudian approaches to dreamlike states—Freud telling us that dreams are the royal road to the unconscious—but we have literary critics, like Lionel Trilling, who say that you really need to put an author on the couch as much as you can. It's not only the associations in the story that are with the unconscious and dreamlike, but it's also the associations that we might find out are tied to the writer or how they are tied to the writer. That's essentially how you would work psychoanalytically with a story like "Young Goodman Brown."

What's important to remember here, however, is that there's a division in the story, a psychological division. The woods are id-like, unconscious. There are qualities of the mind and the whole world of Boston that represent the outer conscious self. In this way, "Young Goodman Brown" is kind of a harbinger to Freud's famous work in the latter part of his career, *Civilization and Its Discontents* (which one of my friends used to call "Civilization and Its Discotheques.") But that's a work that's really much more anthropological: The view is that civilization is driven and ultimately built by the id, by unfettered drives that are compensated for by the guilt of conscience, or by what Freud called the superego. There's a multivalent message in "Young Goodman Brown" that shows the thin membrane that separates good from evil. It also makes us wonder if Hawthorne is indicting the Puritans or, in some way, implicitly affirming what they believe. One can't help but come away from reading "Young Goodman Brown"—it seems to me—wondering about questions of faith, original sin, and the human propensity for evil.

What other elements really make this story a masterpiece, given its longevity and its status as a masterpiece? The central theme in this work is what Hawthorne saw as the unpardonable sin of divorcing the intellect from the heart. Whether Goodman Brown experienced what he experienced in the woods or actually dreamed it, when he came out, his intellect seemed to take over. Intellect taking over diminishes love or reverence for the human soul; we saw this particularly in the character of Roger Chillingsworth in *The Scarlet Letter*. It seems to me that we see it also, ultimately, in Goodman Brown. This is a story which, right from the opening paragraph, sets the mood and the tone, and both are masterfully sustained. Let me just give you an example of how that works:

> Young Goodman Brown came forth at sunset into the street at Salem village; but put his head back, after crossing the

> threshold, to exchange a parting kiss with his young wife. And Faith, as the wife was aptly named, thrust her own pretty head into the street, letting the wind play with the pink ribbons of her cap while she called to Goodman Brown.

Notice how well-structured the story is: From the beginning of the story, he gets a kiss from his wife; at the end, you remember, he avoids that kiss. The pink ribbons, which are introduced in the beginning of the story, are reintroduced at the end of the story. There's a wonderful symmetry to the story; it's well structured. But there's also that sense, initially, of a kind of foreboding, of a mood that's cast early on in that first paragraph. His wife is asking him, "Don't stay too long." She's not questioning why he's going in there, but she wants to know that he'll return, that things will go all right, and that they'll have the life that they had up until the time when he felt—for whatever reason—compelled to go into the woods and enter into this dark sphere.

The language is really rich and sometimes prosaic, but it's nevertheless Puritan speech that we hear as vernacular. There are combined elements, in this story, of Realism, Surrealism (tied to this evocation of the unconscious), and Fabulism—that is, fable-like effects—within the allegorical frame that move us from out of the forest, or woods, to inside the forest, and then, once again, outside to the town. The story represents a spectacular life-transformative journey into what Joseph Conrad many years later would call the "heart of darkness." There is—make no mistake about it—a mesmerizing effect on readers, as we become increasingly drawn into a world of fear, horror, and loss of faith and see and feel the palpable evil of humanity and the evil communion of the human race.

This story, I believe, ultimately compels us to reckon with larger questions of how we choose to live our lives, for Goodman Brown is left hopeless and in gloom at the end. Here's a story that combines galvanizing and frightening effects with this great allegorical ambiguity, didacticism, teaching us—even though Hawthorne may have had his own ambiguous sense of what was to be taught—but certainly providing a kind of moral compass for a rich harvest of great and rewarding reading.

I strongly urge more Hawthorne. The novels as well as other masterful short stories, like "The Birthmark," the story of Aylmer, the scientist who thinks his wife is perfect, but then again, intellect takes over because she has a birthmark and he wants to remove it. You know what that leads to: Never tinker with Mother Nature. And his story of sinister and gloomy guilt, "The Minister's Black Veil." One can understand the nature of Hawthorne's truly extraordinary and riveting gifts as a storyteller by, of course, reading other works of his, including his novels, such as *The Scarlet Letter* and *The Blithedale Romance*. One can understand more completely the thrust of the story's development in the 19th century by reading the stories of Herman Melville, whom I said was a great admirer of Hawthorne's and who also, in his stories that I selected from *The Encantadas*—that's a collection—"Bartleby the Scrivener" and *Billy Budd,* takes us into deep psychological territory, as well.

Hawthorne is the father of this deeply psychological storytelling. It extends into the present century, into stories like "The Yellow Wallpaper" by Charlotte Perkins Gilman or stories by the ever-prolific Joyce Carol Oates. We're going to follow this path that Hawthorne provided in "Young Goodman Brown" as we head, in our next lecture, to Russia and another famous and seminal story by the Russian master Nikolai Gogol. Like Poe, Gogol was born, coincidentally enough, in 1809—five years after Hawthorne—and was a seminal figure in the production of the short story far away on another continent, in Russia, where it also came into prominence and flourished. Gogol's story is another tale cast in Realism but with strong elements of satire and, at story's end, the haunting presence of one of the original little men of fiction, a man of seemingly no consequence who wants nothing more in life than a better overcoat to have against the freezing cold of Saint Petersburg. Next: one of Russia's most famous and revered short stories, Nikolai Gogol's "The Overcoat."

Lecture Three
Under Gogol's "Overcoat"

Scope:

We begin this lecture by looking at the framework of "The Overcoat" and what it yields to even the casual reader. Gogol is of singular importance in that he introduces into fiction a low man—a powerless figure of no apparent consequence. Despite the story's satiric vein, Gogol's Akaky is a man with whom we feel a human connection. We briefly discuss Gogol's own possible biographic link to his character and the ways in which Akaky reaches mythic dimensions. We then focus on Gogol's life, as well as the czarist Russian milieu of his time. We use the approach of contemporary literary critic Terry Eagleton to look at Gogol's story via the concept of the "superstructure." We then explore some of the story's universal and lasting motifs of isolation, suffering, and compassion and conclude with an appraisal of Gogol's more conspicuous gifts demonstrating his mastery of craft: use of setting, his nuanced character portrayals, and his extraordinary command of detail.

Outline

I. Nikolai Gogol's "The Overcoat" is another 19th-century allegorical tale of horror, but this time based on czarist Russia's bureaucracy, corruption, and rigid hierarchy.

- **A.** The story is framed by the real and the supernatural. Gogol is considered the father of Russian Realism: He employs mimesis and verisimilitude in the service of creating a story that reflects real life.
- **B.** The story has comedic elements, as well as Surreal and Fabulist dimensions that contribute to its scathing satire of Russian bureaucracy and the byzantine hierarchies of power and position.
- **C.** "We all came out from under Gogol's 'Overcoat,'" a statement attributed variously to Turgenev, Tolstoy, and Dostoyevsky, reveals the impact this story had on Russian writers. But it also had a great impact on Western storytelling in general and continues to hold sway as one of short fiction's masterpieces.

II. Akaky Akakievich, whose name means "dung on the shoe," is a common man, similar to Hawthorne's Goodman Brown. However, as author Frank O'Connor has noted, Akaky is perhaps "the first Little Man" in fiction: a Russian *schlemiel*, the kind of archetypical character upon whom the soup is accidentally spilled.

- **A.** The story resonates with the humanity of Akaky, to whom a fellow worker says, "I am your brother," and for whom the reader, experiencing the tedious and joyless life of the clerk and the nightmarish theft of his overcoat, cannot help but feel pathos.
- **B.** Gogol, who was ridiculed as a child and disparagingly called "the mysterious dwarf," projects something of himself onto Akaky by making his character a writer (though merely a copier, like Melville's Bartleby).
- **C.** Gogol creates a mythic little man, virtually unnoticeable throughout his life—a man whose lot in life is illustrated comedically by the sour visage he exhibits at his christening.

III. We can perhaps best understand "The Overcoat" by looking at it from the perspective of the Neo-Marxist literary critic Terry Eagleton.

- **A.** For Eagleton, a character such as Akaky signifies a victim of what he called the "superstructure." The superstructure comprises the institutions that make up the social, economic, and cultural fabric of a time and place.
- **B.** The idea of the superstructure helps us understand "The Overcoat" by providing a perspective from outside the text, bringing in the institutions and cultural *zeitgeist* of the historical period during which Gogol wrote his masterpiece.

IV. We find universal and lasting motifs in "The Overcoat."

- **A.** Akaky is isolated, but that isolation shifts briefly when he enters the world and finds an identity with his new coat.
- **B.** Akaky's self expands briefly to explore the richness and color of objects, social life, and even eroticism, as we see when Akaky has a couple of drinks and entertains the impulse to run after a lady.
- **C.** Akaky transitions, in his new sartorial self, from the *schlemiel* to a swift experience of happiness and triumph.

D. Ultimately, "The Overcoat" is a story about human suffering and sacrifice for a goal that is tenuous at best and held all too briefly.

E. The story is psychologically prescient, probing—as Hawthorne did in "Young Goodman Brown"—the kinds of behaviors that exist under the surface of civilized and cultured politeness.

V. Gogol's genius—his mastery of craft—deserves special emphasis.

A. The setting of the story is a crucial element; with great immediacy, the reader experiences the deprivation and cold of Saint Petersburg.

B. Characterization and sketches of individual characters are both extraordinarily detailed.

1. The narrator is a self-conscious, fastidious, and obedient character in his own right. He feels obligated to follow the rules of storytelling, whether eschewing the indecency of mentioning undergarments or complying with the supposed dictate that characters in novels must be completely described.

2. The one-eyed, pockmarked tailor, Petrovich (whose surname indicates that he is no longer a serf), is a man whose self-image is based on the feeling that he is a special tailor, just as the person of consequence furbishes his own self-image. These portraits richly reveal to us the nature of characters who reflect the absurdity of the hierarchical social structure in which they live and work.

C. Details in the story are remarkable and fantastic. The tailor's misshapen nail and the portrait of the general on the snuff box are good examples of Gogol's sure touch with detail.

D. Gogol alludes to the "fantastic ending" of "this perfectly true story," which Vladimir Nabokov called a tale for the "creative reader." "The Overcoat" is also a story of social protest for the Bolsheviks, as well as a comedic tale of horror and the supernatural that paradoxically creates a feeling for humanity at the same time that it spells out in detail the futility of human existence.

Suggested Readings:

Eagleton, *Base and Superstructure.*

Forster, *Aspects of the Novel.*

Gogol, "The Nose."

———, "The Overcoat."

Nabokov, "Gogol's Genius in 'The Overcoat.'"

Questions to Consider:

1. How much pathos do we feel for Akaky as opposed to seeing him as a ridiculous or cartoon character?
2. How can we best characterize the narrator's view toward his fellow Russians? Toward Germans?
3. Do the supernatural appearances at the end of this story diminish its overall effectiveness or make it more powerful?

Lecture Three—Transcript

Under Gogol's "Overcoat"

"The Overcoat" by Nikolai Gogol is another 19th-century allegorical tale of horror, like Hawthorne's "Young Goodman Brown," but based on czarist Russia's bureaucracy, corruption, and rigid hierarchy. There was a heightened awareness in Russia during Gogol's time not only of the plight of the downtrodden but of an increased sense of the importance of helping lowly clerks by making their work more efficient and, in that way, diminishing the overwhelming nature of the bureaucracy which stifled their efficiency and productivity. Gogol's protagonist in the story is a little man who relishes—really even loves—his work as a copier and only faces obstacles when they are thrust upon him by the lawless who prey upon him or by the higher officials who are supposed to help him.

The story is framed by the real and the supernatural. Gogol is considered the father of Russian Realism, that is, employment of mimesis and verisimilitude, or creating a story that reflects real life. However, this story has comedic elements, as well as Surreal and Fabulist dimensions. It's also a scathing satire of Russian bureaucracy and its byzantine hierarchies of power and position.

"We all came out from under Gogol's 'Overcoat.'" That's a statement that has been attributed variously to Turgenev, Tolstoy, and Dostoyevsky, though it's actual source may have been a turn-of-the-century French critic. What it shows, however, is the impact this story had on Russian writers, and it had a great impact on Western storytelling in general and continues to hold sway as one of short fiction's masterpieces.

One can best understand a story like Gogol's not so much from a doctrinaire Marxist view but more [from] what we would call a Neo-Marxist perspective, like that of the British literary critic Terry Eagleton, who saw a character like the downtrodden one in "The Overcoat" as signifying someone victimized by what Eagleton called the "superstructure." Superstructure means, simply, the institutions that existed and made up the entire social and economic fabric, as well as the cultural gestalt—that is, the parts of the system, as well as the entire system itself—and all of that really created history.

This takes us—the idea of the superstructure—into an understanding of a story like "The Overcoat," because we can look at this story from the perspective outside of the text to the institutions, to the *zeitgeist*—which means "the spirit of the times"—to the historical period in which Gogol lived and wrote this masterpiece of a story. This is at the core of understanding much great Russian fiction—I should add—whether it's by Tolstoy, Dostoyevsky, Pushkin, Turgenev, or Chekhov, the most important figure of them all, as far as the short story.

A major critical way into a story like "The Overcoat" is by looking at the superstructure, which carries with it a view of the historical period and what amounts to a dialectical analysis ("dialectic" originally being a term from Hegel but ultimately identified more with Marx, who wrote about feudalism as the thesis in conflict with capitalism—as the antithesis—and for Marx, the synthesis was Socialism). The system of feudalism and, at its core, serfdom would be emancipated under the more egalitarian reforms of Alexander II, 21 years after Gogol wrote "The Overcoat." But the liberal reform movement in Russia began under Peter the Great and was making headway in Russian consciousness onto the canvas of Russian writers. Suddenly, seemingly inconsequential and lowly people are protagonists in fiction by authors like Gogol and Chekhov.

Pushkin, who is usually deemed the father of modern Russian literature and who was a strong believer in social reform—in fact, he was exiled because of his beliefs in social reform and his action on their behalf—was an enormous influence on the Russian *zeitgeist* and on Gogol, as was the fact that he wrote under the reign of the autocratic Nicholas I, who refused to abolish serfdom. Gogol's 1836 satire of Russian provincial bureaucracy was supposedly staged thanks to the personal intervention of Czar Nicholas, the autocrat, perhaps because autocrats wanted a more efficient bureaucracy; certainly, Nicholas did.

Let's look at the central character or this protagonist in Gogol's famous story, Akaky Akakievich. His name means actually "dung on the shoe." He's a common man, like Hawthorne's Goodman Brown, but perhaps—as the author and short story writer Frank O'Connor has noted—"the first Little Man" in fiction, a Russian *schlemiel*, the kind of archetypical character upon whom the soup accidentally spills. (This is a Yiddish folk hero; they used to distinguish between the *schlemiel* and the *schlimazel*. In fact, the great pitcher Sandy Koufax refused to pitch on Yom Kippur, the high holiday of the Jewish religion, because, [as] he said to Joe Garagiola, the interviewer and former catcher, "Call me a *schlemiel*.")

This character is very familiar to us. It's familiar to us in Charlie Chaplin and Woody Allen; it's usually a character whom, as I said—as opposed to the *schlimazel* who usually spills the soup—the soup spills on. The origin of this story—its genesis—was at a tea party that Gogol was at in Saint Petersburg. The story was told there, and those who heard it laughed, but it had the opposite affect on Gogol. He was supposed to have responded to hearing it with a most pensive seriousness from everything we've heard. Akaky, Gogol's protagonist, is just a poor document copier, someone who would never even be noticed in this Russian bureaucratic world, a civil servant who lives and works in Saint Petersburg, a man who is dedicated to his habitual and dull work routine but invisible. In fact, the only way he's really visible is that he's teased by the younger clerks who work with him.

Let me begin the story, "The Overcoat," and give you a sense not only of Gogol's prose style but also of how he writes in so many ways that are really masterful and curious at the same time. He begins by saying, "in the department of," and there's an ellipsis. He says, "but I had better not to mention which department." You can see in an autocracy how one can be afraid, perhaps, of mentioning a department; one can be afraid of bringing attention to oneself. He's also bringing attention to the kind of fiction that was making itself apparent at this particular time in Russian history and really throughout Europe and the Western world. He goes on to say, "There is nothing in the world more touchy than a department, a regiment, a government office, and, in fact, any sort of official body." It's as if he wants to impress upon us just how important these departments are in terms of how they see themselves, and that kind of self-importance really manages to play its way into the story in a way that we find particularly compelling. It's not to say that Akaky is self-important; Akaky is just the opposite. Akaky is a man who has really no self-importance at all: All he does is copy, goes home, eats, and sleeps. That's his whole life, and he's happy with it, for the most part, until he finds out how cold he is in the Saint Petersburg winter.

Here's this omniscient narrator—this narrator who knows really everything—who says,

> Nowadays, every private individual considers all society insulted in his person. [There's Gogol again, coming in with a kind of commentary about his own period.] I have been told that very lately a complaint was lodged by a police inspector of which town I don't remember, and that in this complaint he set forth clearly that the institutions of the State were in danger and that his sacred name was being taken in vain; and, in proof thereof, he appended to his complaint an enormously long volume of some romantic work in which a police inspector appeared on every tenth page, occasionally, indeed, in an intoxicated condition. And so to avoid any unpleasantness, we had better call the department of which we are speaking "a certain department."

All of that detail—all about the police inspector, all of that circuitousness and everything—to get us to the fact that we're not going to name this department; we're going to call it a "certain department" out of fear and apprehension, the police, and the authorities.

> And so, in a certain *department* there was a *certain clerk*; a clerk of whom it cannot be said he was very remarkable; he was short, somewhat pockmarked, with rather reddish hair and rather dim, bleary eyes, with a small bald patch on the top of his head, with wrinkles on both sides of his cheeks and the sort of complexion which is usually described as hemorrhoidal … nothing can be done about that; it is the Petersburg climate. [This is the first time he introduces the climate, which plays a very central role as a kind of antagonist in the story.] As for his grade in the civil service (for among us a man's rank is what must be established first) he was what is called a perpetual titular councilor, a class at which, as we all know, various writers who indulge in the praiseworthy habit of attacking those who cannot defend themselves jeer and jibe to their hearts' content.

There we have a little bit of jeering going on [by] the writers, and there's this self-consciousness of the narrator coming in and saying things to us in a way which we find later on in the novel—and in

Fielding, Richardson, and really the birth of the English novel—to be commonplace—a "now, gentle reader," that sort of thing.

But here's a character who needs a new overcoat, and he goes to his tailor. The tailor's name is Petrovich, and Petrovich tells him his coat can't be repaired and urges him to purchase a new one. After much privation, sacrifice, and the benefit of a holiday bonus, Akaky is able to buy the overcoat, which takes on a central and preeminent importance in his life. In fact, the clerk above him throws a party—if you can imagine this—in honor of the fact that he has a new overcoat. They're honoring the acquisition of the overcoat, but it's a luxurious one. Akaky, living a very isolated life—utterly isolated, removed from any kind of social life—attends this party. On his way home via an unfamiliar route, he's accosted—robbed—by a pair of brigands—thieves—who rough him up and leave him unconscious in the snow. The authorities are of no help to Akaky in recovering his overcoat, and ultimately, he goes, at the recommendation of the fellow clerk, to see a very important person, a general—"a person of consequence," Gogol calls him—who winds up excoriating Akaky for not following a hierarchal chain of power and showing off, in fact, in front of one of his friends how powerful and authoritative he can be. Akaky falls sick, and soon after, he dies.

The story concludes with what is Akaky's ghost—or corpse, depending on the translation—taking peoples' overcoats and, ultimately, confronting this person of consequence to take his overcoat. The narrator, at the end of the story, tells of another ghost with immense mustaches, like those of Akaky's attackers.

We have a story of a little man—a satire—an insignificant man facing a world of government jobs, rank, police, the district commissioner, and corruption. Like Hawthorne's Goodman Brown, Akaky is an everyman. He's small, humble, meek, and an underdog, but his life changes and is transformed—though only temporarily and ephemerally—with the acquisition of the overcoat. What makes this such a powerful story—what makes it such a meaningful story and has made it that way lo these many years—is that it resonates with the humanity of Akaky. A fellow worker early on in the story says, "I am your brother," and the reader experiences this tediousness—this joyless life of the clerk—and also experiences, in a rather singular way, the nightmarish theft of the overcoat, and the aftermath of that, and [the] trying to seek what he has really put so much of his life into acquiring, to get it back or get some sense of justice. It's a story for which it's almost impossible not to feel pathos.

Gogol was often ridiculed—in fact, he was disparagingly called "the mysterious dwarf"—and I think he projects some of himself on to the little man Akaky. He makes his character a writer—a man of words—though a copier. In Herman Melville's famous story, Bartleby the Scrivener is also a copier, though he is the character who simply says, "I prefer not to," says it over and over again, and finally becomes almost catatonic. Akaky, when he has that overcoat, feels joy, maybe for the first time in his life. Not to say that he doesn't like being a copier—because he does; he actually takes great pleasure in copying—but what we see is, in both these stories, a kind of parody of the role of the writer. "Bartleby the Scrivener" was published 11 years after "The Overcoat," in 1853, but it mirrors "The Overcoat" and probably, in some ways, as famous a story as "Bartleby" is, couldn't have been written had it not been for "The Overcoat."

What Gogol creates in this story is a mythic little man for us—a man virtually, as I said, unnoticeable throughout his life—who, even when he initially began his life, did so with a sour visage at his christening. The story set up the contrast: a little, seemingly inconsequential man to the general, the man of consequence, in other words, the dichotomy of the powerless and the powerful. The powerful treats Akaky scornfully, unconscionably, but then experiences regret and guilt and must face Akaky's ghost or corpse before the story concludes.

Let's look at Gogol. Let's look at who he was, and then we can assess more meaning in the story and the importance of the story beyond what I've said. Nikolai Gogol was born in the Russian Ukraine in 1809 to a fairly prosperous family. His father was educated and was a writer. The family name was originally Ianovskii, but Gogol's grandfather changed it in order to claim noble Cossack ancestry. Gogol was sent off as a boy to boarding school, and we know that he was physically so unattractive that he was—as I said—teased by his classmates, called "the mysterious dwarf." Some of those earlier experiences probably helped shape and account for his empathy for a character like this hapless and much-ridiculed Akaky, who was teased by his fellow clerks.

Gogol—like many writers in short fiction we're going to be studying—wanted initially to be a poet, and one can see poetic intensity in his work, especially in "The Overcoat." He had a close relationship with the great Russian writer Aleksandr Pushkin and was deeply affected by Pushkin's death only three years before the publication of "The Overcoat." Gogol settled in Saint Petersburg, Russia's capital city, and there is much in the story "The Overcoat" tied to that city and its mythology, as well as to the experiences Gogol had working there at a number of minor governmental jobs. Gogol went on to work as a teacher and as a private tutor and published a volume of short stories in 1835 called *St. Petersburg Stories*. "The Overcoat" was part of a collection called *The Overcoat and Other Stories of Good and Evil*, published in 1842. There again in the title, you see reflected a concern about good and evil that we saw in Hawthorne and Poe.

Gogol had enormous influence on short fiction, like Poe and Hawthorne, and he produced novels, drama, and satires, as well as short fiction. One sees in "The Overcoat" a wealth of detail and a self-conscious narrator who makes us aware of the fact that he's telling a story and feels bound to follow certain specific rules that he believes apply to the craft of novel writing. As far as the detail, when we meet Petrovich, the tailor, we find out that he had a plaster kitten with a nodding head, or we find out that there's a general's picture on a snuff box and one of the eyes is poked out. These kinds of details one doesn't see in earlier stories, but one begins to see in stories by Gogol and Chekhov, stories that were written by Russian writers.

One also doesn't necessarily see until now this sense of trying to follow specific rules; that is, "I should mention a character," the author says to us, or the narrator says to us, "but if I do, I feel duty-bound to say something about that character that's specific." There even may be a hint of satire about writers in Gogol's making his narrator so overly concerned about keeping some data confidential and following certain strictures about what should or shouldn't be included about a character.

Let's get a feel again of "The Overcoat," particularly as we come to the conclusion. I read the first few opening paragraphs, but when we get to the end, we've moved into the supernatural realm, and here again is the sense of the narrative voice that's very strong. It's not like the voice of Poe's Montresor, who is a character who plays a role in the story, or it's not even like Hawthorne's voice, although that is an omniscient voice, as well. See if you can hear the language here—despite the fact that it's translated—and what it summons and evokes:

> What was even more remarkable is that from that time on the apparition of the dead clerk ceased entirely; [That is, from the time that he took the person's of importance overcoat from him.] apparently, the general's overcoat had fitted him perfectly; anyway, nothing more was heard of overcoats being snatched from anyone. Many restless and anxious people refused, however, to be pacified, and still maintained that in remote parts of the town, the dead clerk went on appearing.

Notice again how this sounds almost reportorial; it sounds almost journalistic: People are reporting. Remember we began the story talking about the concern about policemen, so there's symmetry again:

> One policeman in Kolomna, for instance, saw with his own eyes an apparition appear from beyond a house; but, being by natural constitution somewhat frail—so much so that on one occasion an ordinary grownup suckling pig, making a sudden dash out of some private building, knocked him off his feet to the great amusement of the cabmen standing around, whom he fined two kopeks each for snuff for such disrespect—he did not dare to stop it, and so followed it in the dark until the apparition suddenly looked around and, stopping, asked him: "What do you want?" displaying a huge fist such as you never see among the living. The policeman said: "Nothing," and turned back on the spot. This apparition, however, was considerably taller and adorned with immense mustaches, and directing its steps apparently toward the Obukhov bridge, vanished into the darkness of the night.

Notice that even though we've got apparitions, ghosts, and all that, we have, nevertheless, the sense of it being reported in a realistic way—in a plausible way—as if it actually occurred. It's recounted in that way. And notice the kind of detail that you get, even in the policeman being embarrassed and humiliated and charging them for embarrassing him—these two people—so he can buy snuff with what he charges them. There is, again, the power of the law—the kind of corrupt power of the law—but the policeman himself is afraid and with good reason. These apparitions are something to be afraid of; they're out there haunting the Russian landscape or, at least, haunting Saint Petersburg's landscape.

There are universal themes in this story. The character is isolated, and that isolation shifts briefly to his entering the world and finding an identity with his new coat. When he has that new coat, the self expands briefly beyond to a sense of richness of objects, color, social life, and even eroticism: Akaky has a couple of drinks and the impulse to run after a lady. What I mean by universality in this is the sense that one can suddenly come from a low position and have a moment that seems triumphant—seems joyful—that can open up the senses and open up one to life as one has never been opened up before; really, Gogol captures this masterfully.

Akaky goes in his new sartorial self—that is, outwardly dressed in his overcoat—from being the *schlemiel* that I mentioned before to a swift experiencing of happiness, as opposed to being this unlucky character. Some of you with a good memory for the comic strip *Li'l Abner* may remember that there was a character that Al Capp—the creator—gave us, who had a cloud constantly over his head. Certainly Akaky was that type of character: His life before the overcoat was defined by having garbage thrown on him, chimney soot swept on him, or plaster falling upon his head. Those things happened to him just by dint of his existence. They happened to him because—for the same reason as I said—certain characters in Yiddish literature or folktales that go back to a lot of Russian folklore have the soup spilled on them. There is, [for] Akaky, that moment of sheer triumph when he has the overcoat. He sacrificed enormously for it; he has gone through great self-sacrifice when he wears it, and then what happens? He's accosted; he's beaten. The overcoat is stolen.

Ultimately, "The Overcoat"—notwithstanding its wry humor and its satire of Russian life and Russian bureaucracy—is really a story about human suffering and sacrificing for a goal that is tenuous and evanescent at best, held all too briefly, though happily, but also lost all too easily because of the evil men do. How profoundly sad that the acquisition of a coat made of cat fur should represent the most triumphant day in this poor clerk's life.

It's also a tale of universal humanity on yet another level. It's a nightmarish arabesque of a man—an everyman, as I said, like Goodman Brown—who confronts evil and is destroyed, not only by the evil of having what means the most to him taken away from him by robbers, but also by a kind of banality of evil. (That was a great phrase that the philosopher Hannah Arendt gave us. She was talking essentially of Nazis, who sent people off to their death in the death camps, went home, put on their slippers, petted their dogs, and were banal. Eichmann sending people to the gas chambers, marking them down one after another, [was] just counting beans really—banality of evil.) There's a banality of evil in the general—in the man of consequence—because of all his inflated self-importance, his vanity, really. He terribly mistreats this poor clerk.

However, even the person of consequence reveals his humanity because he feels guilty and regretful, and here in "The Overcoat," we find the story of great compassion. That's why so many writers were moved by it; that's why so many writers were influenced by it. It seemed that in Akaky's pitifulness and in the change also in the person of consequence—his pride and his concern about his image make him act in a way to his old friend to impress at Akaky's direct expense. But upon Akaky's death and being haunted by Akaky, of course, his humanity is compelled forth—and even before that—because he feels guilty.

This is a psychologically prescient story. It probes, just as Hawthorne did in "Young Goodman Brown," what kind of behaviors can exist under the surface of civilized and cultured politeness. All of these first three stories really bring us into a world underneath the world of appearances to a deeper sense of reality. What lies underneath appearances is often—we're told by Gogol, Hawthorne, and Poe—evil or, certainly, destructiveness in men's behavior toward other men.

Gogol's mastery—his genius of craft—is really something that needs to be emphasized. The setting is heralded forth as a crucial element and has great immediacy, just as the reader experiences the deprivation and the cold of Saint Petersburg and the mighty antagonism of the northern frost. The characterization and sketches of individual characters are really extraordinarily detailed, as we've never seen before. The narrator [is] self-conscious, fastidious, obedient, a character in his own right, a kind of Greek chorus almost, in some sense, who feels obligated to follow these rules of how to write, whether he's eschewing the indecency of mentioning undergarments—which he does—or complying with the supposed rule in novels that character be completely described.

What details we get: We have a one-eyed, pockmarked tailor, Petrovich. (The surname is used, by the way, to indicate [that] he's no longer a serf.) He's a man whose self-image is based on feeling himself to be a special tailor—just as the person of consequence furbishes his self-image—and these [details] richly reveal to us the nature of characters who reflect the absurdity of the social hierarchical structure in which they live and work. All in Gogol's story is hierarchically static and fixed; it's a stratified world of clerks, tailors, and those holding government posts. Details of the story are really nothing short of remarkable, fantastic. The tailor's misshapen nail, the portrait of the general on the snuff box: good examples of the sure touch that Gogol has with the tale.

The "fantastic ending" Gogol alludes to of what he calls "this perfectly true story"—he insists on it being true—is what Vladimir Nabokov called a

> tale for the creative reader and [one] of social protest for the Bolsheviks, Communists, a comedic tale of horror and the supernatural that paradoxically creates a feeling for humanity at the same time that it spells out in detail the futility of human existence.

The greatness of this story, like Hawthorne's "Young Goodman Brown," has much to do with its ambiguity of meaning. There have been many debates over the years about whether Gogol intended the small clerk Akaky to be a ghost or a corpse after his death. Ann Charters, who edited the much-prized collection called *The Story and Its Writer: An Introduction to Short Fiction*, argued that Constance Garnett, the famed translator of this story and much great Russian literature, was true to Gogol's intentions in using "corpse" rather than "ghost" to describe the posthumous Akaky. However, the apparitions that appear at the end of the tale—Akaky's and the mustached figure whom we meet in the encounter with the policeman—remain part of a fantastic tableau of the phantasmic work.

Pushkin, Gogol's mentor, may indeed deserve the laurel of being the father of modern Russian literature and its greatest poet, but Gogol established a different form and voice for the short story with "The Overcoat" and was a figure of colossal importance and influence on all of the great Russian writers who followed and stood on his shoulders. We leave Gogol and that apparition vanishing into the darkness to move on to one of the great 19th-century stories of Realism and irony that also calls attention to the plight of lesser people, or common folk, who seem inconsequential, but who nevertheless experience the strange turns of destiny and the vicissitudes of life and give us much universality. Our next story: Guy de Maupassant's famous, well-made tale "The Necklace."

Lecture Four

Maupassant's "The Necklace"—Real and Paste

Scope:

Guy de Maupassant, is one of France's most well known writers and is often credited as one of the fathers of the short story. In this lecture, we examine the effectiveness of plot and irony in his story "The Necklace" and discuss Maupassant's role as a 19th-century Realist writer influenced by the birth of Naturalism. As we will see, the necklace is a representation of the real that is not real. We touch on the concept of the intentional fallacy in literature, then move to the story's meaning and its connections to morality, materialism, and the ephemeral experience of a joyous, triumphant moment that is ultimately transformed into a life of loss and hardship. An analysis of the two chief characters and their links to meaning in the story follows along with our interpretation of the story as a social commentary and a revelation of fate's capriciousness. The lecture concludes with a focus on the story's dramatic denouement, the Sunday meeting with Mathilde and the still beautiful and youthful-looking Mme. Forestier.

Outline

I. "The Necklace" is essentially a Cinderella story—one of uniquely palpable poignancy and darkness—that is woven carefully with realism and abides by the rule that every detail should contribute to the fabric of the tale.

- **A.** The story concerns a woman of great charm and physical attractiveness named Mathilde Loisel, who with no dowry and no social position to offer a prospective husband, marries a "little clerk"; in the ensuing years, she suffers from a kind of poverty compared to the dreams that possess her.
- **B.** A discernible link to Gogol's protagonist in "The Overcoat" can be seen in Maupassant's characters, clerk Loisel and his wife, Mathilde, who are lower class and as saddled with the necessity of self-sacrifice for the cost of a necklace as Akaky is for the overcoat.
- **C.** The story is built on plot and irony—much of the reason for its endurance.

D. Maupassant brings the craft of 19th-century Realism and verisimilitude into fruition, along with what Joseph Conrad called "the importance of the factual."

E. Before the birth of Naturalism with the work of Darwin and others, we find a kind of social Darwinism enveloped by Realism in Maupassant, who wanted to move us by reproducing "the spectacle of life."

F. "The Necklace" is a remarkably popular story, though viewed by some as more of an anecdote and one of the least artistic of the short fiction masterpieces we will study in this course.

G. To create the appearance of reality, Maupassant believed in the necessity of creating a complete illusion of reality, symbolized in the story by the necklace.

H. Maupassant spoke of his intent to show that "life is unpredictable, disparate and disconnected—full of inexplicable, illogical catastrophes." In literature, however, we must always account for the intentional fallacy, the idea that even the author can't truly know what his or her intentions might have been.

II. Meaning in the story is tied to morality, just as Mathilde's dreams are tied to vanity and materialism.

A. Mathilde's triumphant night at the ball, a kind of Cinderella fairy tale, represents a threat to class divisions.

B. The story is a *tranche de vie* ("slice of life") but also a fable of a 10-year plight in which an ephemeral moment of joy and triumph becomes suffering and privation because the illusory is taken to be the real.

C. Mathilde's transformation into an old-looking, impoverished woman carries with it a strong allegorical resonance. She loses her beauty while Mme. Forestier remains young and attractive.

D. The characters Mathilde and Loisel reveal meaning in the story.

1. Mathilde doesn't want to relinquish the jewels of her girlhood convent friend Mme. Forestier at the first selection and is "lost in ecstasy" at the sight of the

necklace; she kisses her friend "passionately" before "fleeing with the treasure."

2. Mathilde envies her friend but has changed irrevocably by the time she returns the substitute necklace to Mme. Forestier, who acts "chilly" when she receives the replacement.
3. Loisel strikes us as a simple, good man (like Hawthorne's Goodman Brown) whose intentions lead him on a trajectory from hope and enthusiasm to anguish and misery.

III. The story's dramatic denouement is the final meeting of Mathilde and Mme. Forestier in the Champs-Elysees.

A. Mathilde uses Mme. Forestier's first name and says that her hard days and wretchedness are "because of you"; in some ways, she seems to be justifying her life over the past 10 years.

B. The ultimate irony of the necklace having been "paste" and "worth at most 500 francs" reveals also that the reader has been in the hands of a masterful storyteller all along—one equally accomplished in the use of Realism, detail, and dramatic revelation.

Suggested Readings:

Chopin, "How I Stumbled upon Maupassant."

Flaubert, *Madame Bovary.*

———, "A Simple Heart."

James, "From Guy de Maupassant."

Maupassant, "The Necklace," translated by Marjorie Laurie.

———, *Stories.*

———, "The Writer's Goal."

Questions to Consider:

1. The story has been criticized as not being nearly as artful as other short fiction masterpieces. Does it deserve the mantle of masterpiece?
2. Is Maupassant rendering a final judgment on class divisions and their rigidity?

3. Is it appropriate to characterize Mathilde's and her husband's sacrifices on behalf of paying off the cost of the necklace as heroic?

Lecture Four—Transcript

Maupassant's "The Necklace"—Real and Paste

We now move on to Guy de Maupassant's "The Necklace," first published in a Paris newspaper in 1884 and included in an anthology called *Tales of Days and Nights*. A novelist, an editor, an author of travel books and poetry, and a newspaper reporter, Maupassant was the author of almost 300 short stories, some of them horror-type stories inspired and greatly influenced by Poe. Maupassant was born Henri René Albert Guy de Maupassant in 1850 to a noble and old Lorraine family that settled in Normandy.

Maupassant is often described as one of France's most famous writers and one of the fathers of the short story, along with such figures as Émile Zola, who is also known as one of the fathers of Naturalism. He was a protégé of Gustave Flaubert, the author of *Madame Bovary*, who was a childhood friend of Maupassant's mother and Uncle Alfred. Maupassant's maternal grandfather was, in fact, Flaubert's godfather, and Flaubert was a literary godfather to Maupassant, mentoring him and helping him meet other distinguished literary figures of his day and helping him establish himself as a career writer.

Maupassant's parents separated when he was quite young, and as a young man—before he established himself as a writer of wide fame and fortune—Maupassant was expelled from a seminary; [he] went to Paris at age 21, in 1871, where he worked as a civil servant. He died of syphilis before his 43rd birthday and left a dark and revelatory epitaph that he wrote for himself: "I have coveted everything and taken pleasure in nothing." This reflects a different kind of dark view of life than the Calvinism we found in Hawthorne or the heavy Russian tragic sense we found in Gogol.

Maupassant was influenced by the naturalists, and his work is a guidepost for us of Naturalism, which was beginning to make its headway into short fiction. The ideas of the naturalists—particularly Darwin—were linked to the notion that we, as a species, are driven by a kind of natural selection that makes for a determinism that is often interpreted by fiction writers who call themselves "Naturalist" as being imprinted in our natures. Thus, you had Zola, who believed humans are creatures who can be put under the microscope by a fiction writer and understood scientifically in terms of predictability of human behavior being like the predictability of other animals. Or you have the great American novelist and turn-of-the-century Naturalist writer Theodore Dreiser, who believed that under certain environmental stimuli, an effect on human behavior could be determined.

We see the influence of Naturalism and this dark view of Maupassant in his most famous, widely read, and frequently anthologized story, "The Necklace." It's a story which has a twist at the end of careful plotting, not characteristic of most of Maupassant's other stories but paving the way for the celebrated stories of writers like O. Henry—real name William Sydney Porter—and Somerset Maugham, who both became immensely popular writers of short fiction, often identified, like "The Necklace," with a surprise or even a shocking twist of an ending.

"The Necklace" is essentially a Cinderella story, and that famous fairy tale can be traced back centuries before in nearly every culture. There are, in fact, nearly 1,500 variations of the Cinderella story, but none has the twisted end nor the palpable poignancy and darkness of Maupassant's tale. It is also a story woven carefully with Realism, abiding by the rules of every detail contributing to the fabric of the story.

We can and should also understand this particular story—as we can in all of Maupassant's stories—by delving into the author's background and the culture he grew up in and wrote from and about. "The Necklace" concerns a woman of great charm and physical attractiveness named Mathilde Loisel, who with no dowry and no social position to offer a prospective husband, "let herself be married"—and that's the exact language—"to a little clerk at the Ministry of Public Instruction." Mathilde suffers—she lives in a kind of poverty compared to the luxury, elegance, and affluent dreams that possess her.

> She was one of those pretty and charming girls who are sometimes, as if by a mistake of destiny, born in a family of clerks. She had no dowry, no expectations, no means of being known, understood, loved, wedded by any rich and distinguished man; and she let herself be married to a little clerk at the Ministry of Public Instructions.
>
> She dressed plainly because she could not dress well, but she was as unhappy as though she had really fallen from her

> proper station, since with women there is neither caste nor rank: and beauty, grace, and charm act instead of family and birth. [Notice how we have these kinds of sweeping and facile generalizations about women at the time that the story was written by Maupassant.] Natural fineness, instinct for what is elegant, and suppleness of wit are the sole hierarchy and make from women of the people, the equals of the very greatest ladies.
>
> She suffered ceaselessly; feeling herself born for all the delicacies and all the luxuries. She suffered from the poverty of her dwelling, from the wretched look of the walls, from the worn-out chairs, from the ugliness of the curtains. All those things, of which another woman of her rank would never even have been conscious, tortured her and made her angry. The sight of the little Breton peasant, who did her humble housework aroused in her regrets which were despairing, and distracted dreams. She thought of the silent antechambers hung with Oriental tapestry, lit by tall bronze candelabra, and of the two great footmen in knee breeches who sleep in the big armchairs, made drowsy by the heavy warmth of the hot-air stove. [Notice again the attention to detail here.] She thought of the long *salons* fitted up with ancient silk, of the delicate furniture carrying priceless curiosities, and of the coquettish perfumed boudoirs made for talks at five o'clock with intimate friends, with men famous and sought after, whom all women envy and whose attention they all desire.

This is a woman who is really quite unsettled and in despair because of what she has pretty much accepted—but not really accepted—as her allotment in life, to which she has been consigned.

> When she sat down to dinner, before the round table covered with a tablecloth three days old, [notice again the detail] opposite her husband, who uncovered the soup tureen and declared with an enchanted air, "Ah, the good *pot-au-feu*! I don't know anything better than that," she thought of dainty dinners, of shining silverware, of tapestry which peopled the walls with ancient personages and with strange birds flying in the midst of a fairy forest; and she thought of delicious dishes served on marvelous plates, and of the whispered

> gallantries which you listen to with a sphinx-like smile while you are eating the pink flesh of a trout or the wings of a quail.
>
> She had no dresses, no jewels, nothing. And she loved nothing but that; she felt made for that. She would so have liked to please, to be envied, to be charming, to be sought after.

Maupassant pretty much sketches the character here in a very detailed way. What she wants out of life is not what she has: She's very unsettled; she's a dreamer; she thinks magically. Then fate enters in the form of an invitation to a ball that her husband brings home, and Mathilde, you would think, might be happy going to a ball. No, she despairs because she doesn't have a dress. It turns out her husband has saved just the minimal amount she feels she needs to buy a dress; he put the money aside to buy himself a gun to use in a planned lark-hunting trip with friends. They're able to buy a dress, but then she despairs over not having jewels to wear to the ball. Loisel, her husband, suggests that she borrow jewels from a rich girlhood friend, Mme. Forestier. She takes her husband's advice and goes to Mme. Forestier, who gives her carte blanche to choose from the large jewel box. Mme. Loisel looks at these jewels only to discover in another black satin box "a superb necklace" that she wants above all the other jewels that belong to her friend. When her friend loans her that necklace, she's ecstatic.

Thus, Mathilde—Mme. Loisel—is able to go to the ball dressed way above her economic station in life and to become the belle of the ball, the object of great admiration and attention by men of higher station than her lowly clerk husband, to live these dreams and this magic that she was really tortured by. Her appearance is an absolute triumph. Does this sound familiar in some ways, an echo to "The Overcoat": that one moment of triumph, that moment of building up to it, of feeling despair of not having the outer semblance to be recognized in some different way, and then having all of it?

What happens next in the story is at the significantly named Rue des Martyrs, where she and her husband live: She discovers she has lost the necklace. The Loisels need to replace the necklace, and they find one in a shop that costs them 40,000 francs. They borrow, scrimp, save, and they endure what Maupassant describes as "black misery" to repay the debt. Mathilde works like a peasant doing—again,

Maupassant's description—"heavy housework" and "the odious cares of the kitchen." Her husband works nights, and for 10 years, this goes on.

Let me go back to the text:

> So they begged the jeweler not to sell it for three days yet. And they made a bargain that he should buy it back for thirty-four thousand francs, in case they found the other one before the end of February.
>
> Loisel possessed eighteen thousand francs which his father had left him. He would borrow the rest.
>
> He did borrow, asking a thousand francs of one, five hundred of another, five louis here, three louis there. He gave notes, took up ruinous obligations, dealt with usurers and all the race of lenders. He compromised all the rest of his life, risked his signature without even knowing if he could meet it; and, frightened by the pains yet to come, by the black misery that was about to fall upon him, by the prospect of all the physical privation and of all the moral tortures which he was to suffer, he went to get the new necklace, putting down upon the merchant's counter thirty-six thousand francs.

[That amount]—36,000 francs—was really a fortune, especially for people in these straights. It's not to say they were poor before the necklace was lost—they were certainly poor by the standards of what she wanted to live by—but certainly in terms of the privation of what they suffered as result of trying to make up and compensate for the cost of the necklace, they were poor. They lived an impoverished life, destitute.

> When Mme. Loisel took back the necklace, Mme. Forestier said to her, with a chilly manner:
>
> "You should have returned it sooner; I might have needed it."
>
> She did not open the case, as her friend had so much feared. If she had detected the substitution, what would she have thought, what would she have said? Would she not have taken Mme. Loisel for a thief?

> Mme. Loisel now knew the horrible existence of the needy. She took her part, moreover, all of a sudden, with heroism. That dreadful debt must be paid. She would pay it. They dismissed their servant. They changed their lodgings. They rented a garret under the roof.

Again, this is destitution, but it's also suffering because of a kind of honesty. They felt the duty and the obligation to replace what was lost and, as a result, went destitute and went into this poverty, suffering, and misery in order to do that right thing, the proper and honest thing. But here's what her life becomes:

> She came to know what heavy housework meant and the odious cares of the kitchen. She washed the dishes, using her rosy nails on the greasy pots and pans. [Even there, you have a nice touch of those rosy nails, right? She still has rosy nails.] She washed the dirty linen, the shirts, and the dishcloths, which she dried upon a line; she carried the slops down to the street every morning, and carried up the water, stopping for breath at every landing. And dressed like a woman of the people, she went to the fruitier, the grocer, the butcher, her basket on her arm, bargaining, insulted, defending her miserable money, sou by sou.
>
> Each month they had to meet some notes, renew others, obtain more time.
>
> Her husband worked in the evening, making a fair copy of some tradesman's accounts, and late at night, he often copied manuscript for five sous a page. [Like Gogol's "Overcoat" hero, he's a copier as well.]
>
> At the end of ten years, they had paid everything, everything, with the rates of usury, and the accumulations of the compound interest.
>
> Mme. Loisel looked old now. She had become the woman of impoverished households, strong, and hard, and rough. With frowsy hair, skirts askew, and red hands, she talked loud while washing the floor with great swishes of water. But sometimes, when her husband was at the office, she sat down near the window, and she thought of that gay evening of long ago, of that ball where she had been so beautiful and so admired.

It's still there in her memory for her to have, in these ephemeral moments, that sense of triumph. But 10 years! Think of that: 10 years of really hard work, of doing without, of impecuniousness, that is, poverty.

> And what would have happened if she had not lost that necklace? Who knows, who knows? How life is strange and changeful. How little a thing is needed for us to be lost or to be saved.

There is Maupassant's philosophy almost epitomized in those lines: Something can take a different turn, and life can change irrevocably.

The twist in this story comes at its end, when Mathilde meets her old friend Mme. Forestier on the Champs-Elysees and discovers that the necklace, the one that she had taken—the one that she was so ecstatic about—was fake. It was paste; it was worth, at the most, 500 francs.

First of all, you can see the link to Gogol and the little man. In this case, it's Loisel and his wife who are the little people like the clerk Akaky. They're lower class; they're saddled with the necessity for self-sacrifice to make up for the cost of the necklace, just as Akaky is compelled to self-sacrifice and go[ing] without, privation—not that his life was not without privation even before that—for the cost of the overcoat. This story, like Gogol's masterpiece, is a story of life's essential cruelty, of an evanescent moment of triumph which becomes overshadowed by life's cruelty.

You might be asking yourselves: Why are these early stories so mordant, or so tied to a sense of cruelty? (Tragedy, really, if you choose to see it as such.) These were realistic writers; these were writers who really wanted to brook no quarter as far as giving us a sense of what they saw as reality. Remember that Poe, Hawthorne, Gogol, and Maupassant were men who had experienced a lot of the harshness of life; they are artists and, therefore, certainly had a vision that was not exactly euphoric or anything that we would tie to happiness, except for those rare moments that come, [as] when Gogol's Akaky has his overcoat or when we see and experience what Mme. Loisel experiences at the ball.

This story really is built on plot; it's also built on a poignant sense of irony, which is much of the reason for its lasting endurance, and it also has social commentary. Maupassant, when he was a boy, spoke Norman with the peasants and developed a real sympathy for poor folk like the Loisels, even poorer than the Loisels, from what we know. But he also seems, given his own noble ancestry, aware of the necessity of keeping the social hierarchy intact. On some level, this story seems to suggest that Mathilde should have stayed in her own social station, for that, ironically, is where she winds up—in fact, as I said, maybe even in a lower social station. She has descended to a lower economic and class rung at the story's end as a woman of impoverishment. This is also a story of the capriciousness of fate, about how something as seemingly simple as losing a necklace can mean being lost or saved.

Maupassant brings the craft of 19th-century Realism and verisimilitude into fruition, along with what Joseph Conrad called "the importance of the factual," something he learned a great deal about from his mentor, Flaubert. The much-respected 20th-century Irish short story writer and literary critic Sean O'Faolain called Maupassant "the relentless realist." Maupassant wanted to move us by reproducing "the spectacle of life." To create the appearance of reality, Maupassant believed in a necessity of creating a complete illusion of reality, symbolized in the story by the necklace. As we'll see in Henry James's great story "The Real Thing," at the heart of this, and [of] James's story, is the question: What is the real thing, the object or the illusion of reality that represents it? What is more relevant to art, putting the mirror up to life or the life that is represented by asking that same question? Is art real in its representation of life, or is the reality what is being represented?

Maupassant spoke of his intent, though in literature we must always bear in mind what would come to be known as the intentional fallacy from a couple of literary critics named [Monroe] Beardsley and [W. K.] Wimsatt; that is, the idea that we really don't know an author's intent because the author himself or herself can't know truly what the intention might have been. There's the unconscious; there's a text yielding different meetings. But Maupassant said that his intent was to show how "life is unpredictable, disparate, and disconnected, full of inexplicable, illogical catastrophes." A direct quote from the master.

"The Necklace" is a remarkably popular, successful, and influential story, though some have characterized it as being largely an anecdote or not having the artistic merit of many of the other short stories that have been classed as great short fiction or short story masterpieces.

Anecdotes—by the way—are short tales, usually biographic and based on real life, often designed to reveal a truth or make a point. Anecdotes, like myths and fables, are often turned into short fiction, but it's a word that can be used dismissively about short fiction to undercut its literary or artistic seriousness of purpose.

Maupassant has also been criticized for writing in "The Necklace" a story that seems too implausible. A writer deeply committed to Realism seems an odd candidate for the charge of being implausible, but it's not terribly difficult to see why some choose to see this story that way or to even deem it anecdotal. Say what one wants about "The Necklace," it is a story of inestimable importance and much enjoyed and loved now for over a century. It's what we call a *pièce-à-thèse*—a thesis story, a "well-made tale," as well.

Meaning in the story is tied to morality, and Mathilde's dreams are tied to vanity, materialism, and her belief that she was made for dresses and jewels and not for the class she was born into—to her thinking, a mistake of destiny. A perversion of class lines, therefore, occurs when she attends the ball and appears to be of the class she is not. Reality is distorted. Her triumphant night at the ball—the Cinderella fairy-tale element of the story—represents a threat to class line divisions and hierarchy.

The story is ultimately what we call a *tranche de vie*—a slice of life—but it's also a fable of a 10-year plight after an ephemeral moment of joy and a transformation that turns into suffering and privation. Why? Because the illusory is taken to be the real. And there's a strong allegorical resonance as Mathilde turns into an old-looking woman. She loses her beauty, while Mme. Forestier remains young and beautiful. Maupassant appears to be showing us that wealth can preserve beauty—even in an era long before Botox—while poverty, and the struggle that goes with it, ensures a loss of beauty.

The characters, both Mathilde and Loisel, reveal meaning in the story. Mathilde, early on, doesn't want to relinquish the jewels of her girlhood convent friend Mme. Forestier at the first selection and is "lost in ecstasy" at the sight of the necklace. She kisses her friend "passionately"—Maupassant tells us—before "fleeing with the treasure." At the ball, we witness Mathilde crazed with pleasure and joy, triumphant, until confronted when leaving with her "common" wrap, mindful of the other women with their costly furs. This makes her want to escape.

Mathilde envies her friend Mme. Forestier but has changed irrevocably by the time she returns the substitute necklace to her friend, who—as we said—acts "chilly" when receiving the replacement necklace. Mathilde took her part in life with a kind of stoic heroism, while her friend remains immune, through her riches, either to struggle or to misery.

Loisel is not a major, strong character, but he strikes us as a simple, good man, like Hawthorne's Goodman Brown, who follows a trajectory from hope and enthusiasm to aging, five years after the first week of their ordeal following the loss of the necklace. He wants to please his wife, first selling his gun and then sacrificing himself for every franc and sou he can to pay their staggering debt. He has to give up his paternal inheritance, deal with usurers and what Maupassant's narrator refers to as "the race of lenders," a possible anti-Semitic allusion. Loisel, the small clerk, winds up anguished and in misery because he wanted to bring pleasure and happiness to his wife, to make her feel, even if briefly, above her station in life and above the role to which by class she was destined.

The story's dramatic denouement, the final resolution of the plot, is the final meeting of the two women. Let's go to that:

> [But], one Sunday, having gone to take a walk in the Champs-Elysees to refresh herself from the labor of the week, she [Mme. Loisel] suddenly perceived a woman who was leading a child. It was Mme. Forestier, still young, still beautiful, still charming.
>
> Mme. Loisel felt moved. Was she going to speak to her? Yes, certainly. And now that she had paid, she was going to tell her all about it. Why not?
>
> She went up.
>
> "Good-day, Jeanne."
>
> The other, astonished to be familiarly addressed by this plain goodwife, did not recognize her at all, and stammered:
>
> "But—madame!—I do not know—you must be mistaken."
>
> "No. I am Mathilde Loisel."
>
> Her friend uttered a cry.
>
> "Oh, my poor Mathilde! How you are changed!"

"Yes, I have had days hard enough, since I have seen you, days wretched enough—and that because of you!"

"Of me! How so?"

"Do you remember that diamond necklace which you lent me to wear at the ministerial ball?"

"Yes. Well?"

"Well, I lost it."

"What do you mean? You brought it back."

"I brought you back another just like it. And for this we have been ten years paying. You can understand that it was not easy for us, who had nothing. At last it is ended, and I am very glad."

Mme. Forestier had stopped. "You say that you bought a necklace of diamonds to replace mine?"

"Yes. You never noticed it, then! They were very like."

And she smiled with a joy which was proud and naïve at once. Mme. Forestier, deeply moved, took her hands.

"Oh, my poor Mathilde! Why, my necklace was paste. It was worth at most five hundred francs!"

What a moment of sheer drama. That's at the core of the story: that sense, again, of suffering for an unknown fact, an unrecognized fact, trying to do the right thing. The use of the first name here and the revelation of the hard days and wretchedness "because of you" is, in a way, perhaps, something of her saying, "It's justified what I did because I did the right thing." But there's a real irony here of the diamonds (you know, "Diamonds are a girl's best friend," as the old saw would have it from the movie) being paste worth at most 500 francs. One reads Maupassant and realizes, ultimately, that he or she is in the hands of a realistic storyteller who compresses the story, builds it on plot, and has this climactic ending that comes to us with such force. He's not only the heir of the great Gustave Flaubert—whose most famous novel is *Madame Bovary* and his best known short story is "A Simple Heart"—but also writers like Joseph Conrad and Henry James.

The realism that I really keep emphasizing in Maupassant was something that James and Chekhov learned from. They both learned a lot about plot, as well, although when we meet Chekhov, we see a writer who forgoes plot a great deal for the sake of character. James learned from both Maupassant and Chekhov, but as we'll see, he went on his own way.

The sense of Realism in the 19th century can't be underscored enough. The short fiction masterpieces that we're studying—whether they're realistic or naturalistic or Naturalism as viewed with a sense of Realism; whether they move up into the supernatural, [as in] Hawthorne and Gogol; whether they have a twist of an ending that seems almost implausible, [as] in Maupassant—nevertheless represent writers who are trying to be true to life and who are trying to show life as it really is. Maupassant, as you can see, as well as Gogol and Hawthorne, also interweaves a kind of morality. In this story, [the lesson is that] people shouldn't necessarily try to be something that they're not; they should value what's real as opposed to what's illusory. They should not be caught up in or compelled by the fake, because the fake is immaterialism: going to the ball and pretending to be somewhat of a higher station, as well as in just the jewels or the necklace themselves being fake.

When we move on to another 19th-century short fiction masterpiece, we're going to continue with the sense of realism but with a different kind of story. Anton Chekhov's "The Lady with the Dog" is a realistic story, to be sure. It's also a love story which takes place, like Gogol's "The Overcoat," in 19th-century Russia, but unlike that classic tale, this one has no elements of the supernatural; it has nothing resembling walking corpses stealing overcoats or corpses with moustaches. This is a story more about character than plot. It is a story of adultery and passion by one of the world's great master storytellers, in fact, by someone who is often regarded as the greatest master storyteller of them all. We move from Gogol at mid-century with "The Overcoat" in 1840 and Maupassant with "The Necklace" in 1884 to the end of the 19th century, when Chekhov created what many regard as his greatest masterpiece of the short story (and remember that he also was a dramatist). "The Lady with the Dog," also called "The Lady with the Little Dog," first appeared in 1899. We're headed there to that story and Chekhov next.

Lecture Five

Chekhov, Love, and "The Lady with the Dog"

Scope:

Anton Chekhov, one of our greatest and most humane writers, was of serf lineage and wrote stories that were grounded in 19th-century Russia. His story "The Lady with the Dog" is unconventional in this sense, dealing with an extramarital affair at a time when the Russian Orthodox Church held sway over the morality and decisions of ordinary people. In this lecture, we discuss Chekhov's unique contribution to the genre of the short story, his wide influence on an assortment of other important fiction writers, the nature of his reading audience, and his ability to write fiction that avoided moralizing. We also focus on the changing setting and four-movement structure of the story, as well as on the characters and their relationships to one another. The lecture then explores Chekhov's remarkable deftness in the use of realistic details and concludes with a discussion of the story's meaning and modes of interpretation.

Outline

I. Grounded in the culture of 19th-century Russia and himself of serf lineage, Anton Chekhov had a deep and abiding empathy for people shackled by adversity.

- **A.** Chekhov was one of our greatest and most humane storytellers, as well as a dramatist and a physician.
- **B.** He produced hundreds of short stories and was a major influence on a score of fiction writers.

II. "The Lady with the Dog" was written toward the end of Chekhov's life and is considered one of his masterpieces.

- **A.** It is an unorthodox tale defined best by Vladimir Nabokov, who said, "All the traditional rules of storytelling have been broken in this wonderful story."
- **B.** The story has no problem or conventional climax; nevertheless, Nabokov called it "one of the greatest stories ever written."

III. The story begins with the characters Gurov and Anna meeting in Yalta by the Black Sea—a resort associated with immorality and adventure, zipless sexual encounters that, we discover, are perhaps greatly exaggerated.

- **A.** After the love affair begins, Chekhov moves us to Moscow, where we see Gurov's family life along with the big-city whirl of the bank and the club.
- **B.** In contrast, the provincial town by the Volga where Anna and her husband live is pictured as gray and drab. Ironically, a play called *The Geisha* is being performed at the local theater.
- **C.** The story is divided into four movements—the first two in Yalta; the third in Moscow and the small town where Anna and her husband, von Dideritz, live; and the fourth encompassing Anna's visits to Moscow.

IV. Character—and, more important, the roundness of character—is vital to consider in Chekhov's work.

- **A.** Gurov's wife is seen by us through his eyes: intellectual and dignified on the outside but, from his point of view, unintelligent, narrow, and inelegant. This division between selves is an important theme in the story as a whole, especially with respect to Gurov.
- **B.** We see Gurov through a sympathetic lens supplied to us by Chekhov's point of view. Gurov is afraid of his wife and regards women as "a lower race"—a misogynist—yet he is more at ease with women and, indeed, cannot live without them.
- **C.** Anna is childlike, identifiable with Gurov's young and naïve school-age daughter. She is pious and unhappy and feels sinful for her transgressive behavior but also wants desperately to live and to experience life. Like Gurov, she is trapped by marriage and the dicta of the Russian Orthodox Church.
- **D.** Von Dideritz is presented by Anna as a flunky, and when we see him at the theater, he bows repeatedly as if he is one. He has vague German associations, no great calling card to many Russians, and we can understand why Anna is unhappy.

V. The realistic details in the story reveal to us Chekhov's genius.

A. The initial link made by Gurov with the dog and the humorous dialogue about Grenada that follows are splendid examples of realistic touches.

B. In the first section, Anna loses her lorgnette; we later see her with one in hand at the provincial theater, used by Chekhov as a sign of her ordinariness.

C. Again, we note the understated power of the details in the scene in which Gurov eats a slice of watermelon while Anna wallows in her feelings of sinfulness after the two have become lovers.

D. Gurov is moved to reveal his feelings for Anna to a fellow club member but receives a response about the sturgeon being "off"; this scene is a turning point for him and a catalyst to go see Anna. It also reminds the reader of the earlier image of fish scales with which Gurov identifies women's underthings when love affairs go south.

E. When Gurov goes to see Anna, we see the drabness of her life in the gray carpet made of military cloth, the inkstand gray with dust in the hotel, and the dark-gray fence around Anna's house.

VI. "The Lady with the Dog" is not just a story of infidelity.

A. It is a story of love, the vagaries of marriage and caged destiny, and the ways in which love can change ordinary people, like Gurov and Anna.

B. It is also a story of passion and morality—Chekhov was lambasted by the critics of his day for not being moral enough, though he stated clearly in one of his letters that the writer's obligation is to portray through actions, not through depiction of state of mind.

C. It is a story about beauty—best seen in the contemplative scene in Oreanda, a meditation by a slightly more obtrusive Chekhov on the beauty of nature and life and the eternal nature and possibility of humanity and human dignity.

D. It is a story about secret lives and Gurov's realization that another life lurks beneath the one in which we live—the mundane and quotidian versus a hidden or real life that can be authentic and concealed.

E. "The Lady with the Dog" is a tragic but ennobling story that profoundly captures, without a conclusive ending, empathy for lives bounded and roads not taken.

Suggested Readings:

Chekhov, *Four Plays*.

———, "The Lady with the Dog," translated by Constance Garnett.

Malcolm, *Reading Chekhov: A Critical Journey*.

Nabokov, "A Reading of Chekhov's 'The Lady with the Dog,'" from *Lectures on Russian Literature*.

Questions to Consider:

1. Is Chekhov being too easy on adultery by not being judgmental about it or causing it to result in harsher consequences?
2. How central is Gurov's age or the age of his daughter to his falling in love with Anna?
3. Are Chekhov's omniscient remarks and observations about life and love a form of moralizing?

Lecture Five—Transcript

Chekhov, Love, and "The Lady with the Dog"

We move on now to Chekhov and a famous story of his called "The Lady [with] the Dog." Let's first talk about Chekhov, who comes from serf lineage and writes stories that are really grounded in—as this story is—19th-century Russia. His grandfather was [the] grandson of a former serf, and though serfdom was officially abolished in 1861—the year following Chekhov's birth—peasants remained woefully unequal, both socially and economically, in Russia throughout Chekhov's lifetime. Chekhov had a deep and abiding empathy for this class of people, who were still shackled by poverty, quite possibly due, at least to some degree, to his own lineage.

One of our greatest and most humane storytellers but also a dramatist and a physician, Chekhov treated scores of poor people for free. He once said, "Medicine is my lawful wife, and literature is my mistress." He produced hundreds of short stories, four plays, and a novel and was a major influence on a score of fiction writers. The great 20th-century short story writer Eudora Welty once said that reading Chekhov was "just like the angels singing to me." Many writers feel that way about Chekhov: that his language, prose, and really his stories have a kind of singing and poetic quality to them. He revolutionized the story. He cast it more in terms of drama and character revelation than plot, but his output was prodigious and really remarkable, especially considering that he also practiced medicine and wrote plays. All those plays, by the way, have endured the test of time: *The Seagull*, *Uncle Vanya*, *Three Sisters*, and *The Cherry Orchard*. He found a different audience than Gogol had in Russia, because his stories are more of the quotidian—the everyday—and take on the whole panoply and range of human character and emotion.

The story "The Lady with the Dog" was written toward the end of his life and is considered one of his masterpieces. Chekhov had tuberculosis and was at a clinic—a health spa—in Yalta in 1897. The following year, he built a villa near Yalta and, in 1899, published "The Lady with the Dog," or "The Lady and the Dog." Sometimes, depending on the translation, it's also titled "The Lady with the Little Dog" or "The Lady with the Lap Dog." In fact, there have been all kind of disputations as to whether the dog was a Pomeranian or a

Spitz; a lot of this doesn't really matter. The story is initially set in Yalta, but the idea that an anonymous lady walks by with a dog and becomes so central in the life of this character is really at the heart of this story.

Chekhov was able to move to Yalta after he sold his estate and the publishing rights to all his collected works for what, by today's standards—or, for that matter, his day's standards—would be considered a paltry sum: 75,000 rubles. His stories were unknown internationally until after the First World War. They didn't become part of the English-speaking and -reading world until the famous Russian translator Constance Garnett translated some 13 volumes of them. That was done between 1916 and 1922, though she worked randomly, rather than chronologically. His work, once it became recognized—once people became aware of it—was extraordinarily far-reaching and singular in its impact and influence.

One of the true masters of the modern short story, Chekhov wrote about ordinary people living ordinary lives, like the characters in this story, "The Lady with the Dog." Gurov and Anna are both living what Thoreau might have called "lives of quiet desperation"; both are unhappily married, and both find each other and find passionate love in Yalta.

This is an unorthodox story. Vladimir Nabokov—the author of *Lolita*, *Pale Fire*, and so many great works—said in a 1981 essay, "All the traditional rules of storytelling have been broken in this wonderful story." By the way, Nabokov was not necessarily all that keen on many of Chekhov's stories, but [with] this one, he felt that it was one of the greatest stories. I'll give you a quote in the book, obviously, that really kind of qualifies that.

There are no unities, in this story, of time or space; it's really the story of an affair that takes place in three different locales over an entire year. There is no problem, regular climax, or even point at the end of the story. Novelist Richard Ford said "It's a story of non-events." Nevertheless—and here's the Nabokov quote—Nabokov said it is "one of the greatest stories ever written."

Let's talk about what Chekhov believed the role of the artist was before we get into the story. He believed that the artist was really to ask questions in his role, not to answer them. It was his duty to ask questions, and Chekhov went to great lengths in this and other works that he produced to avoid what we would call moralizing. This is essentially a tale of two adulterous lovers.

Let us consider what takes place in the story. Gurov, a man who has had a number of affairs, meets a comely lady with a dog. Her name is Anna, and they become acquainted and soon take up with one another as lovers. Anna is filled with self-loathing and feelings of sinfulness. She's a religious woman, and she certainly feels, in the sense of this Russian Orthodox Church background that she has, [that she is] an adulterer. They part after becoming lovers: she to return to her husband, whom she calls a "flunky," and Gurov to his harsh and rather severe wife. Gurov beings to realize, following their parting and while he's back at his home in Moscow, that he has fallen in love with Anna, who has elevated him.

His memories are very intense of her, and he really can't stop thinking about her, even though when he leaves—when he departs—he thinks it's just going to be a memory like these other affairs that he has had. But when he's away from her, the memories not only become more vivid, [but] his longing for her becomes more passionate, and he realizes that what has come upon him in his midlife crisis is love. She has seen him, to a great degree, as being far more good and finer than he deems himself worthy of being seen. As a result, he longs for her and for that feeling of elevation that she gave him. Everything in Moscow seems superficial to him while they're separated, while everything about his emotions and attachment to Anna feel real.

> He was tormented now by his strong desire to tell someone his memories. But at home, it was impossible to talk of his love, and away from home there was no one to talk with. Certainly not among his tenants nor at the bank. And what was there to say? Had he been in love then? Was there anything beautiful, poetic, or instructive, or merely interesting, in his relations with Anna [Sergeevna]? And he found himself speaking vaguely of love, of women, and no one could guess what it was [all] about, and only his wife raised her dark eyebrows and said:
>
> "You know, Dmitri, the role of fop doesn't suit you at all."

> One night, [as] he was leaving the Doctors' Club together with his partner, an official, he could not help himself and said:
>
> "If only you knew what a charming woman I met in Yalta!"
>
> The official got into a sleigh and drove off, but suddenly turned around and called out:
>
> "Dmitri Dmitrich!"
>
> "What?"
>
> "You were right earlier: the sturgeon was a bit off!"

Suddenly these words—which seem so mundane because they are talking about the sturgeon, the fish, being off—have an extraordinary affect on Gurov. He feels he has to go to Anna; he has to see her. Everything around him seems too dull—uninteresting and unstimulating—and without life to it.

What happens in the course of the story is that the two lovers continue to see each other, and that's the basic outline of the story, which on the face of it, hardly justifies its greatness. The greatness lies in the way that it's told and the way we come to know the characters and care profoundly about them. It also lies in the greatness of Chekhov's craft, his inimitable compassion for people, like the characters he portrays in this and his other stories and plays. It's ironic that he began writing stories largely to make money to support himself in medical school and help support his family—ironic because he was destined to become one of the greatest of storytellers.

Back we go to the story itself. "The Lady with the Dog" begins in Yalta by the Black Sea, and it's a resort associated with immorality, adventure, and zipless sexual encounters that we discover are perhaps greatly exaggerated. Nevertheless, it's an important initial meeting place for Gurov and Anna, and it's a place Chekhov knew well as a resort. It inspired a desire in those who were bored or looking for more to fill the emptiness in their lives, and certainly, Chekhov captures exactly that within this story.

After the love affair begins, Chekhov moves us to Moscow, where we see Gurov's family life but also the big-city whirl of the bank and the club. Gurov, we're told, at one time had higher aspirations, perhaps to being an artist, but he's living a pretty mundane life—the life of a family man, the life of a businessman—but not necessarily the life that appeals to his inner life, which is brought out to a great extent in the love affair. The provincial town by the Volga where Anna and her husband live is where Gurov goes off to see her. We're given a different picture, but in some ways, they're parallel—that is, his life and hers. Her provincial town is gray; it's a drab, small town. It's certainly not Moscow, the big city, but we get a picture of dullness again, ordinariness. The local theater is having a performance of a theatrical production, ironically, of something called *The Geisha*.

The story is divided in four movements: The first two are in Yalta; the third is in Moscow and the small town where Anna and her husband, von Dideritz, live; and then [the fourth concerns] the visits to Moscow by Anna.

I want to talk with you about the characters, because character is so important in Chekhov—more important, probably, in terms of the roundedness of character. I ought to mention that the great novelist E. M. Forster—the author of *Passage to India*, among some of the other works—wrote a book called *Aspects of the Novel* in which he said there are round characters and there are flat characters. Flat characters are one dimensional, maybe even cardboard, and stereotypical; round characters are characters who have nuance, depth, and multidimensionality. Certainly, Gurov and Anna are presented to us very much as what Forster would have called round characters.

We see Gurov, and we see his wife, and his wife is seen by us through his eyes. She is intellectual and dignified on the outside, but from his point of view, she is unintelligent, narrow, and inelegant, kind of a dowager, really. This division between selves is an important theme in the story as a whole—especially with respect to Gurov—because we discover early on, when we meet his wife, that he has been steadily unfaithful; he has been leading the life, essentially, of a serial philanderer. Nevertheless, we see Gurov through a sympathetic lens supplied to us by Chekhov's point of view and the kind of closeness he has to his protagonist. Gurov is a man who is afraid of his wife and who regards women as a "lower race"—that's the phrase that's used—yet he's more at ease with women. He needs them; he really can't live without them. He's a misogynist—that's a man who is fearful of and maybe even hates women—and he's a man who's in a midlife crisis, who really needs something more in his life and has been searching for something more in his life through all of these serial affairs, which all really ended badly.

We also get a picture of Anna's marriage and, certainly, a very rounded sense of Anna's character. She's childlike, schoolgirlish, and identifiable in a number of ways with Gurov's young and naïve school-age daughter, which is a little bit daring of Chekhov in some ways. She's pious, unhappy, and—as I said—feels sinful for her transgressive behavior, but she also wants desperately to live. It's that desperate sense of wanting to experience life, that sense of being trapped, that brings them together and that they both share. Both are trapped by marriages which are unhappy, by the dicta of the Russian Orthodox Church, which says, of course, that any kind of moral transgression is unforgivable and punishable in hell.

We have, perhaps, in some ways, a situation with Anna that's reminiscent of another famous Anna, Anna Karenina, but could also be likened to Emma Bovary in Flaubert's famous novel of adultery or Kate Chopin's novel *The Awakening* and the character of Edna Pontellier. These are all women who are trapped by morality, their marriages, bourgeois shibboleths—by which I mean sort of sacred cows—and by the desire to move against those sacred cows and find themselves and find, through experience, some sense of life and adventure.

Von Dideritz, Anna's husband, is presented to us by Anna as being a flunky. When we see him at the theater where *The Geisha* is being performed, he is repeatedly bowing like one over and over again. His name and the associations that Chekhov builds up about him have vague German associations, which of course, was no great calling card to many Russians. We can understand, as with the perception we get of Gurov's wife and her effect on Gurov, why Anna is so unhappy. By the way, there's a tendency in Russian writers to poke fun or ridicule Germans; we see this in Gogol's "The Overcoat," as well.

In the story, there are realistic details which really bring us into Chekhov's genius. There's an initial link made by Gurov with the dog and a humorous dialogue that ensues about Grenada. Anna is amused; there are splendid touches, in other words, of Realism in this. It's very difficult to get dialogue and get it down in a way that it seems real, especially the initial kind of electricity or chemistry—or whatever you want to call it—between two people, and to make the dialogue not only credible but to make it have a kind of amusing flair to it, where a man would indeed be charming or attractive to a woman. Yet Chekhov brings this about and brings it about in a very compressed way.

The kind of details I'm talking about that we see in Chekhov can also be exemplified initially, in the first section, when Anna loses her lorgnette. We later see her with one in hand at the provincial theater, as Chekhov identifies it with her ordinariness. There's real understated power in a scene in which Gurov is eating a slice of watermelon while Anna is wallowing in her feelings of sinfulness after the two have become lovers. What Chekhov manages to do is take us through a whole gamut of emotions, [as] when Gurov is moved to reveal his feeling for Anna to a club member later on in the passage that I read and receives that response about the sturgeon being "a bit off."

It's a turning point for him, because earlier on, when we saw him eating a watermelon, he was really not as involved in thinking about her and her feelings, although he manages to turn her character around and they wind up laughing. But there's that sense of her transgressing, her sense of sinfulness, and her sense of idealizing him that comes back to him in Moscow that he can't retreat from. This, by the way, also harkens back to fish-scale imagery that Chekhov gives us earlier on that's identified with, in Gurov's mind, women's underthings when love affairs go south.

When Gurov goes to see Anna, there's a gray carpet made of military cloth. There's an inkstand, gray with dust on it, in the hotel he stays in. There's a dark-gray fence around Anna's house. All of his grayness creates the drabness of her life, but it also shows us the kind of particular attentiveness, almost meticulousness that Chekhov has about details. The gray fence, especially, is revelatory for being fenced in, and we even have details, like the porter in the hotel pronouncing Anna's husband's name in the wrong fashion, or the headless horseman in the hotel room who waves a lot, and of Gurov's forgetting the name of Anna's dog—all these touches. (By the way, he forgets the name when he goes to the small town called "S" only and not identified. It makes you think of Gogol not wanting to identify places or not wanting to identify things specifically.) But what we have in Chekhov is—a moment, for example, when he forgets the name of the dog because he's so overwhelmed by his emotions and his adrenalin—all of these remarkable touches by a sure master storyteller's hand.

I want to get into the meaning of the story and its themes. It's not just a story of infidelity; it's really a story of love and the vagaries of marriage, caged destiny, and of how love can change ordinary people—like Gurov and Anna—and make them better and more compassionate. It is a story of how it can insinuate itself, as it does in Gurov, at an age when his head is turning gray and memories after his separation are involuntarily glowing and vivid rather than fading. There are some readers that express doubt about Gurov's love, particularly because he's aging, because he's in a midlife type of crisis, [and] because he wants to be in love and maybe falls in love for that reason, as opposed to what we call real love, what, as teenagers, we used to talk about as real and authentic love. But I think that it is love, and I think that one of the reasons that this story has had such an effect and is so remarkable is because it's a very touching, tender, passionate, and moving love story about two people who can't really feel the sense of that love bloom, can't let it out into the open, and have to remain closed and furtive, seeing each other only at very special, delicate moments when they can afford to make excuses to get away. In other words, it's an ongoing affair that seems to have a sense of destiny built into it but a destiny that may not be entirely known or predictable in terms of nuances, in terms of its details, particularly.

It's a story of passion and morality. Chekhov was lambasted by the critics of his day for not being moral enough, though he stated clearly in one of his letters that the writer's obligation is to portray through action and not through depiction of state of mind. Chekhov would have subscribed to Isaac Babel's notion that came to us years after Chekhov—in Babel's stories of Odessa—that passion rules the universe. When these two fall in love, it's described as "a sweet delirium or madness," and it's that madness that really takes them into a higher level, into a level of not only intimacy and compassion for one another but compassion for humanity.

It's also a story about beauty, which can best be seen in the contemplative scene that's described for us by Chekhov in Oreanda.

It's a meditation that takes place there by a slightly-more-than-usual obtrusive Chekhov into the beauty of nature and life, the eternal nature and possibility of humanity and human dignity. Note how much more Chekhov, like Gogol, uses authorial comment, yet Chekhov's is vested more in a kind of lyricism and poetry than it is what we could in any way deem as moralizing. He speaks of lofty and higher spheres associated with the beauty of nature and transcendent human emotion but, for the most part, absents himself from the text, particularly morally. The eternal and a higher celestial level are hinted at in the passage at Oreanda, and it's curious that this is done in a transgressive relationship. It's done as these two people are portrayed for us as lovers who are sinning outside of the boundaries of what was considered morally appropriate or acceptable, not only by the Russian Orthodox Church but by the society that Chekhov is writing about at the time that he was writing about it.

There are higher levels in the story that are also alluded to, [for example,] when Gurov talks with his daughter about cold temperatures and when he talks to Anna at the theater production of *The Geisha*, which is—as I said—a pretty revelatory title, but it's not necessarily meant to be that ironic. The point is that they're talking about upper chambers and upper levels. What we get in all of this imagery is a sense, once again, of how love can elevate the human spirit [you can] call it; how love, even if it's transgressive love, can transform.

Does that sound romantic? In many ways, perhaps it is, although Chekhov was really a Realist and a very hardcore Realist. Nevertheless, there was a belief in love—a kind of faith in love—that comes across in the story; as we'll see later on in a story like "Araby" by James Joyce, certainly romantic love seems to be something that's demolished almost and can be catastrophic, especially in a young man's life. But this is an older man—Gurov—who finds love and discovers love, no doubt for the first time.

It's also a story about secret lives: Gurov's realization that there is a life underneath the one that we live within. The mundane and quotidian exists on the outside, but there's a hidden or real life that's authentic, and it's concealed. Ironically, Anna tells her husband, when they're having the affair and after they're separated from Yalta, that she has to travel to Moscow because of "a female disorder"; it's a wonderfully apt metaphor for what drives her secret life. Intertextually, both of these characters are reminiscent of the Poe and Hawthorne stories. We have writers, again, who point in their stories to a wide and impossible chasm that exists between the outer and inner life.

This is a tragic but ennobling story that profoundly captures, without a conclusive ending, the empathy for lives bounded and roads not taken. What especially emerges from this extraordinary story about ordinary people is Chekhov's compassion and his willingness to remain morally neutral in the face of an adulterous relationship. Chekhov's source of humanity is often attributed to his soft and kind storytelling mother, as opposed to his tyrannical and abusive religious-fanatic father. It's worth noting here that before he married the actress Olga Knipper in 1901, Chekhov had at least one love affair with a married woman that we know about, which probably did provide some autobiographic fuel to this story, even though, at the time, unlike Gurov, Chekhov was unmarried. But the humanity of a doctor who treated the poor for free, who had uncommon insight into the mysteries of the heart and of humankind in general, and who was a master of craft all shine through in this story.

Chekhov died in 1904 of tuberculosis. He was first diagnosed with it in 1897 while in Moscow and spent the years after living in Yalta with his mother and sister and traveling to Moscow, where Olga, his wife, resided. His influence cannot be overstated. If Russian writers came in under Gogol's "The Overcoat," a legion of writers came in under Chekhov, including Virginia Woolf, as well as two writers that we'll be looking at and studying: James Joyce and Katherine Mansfield.

Hemingway, who tended to be pretty competitive with writers living or dead, called Chekhov an amateur and said he really only had six good stories. But he still acknowledged that six of them were really good, and that was difficult for Hemingway to do (that is, acknowledge the talent of any other writer). One of Chekhov's most devoted disciples was a short story writer whom we'll meet later on, whom many consider to be one of the best of the 20th century: Raymond Carver. I mention Carver because Carver wrote a story about Chekhov's death—a famous story called "Errand"—in which he sought really to capture Chekhov's death and give us all of the details of Chekhov with tuberculosis, his suffering, and to capture the sense of who the man was.

Speaking of great masters, we next go to the only fiction writer who has been called—and, to this day, continues to be called—*the* master. Henry James lived a lot longer than Poe, Gogol, Maupassant, and Chekhov, who all died before they were 45 years of age. Perhaps James becoming a man able to pass seven decades and the fact that he devoted his life to literary art and produced a great body of work—including novels, like *The Ambassadors* and *Portrait of a Lady*, as well as literary criticism and short stories—accounts at least in part for his having been beatified as the master.

Here's Chekhov, on the one hand, regarded as perhaps one of the leading figures in terms of the development of the modern short story, certainly one of the central figures in literature as both a dramatist and a short story writer. Then we have James, a central figure in both the novel and the short story: two really remarkable figures in the cannon of literature. We move on next to study Henry James. "The Real Thing" is the story that we'll be focusing on and is the story which will conclude our first cluster of six short fiction masterpieces all based in 19th-century storytelling. This is a story which perhaps brings us to the crest of Realism. Chekhov brings us to a kind of mountaintop in so many ways with what he does with character, with the opening up of plot. But as we move into Henry James—as we move into the work of the master—we'll see a storyteller who nevertheless can focus on Realism and make us very confused about what is art and what is real; where representation comes in, or appearance, and what is indeed reality. On we go, onward and—to echo Chekhov—upward to Henry James and "The Real Thing."

Lecture Six

James in the Art Studio—"The Real Thing"

Scope:

Henry James was a master storyteller and a writer at the crest of Realism. In this lecture, we give proper respect to the important role James played in literature and the creation of psychological realism and to his thoughts about the form of fiction, as seen in the idea of "the figure in the carpet." From there, we move to the story "The Real Thing" and its origins in James's respect for and desire to emulate Maupassant. The lecture then focuses on how the story works as a moral parable on the creation of art, on reality and appearance, and on amateurism and professionalism. We continue with an elucidation of the moral questions raised in the story and the roles of the characters in terms of the social class divide. We also discuss the perspective brought in by the narrator's painter friend, Jack Hawley, which casts the story's ultimate meaning into a kind of ambiguity. The lecture concludes with a discussion of the values and power of human transformation and memory that appear to be implicit in the story, with the caveat that there may yet be another reality underneath that appearance.

Outline

I. Henry James has earned the title of master because of his fictional work and his contributions to literary theory and criticism.

   A. James's brother William was a famous psychologist and the father of American pragmatism. An old saw has it that William was the psychologist who wrote like a novelist and Henry the novelist who wrote like a psychologist.

   B. Many of James's tales are deeply psychological—*The Turn of the Screw*, for example—and tread into nuances of human behavior. James also brings us to the crest of 19th-century Realism.

   C. James advanced the idea of "the figure in the carpet," by which he meant that all the details of a story should be tied in with the greater themes; every fiber of the carpet in a story must contribute to its overall loom, as opposed to a wider canvas.

D. "The Real Thing" came from a story told to James by George du Maurier, which became the premise (*donnée*) for a work of short fiction by James.

E. James had developed a friendship with Guy de Maupassant and wanted to write a story with a lesson, one as "admirably compact and celebrated as Maupassant."

II. The story is a parable on the nature of the creation of art.

A. The Monarchs are the real thing, but art, including the literary art of creating short fiction, is, by its nature, representational. It requires alchemy or plasticity, as well as the artistic imagination, working together with the real.

B. The classic literary theme of the division and interaction between appearance and reality infuses its meaning into the story. We discover that the artist requires the vehicle of imagination to transform reality into appearance, to hold the mirror up to nature in order to make something real from raw material that is not real.

C. The imagination can transfigure a cockney Eliza Doolittle type, like Miss Churm, into a Russian princess or a poor Italian peasant and street peddler, like Oronte, into a gentleman.

D. Subjects like the Monarchs (the name is transparently significant of how they appear) look majestic but cannot be rendered with any imaginative life beyond a kind of photographic replication. Realism needs the vitality of the imagination.

III. The story is also a representation of the social divide between classes, with the embedded irony of the Monarchs being near destitution and having to cede their rank to learn a different reality in the artist's studio. Jack Hawley becomes the "fresh eye" who sees and corroborates the chasm of the social divide and its connection to the failure of art to be ignited with real life.

A. When Mrs. Monarch cries, it is because she recognizes the gap between their appearance as a couple of social class versus their need and willingness to do nearly anything to survive.

B. The class divisions appear obvious, but are they? Miss Churm and Oronte have a talent for imitation and the Monarchs are amateurs. They are types, but types, we discover, are not the real thing.

C. Yet the Monarchs are also noble and dignified people. They are real people, as well as representations of a certain social class of gentlefolk, a gentleman and his lady. Their marriage is "a real marriage." They are types, but they are also individuals.

D. Jack Hawley's enmity against the class system and his image of the Monarchs as types lead him to believe that they don't belong in the artist's studio. But the reality is that they do, because they create for the artist another reality grounded in memory.

IV. Values emerge from the story's lesson about appearance and reality that ultimately elevate the story to an even higher plane.

A. A friendship emerges between the narrator and the Monarchs, and the narrator gains a deeper and more compassionate understanding of the real and the appearance of the real that will enable him to grow as an artist.

B. There is personal growth and transformation in the story, as well—especially in what the narrator learns from the Monarchs. He represents the couple as colossal in his paintings, only to discover the essential humanity in both of them that makes him "content to have paid the price for the memory."

C. The story rises above many of its intricate and well-woven themes to give us a moving sense of all that can occur as a result of human contact and the value of the real memories created in that contact.

Suggested Readings:

Edel, *Henry James.*

James, *The Beast in the Jungle*.

———, *Daisy Miller*.

———, "The Genesis of the Real Thing."

———, *The Jolly Corner*.

———, "The Real Thing."

———, *The Turn of the Screw*.

Questions to Consider:

1. How reliable is the narrator in this story? Can we believe completely in his contentment with memory and his growth as an artist or are there reasons that cast doubt?
2. How does the opening paragraph of the story reveal to us many of its essential paradoxes with respect to understanding character?
3. Did James succeed in providing us a "magnificent lesson" in this story?

Lecture Six—Transcript

James in the Art Studio—"The Real Thing"

Henry James has earned the title of master because of his oeuvre—his body of work—and the contributions he has made to literary theory and criticism. His output was prodigious; one would be hard-pressed to find a more consummate man or woman of letters. James wrote novels, biography, autobiography, journalism, plays, travel accounts, reportage, literary criticism, and 112 stories. He published his first story when he was 21. He was prolific and deeply and passionately committed to the literary life and made a living with the writer's life. He also wrote with considerably more detail and length: He was said to have found the 8,000-word limit typical of his era of short story magazine length to be confining, and he called his short fiction "nouvelles."

The story we will be discussing, "The Real Thing," is over 10,000 words. Of the stories we have discussed or will discuss, only Gogol's "The Overcoat" (which was Lecture Three) and Baldwin's "Sonny's Blues" (which will be Lecture Eighteen) are longer stories. James published "The Real Thing" in 1891, when he was 48; a famous James story, *Daisy Miller*, was published in 1878; and James was still publishing great stories like "The Beast in the Jungle" and "The Jolly Corner" in 1903, when he was 60.

He came from a distinguished and prominent New York family, though he spent most of his early life in Europe. He wound up an American expatriate in Britain, renouncing his American citizenship and becoming a naturalized British citizen after the United States would initially not join Britain and France in the First World War. James's brother William was a famous psychologist and the father of American pragmatism. There is an old saw that William James was a psychologist who wrote like a novelist, and Henry James was a novelist who wrote like a psychologist.

Many of James's tales are deeply psychological—*The Turn of the Screw*, for example, published in 1898—and they tread into nuances of human behavior. James also brings us to the crest of 19th-century Realism. His interest in painting, especially Impressionism, was strong and can be seen in the story "The Real Thing." Much of his work concerned the nuances and subtleties of a kind of drawing-room—or, certainly, upper-crust—world, but as we see in "The Real Thing," James also took great interest in grappling with large questions having to do with aesthetics, art, the role of the artist, and the difference between commercial art or more serious, highly aspiring art. These are central in "The Real Thing," and they deviate from the concerns we have found in Chekhov or even Maupassant, for whom James had a great deal of admiration.

James advanced the idea of "the figure in the carpet," by which he meant that stories needed to have all of the details tied in with the greater themes and every i dotted, every t crossed, every fiber of the carpet in a story contributing to its overall loom, as opposed to a wider canvas. This extended into a debate about the novel called the saturation-selection debate, featuring James's notion of compactness and selectivity, on the one hand, and H. G. Wells's idea that fiction can have a broader and more expansive, less compact canvas. The debate emerged years later when F. Scott Fitzgerald wrote *The Great Gatsby*. For James, it constituted nothing less than a debate about aesthetics.

This story has its genesis and origins in a story related to James of an actual incident, told to him by his friend George du Maurier. It became the *donnée*—or given premise—that he wanted to expand into short fiction. James had developed a friendship with Maupassant and wanted to write a story, like Maupassant, with a lesson, one as—quoting James now—"admirably compact and celebrated as Maupassant."

James was, like Chekhov, not a moralist but deeply interested in realistically portraying moral questions of great seriousness and intellectual weight. In the notebook that included fragments of ideas that he would turn into stories, he wrote that he wanted this particular story to include "a magnificent lesson." The lesson in "The Real Thing" is disconnected from the moral universe of theology and right or wrong behavior or good and evil. It has to do—in many ways—more with art, as well as with humanity, but particularly, with the imagination and, like Maupassant's "The Necklace," the differences between appearance and reality. Essentially, it's a story of an unnamed artist who creates illustrations for potboiling-type cheap books.

The Monarchs are a well-bred, aristocratic couple who come to the artist's studio, and he assumes they want to be painted by him, but it turns out they're indigent; they want work as models. This initial confusion about the appearance of reality versus reality sets up for us the major motif in the story or certainly one of the major motifs. The Monarchs cannot even pose for what presumably they are—an upper-class couple—because the artist draws them as larger than they actually are, and he can't transpose them to fit other roles. We see this in contrast to his other pair of models, a working-class British woman named Miss Churm and an Italian-ice street vendor named Oronte.

Miss Churm, the artist/narrator tells us—he has no name in this story, and as we move into the 20th century, we'll see many more narrators who have no name—"was only a freckled cockney, but she could represent everything, from a fine lady to a shepherdess."

He tells us of Oronte, his other model: "He was sallow but fair, and when I put him into some old clothes of my own he looked like an Englishman. He was as good as Miss Churm, who could look, when requested, like an Italian." Both models are able, somehow, to act as catalysts for what the narrator calls "the alchemy of art." They can pose in ways that allow for representing them as what they are not, while the poor Monarchs, as far as the narrator and his art are concerned, can't be anything but what they are—the real thing—particularly for the illustrations that he's doing. The narrator says, "When I drew the Monarchs I couldn't anyhow get away from them—get into the character I wanted to represent; and I hadn't the least desire my model should be discoverable in my picture."

The story is short but, in James's word, magnificent in its lesson on the nature of the creation of art. The Monarchs are the real thing, but art—including, of course, literary art, creating short fiction—by its nature is representational. It must have that alchemy or plasticity, as well as the imagination, working together with what's real. The classic literary theme of this division and interaction between appearance and reality infuses its meaning into the story, as we discover that the artist requires the vehicle of his imagination to transform reality into appearance, to hold the mirror up to nature in order to make something real from raw material which is not real, what the poet Marianne Moore in 1923 would call "imaginary gardens with real toads in them."

The imagination can transfigure a cockney Eliza Doolittle–type like Miss Churm into a Russian princess or a poor Italian peasant and a street peddler like Oronte into a gentleman. The Monarchs can only look like what they appear to be, though once the narrator imagines the Major as a footman, the Monarchs begin to move from appearance to the reality of their poverty: to being tea servers and appearing noble, heroic, and admirable to the narrator in the process. As Mrs. Monarch fixes Miss Churm's hair and picks up a dirty rag and the Major picks up "breakfast things," models become servants, and servants become models.

Subjects like the Monarchs—the name is transparently significant of how they appear—look majestic, perhaps even regal, but they can't be rendered with any imaginative life beyond a kind of photographic replication, at least not by the narrator in trying to use them as models for his illustrations. Realism, James is suggesting, needs the vitality of the imagination. James appears to be saying it needs that vitality lest it be simply a replication, a photograph that duplicates reality rather than a work of art that infuses it with a life of its own.

Moreover, the Monarchs are the real thing in their appearance, but underneath the surface appearance of gentlefolk of higher social status is a couple out of work, at the end of their economic options, barely surviving hand-to-mouth, and desperate for—though highly unsuitable for most—work. They are a couple who are deeply devoted to one another as well, and we learn that they have a strong marriage. This all takes us into deeper levels beyond the appearance as we begin to understand their humanity in the story through the narrator's eyes. But their appearance is more of the stiff-upper-lip kind of cool and detached British aristocracy. Reality is apart from appearance and can only be captured by the artist's imagination.

The story is also a representation of the social divide between the classes, with the embedded irony of the Monarchs being near destitution and having to cede their rank to learn a different reality within the artist's studio. James had the advantage of seeing the British class system as it was being challenged from within from his unique perspective as an American outsider. Jack Hawley—a character in the story who is the narrator/artist's friend—becomes the "fresh eye" who sees and corroborates the chasm of the social divide and its connection to the failure of the art to be ignited with real life.

When Mrs. Monarch cries, as she does in the story, it's because she recognizes the gap between their appearance as a couple of social class versus their need and willingness to do just about anything they can to survive. The Major says, ironically, that her getting a job as a secretary is like getting a peerage. Mrs. Monarch winces at Miss

Churm's wet umbrella, and Miss Churm makes a scene about serving tea, and the class divisions appear obvious to us. But are they? Miss Churm and Oronte have a talent for imitation, but the Monarchs are amateurs. They are types, but types, we discover, are not the real thing. The real thing seems to be the same thing and not a fluid thing like the appearance of reality projected by Oronte and Miss Churm. But through the course of the story, as we get deeper into understanding the Monarchs and their humanity, they become the real thing in another sense. It's like a lot of Chinese boxes or a kind of labyrinthine world that James presents [to] us between appearance on the one hand and reality on the other, between what can lift something into art as opposed to just potboiling illustrations, types as opposed to distinct individuals, amateurs as apart from professionals. There's all this binary in the story—this division or dichotomy—of so many things that makes for its richness.

The Monarchs are really noble and dignified people, and that's what they appear to be. They're real people, as well as types representational of a certain social class of gentlefolk, a gentleman and his lady, if you will. It turns out that their marriage is "a real marriage." They are types, but they are also individuals, humans. Jack Hawley's enmity against the class system and his seeing the Monarchs as types lead him—and he's a good critic but not so good a painter—to feel that they don't belong in the artist's studio, but the reality is that they do, because they create for the artist another reality grounded in memory.

Values ultimately emerge from the story's lesson about appearance and reality and elevate the story to an even greater plane. Let me get to the beginning of the story because there is certainly distinctiveness about James's style that one recognizes in the way he uses detail and in the way he presents a picture to us. Remember that this is the opening of the story, where the Monarchs come to the unnamed artist's place, but they come not—as he perceives it—to be painted; they come to be models, and they're looking for work.

> When the porter's wife, who used to answer the house-bell, announced, "A gentleman and a lady, sir," I had, as I often had in those days—the wish being father to the thought—an immediate vision of sitters. [Naturally, he's up there; he paints portraits; they announce a gentleman and a lady; and he thinks they've come looking for their portrait to be

> drawn.] Sitters my visitors in this case proved to be; but not in the sense I should have preferred. There was nothing at first however to indicate that they mightn't have come for a portrait. [This allows James to give us a fine description of the couple; notice how he does this.] The gentleman, a man of fifty, very high and very straight, with a moustache, slightly grizzled and a dark grey walking-coat admirably fitted, both of which I noted professionally—I don't mean as a barber or yet as a tailor—would have struck me as a celebrity if celebrities often were striking. It was a truth of which I had for some time been conscious that a figure with a good deal of frontage was, as one might say, almost never a public institution.

Notice the narrator bringing in his own perceptions here, but we're seeing how he thinks—or understanding how he sees things—and that's very important. It's his point of view that takes us through the whole story.

> A glance at the lady helped to remind me of this paradoxical law: she also looked too distinguished to be a "personality." Moreover one would scarcely come across two variations together.

He's talking about types—he's talking about celebrities—as opposed to, again, the way people appear. There's a whole kind of embedded philosophy of observation, if you will, and again, the difference between appearance and reality that come straight to us.

> Neither of the pair immediately spoke—they only prolonged the preliminary gaze suggesting that each wished to give the other a chance. They were visibly shy; they stood there letting me take them in—which, as I afterwards perceived, was the most practical thing they could have done. In this way their embarrassment served their cause. [He's speaking about this with the knowledge that they were there not to have their portraits painted but to get jobs as models.] I have seen people painfully reluctant to mention that they desired anything so gross as to be represented on canvas; but the scruples of my new friends appeared almost insurmountable. Yet the gentleman might have said "I should like a portrait of my wife," and the lady might have said "I should like a portrait of my husband." Perhaps they weren't husband and

> wife—this naturally would make the matter more delicate. Perhaps they wished to be done together—in which case they ought to have brought a third person to break the news.

You see his mind is traveling all over here, thinking: What are they here for? He's trying to get the real picture, the real thing, of what they're doing there.

> "We come from Mr. Rivet," [right as a rivet] the lady finally said with a dim smile that had the effect of a moist sponge passed over a "sunk" piece of painting, as well as of a vague allusion to vanished beauty.

Notice what James is able to do in one sentence there: seeing things from a painter's point of view—like a sponge on a canvas, in terms of the way he's seeing the woman—but also giving us that sense that she was probably beautiful at one time but has aged.

> She was as tall and straight, in her degree, as her companion, and with ten years less to carry. She looked as sad as a woman could look whose face was not charged with expression; that is, her tinted oval mask showed waste as an exposed surface shows friction. The hand of time had played over her freely, but to an effect of elimination. She was slim and stiff, and so well-dressed, in dark blue cloth, with lappets and pockets and buttons, that it was clear she employed the same tailor as her husband. The couple had an identifiable air of prosperous thrift—they evidently got a good deal of luxury for their money. If I was to be one of their luxuries it would behoove me to consider my terms.

Here, again, he's hoping that he's going to be able to draw them. But you notice how he's sizing them up: He's looking at their clothes, their countenances. He's looking at essentially what they're presenting simply in terms of what they look like, what their appearance is. But, of course, as the story moves on, we discover they were recommended to see him by Mr. Rivet, not to be models for him to get money for painting, but to offer themselves as models so that they can get compensated because they need work.

What happens in the story as it evolves is really a friendship that takes place between the narrator and the Monarchs, as well as a deeper and more compassionate understanding of the real—and the appearance of the real—that will enable this narrator perhaps to grow as an artist. He doesn't necessarily want to be doing potboiler illustrations; he wants to be a more serious artist. He wants to be an artist more worthy of being an artist or having the nomenclature "artist."

There is personal growth and transformation in the story, as well, especially in what the narrator learns from the Monarchs, whom he represents initially as colossal in his paintings, only to discover their essential humanity. That makes him, as he says at the end—whether we believe him or not is another story—"content to have paid the price for the memory," that is, the price of hiring them and really having them come and pose when, to some extent, they simply don't work for his imagination. He can't ignite his imagination to do these kinds of illustrations with them because they look like what they are, and yet he understands, in the course of the story, that they're much more than what they appear to be.

He sees much in them and in the transformation that they have for both him and us to admire, in what he describes as their "latent eloquence." They wind up doing servile domestic tasks, holding to the studio for the warmth of the fire like charity cases, but maintaining their dignity, and even as the narrator feels "dreadful to see them emptying my slops," he recognizes that something has occurred here, some kind of transformation has occurred. It's the kind of transformation that frankly could occur as a result of the artistic imagination. Characters are changed from types to something quite different, from the appearance of what they might be—or what they might even *be*—to something that embodies that but that becomes magically different.

This story rises above many of its intricate and well-woven themes to give us a rather moving sense of all that can emerge and all that is real that can occur as a result of human contact and the value of the real memories that are created. Yet there is possibly another paradoxical reality underneath that appearance that we get at the end of the story, in the narrator's point of view, of personal memories to cherish when the Monarchs are remembered in sadness. Jack Hawley is cited in the story's final sentence as telling the narrator that the Monarchs did him "a permanent harm," got him "into false ways."

Let's go to the end of the story and see what James is getting at here, which isn't all that simple, to be sure:

> The Major meanwhile had also been looking for something to do, and, wandering to the other end of the studio, saw before him my breakfast-things neglected, unremoved. "I can say, can't I be useful *here*?" he called out to me with an irrepressible quaver. I assented with a laugh that I fear was awkward, and for the next ten minutes, while I worked, I heard the light clatter of china and the tinkle of spoons and glass.

Before this takes place—and you really get that sense of nuance from James, a subtlety with which he can present character and bring a rounded sense, a full sense, of character out for us—before that, we heard Mrs. Monarch in her sweet voice (it says, "beside, or rather above me"), saying, "I wish her hair were a little better done" (talking about Miss Churm, the model).

I looked up and she was staring with a strange fixedness at Miss Churm, whose back was turned to her. "Do you mind my just touching it?" she went on—a question which made me spring up for an instant, as with the instinctive fear that she might do the young lady a harm. But she quieted me with a glance I shall never forget—I confess I should liked to have been able to paint *that*. There you see that kind of subtlety of James's hand, along with the eye of the artist. Just in one glance, James gives us that whole movement from being afraid that this lady is going to do some harm to Miss Churm to realizing that everything is just fine. Now back to Major Monarch in the last moments in the story:

"Mrs. Monarch assisted her husband—they washed up my crockery, they put it away." Again, they're acting in a way that they need to, to just be useful, but it also reflects their real need for some kind of occupation, for some kind of job or a way to bring in at least some income. This is very difficult because these are dignified people. These are people who we see throughout the story have a sense of not only class about them but real class. They appear to be of the higher class because they are the higher class, but they're also classy people.

> They wandered off into my little scullery, and I afterwards found that they had cleaned my knives and that my slender stock of plate had an unprecedented surface. [Here's the narrator's perception of things.] When it came over me, the

> latent eloquence of what they were doing, I confess that my drawing was blurred for a moment …

It's his slight sense of people just wandering around, doing tasks of this sort—menial tasks—but it really has an effect on this artist with his artistic sensibility. It really penetrates him, at least at this moment, and it becomes so blurred—what he's drawing—that he tells us "the picture swam." This is his perception of the Monarchs, he says,

> They had accepted their failure, but they couldn't accept their fate. They had bowed their heads in bewilderment to the perverse and cruel law in virtue of which the real thing could be so much less precious than the unreal; but they didn't want to starve. If my servants were my models, then my models might be my servants. They would reverse the parts—the others would sit for the ladies and gentlemen, and *they* would do the work. They would still be in the studio—it was an intense dumb appeal to me not to turn them out. "Take us on," they wanted to say—"we'll do *anything*."

But this is his perception, and certainly we believe that perception from everything we've seen of the Monarchs and from the way that they're behaving.

> My pencil dropped from my hand; [Just in that gesture alone, you see the effect and the impact that this has had on him.] my sitting was spoiled and I got rid of my sitters, who were also evidently rather mystified and awestruck. Then, alone with the Major and his wife I had a most uncomfortable moment. He put their prayer into a single sentence: "I say, you know—just let *us* do for you, can't you?" I couldn't—it was dreadful to see them emptying my slops; but I pretended I could, to oblige them, for about a week. Then I gave them a sum of money to go away; and I never saw them again. I obtained the remaining books, but my friend Hawley repeats that Major and Mrs. Monarch did me a permanent harm, got me into false ways. If it be true I am content to have paid the price—for the memory.

We're left with that ambiguity: Did Hawley see things right, or does the narrator see things right? We don't really know when we come to the end of the story, and we don't know because, to a great extent, we have seen the constant fluctuation between what's real and what appears to be real, between the real thing, as the title suggests, and what may indeed be the real thing.

A lot of this has to do with the narrator's creating these potboiler illustrations. These don't seem to be the real thing, and yet they have a reality about them. They're done for commercial or mercantile reasons, if you will, but they're also done with the necessity of the artistic imagination. It's as if James wants to say to us, "Well, you can talk all you want to in a demeaning way about commercial art or art that's done for commercial reasons, but it still requires that quickening of the artistic imagination to make the representation real." Remember that this was a writer who built his life economically around writing. We get that sense, in other words, that the commercial may be the real thing or may certainly have the elements of the real thing where art is concerned. But does that mean that, by contrast, art—the highest kind of art that artists aspire to, that this artist aspires to—may have less than the real thing or may not be real?

It's one of those sort of quandaries that Henry James is so gifted at presenting to readers and making readers grapple with. It's one of the things that makes his art so special in the minds of those who particularly appreciate what he can do as a writer. He brings us into this sometimes confusing world of appearance and reality in ways that probably are inimitable, that we see in perhaps a few other writers, but we don't see with this kind of exacting detail or the kind of concentration that we see in a story like this. Remember that his stories are longer, and his stories have much more detail. We saw that in the early passage I read with all the detail that's given to us that's important, but he nonetheless sounds like a tailor or a barber at one point. He says, "No, I'm not a barber, but you know I size people up for portraits. I have to look at what they're wearing. I have to get a sense of their type. I have to see how they're groomed, what their tonsorial facts are. I have to get a picture of them." That allows James, of course, to give us a picture of the characters—very clever on James's part.

But nevertheless, what he's doing is bringing us into the world of art, bringing us into this artist's studio, making us comfortable in this artist's studio, but making us also realize that an artist's studio is not a place of pure high-art aspirations. It's a place of commerce, particularly if the artist is producing work that's going to be sold and needs to do that kind of work in order to, perhaps, support the real art that he feels, in this case, he wants to be creating and that he's particularly drawn to. We know so many artists who write in order to make what they think are their greater expectations, as far as their own artistic impulses are concerned.

We see in a story like "The Real Thing" the kind of aesthetic battle that goes on, and maybe "battle" was too strong a word, but it is a kind of battle. Nietzsche can talk about the battle of the sexes; I can talk about the battle between aesthetic aspirations, on the one hand, for a higher and loftier art and the world of commercial art and illustrations, because what you begin to see is that they both require a kind of—I'll use the word propinquity advisedly—closeness or intimacy to what is real and what is illusory, what is actual or authentic and what is made up or imagined. They both, in other words, require the essentials of art. You can't write commercial or potboiler art, even if you don't want to call it art, without that same kind of impulse.

I once spent a good deal of time wanting to be a novelist, and I realized I couldn't be the kind of artist that I wanted to be, just having a dearth of talent and missing the kind of talent necessary—I'm only missing that slight ingredient—but I also thought that perhaps I could write a potboiler. I remember reading all these potboilers by potboiler novelists, like Harold Robbins, and Jacqueline Susann, and even later on, Tom Clancy. I didn't have it in me. It needs a drive; it needs an artistic drive or something like the artistic drive. John Grisham has that drive. You may not admire him as much as you admire, say, another novelist, like Scott Turow, who writes detective novels and courtroom novels, too, that aren't nearly as potboiling, but nevertheless, it takes the desire, drive, and whatever it is that puts the words onto the paper.

We leave Henry James and "The Real Thing" for now, and we move on to the 20th century and another cluster of stories. It's almost appropriate in many ways to leave James as we do right at the crest of the 20th century, because we leave a certain kind of storytelling. We move into what is often described as Modernism, and we begin with another initiation story by the famous great Irish writer James Joyce, whom many consider the 20th century's greatest novelist. Like Henry James, Joyce was a prodigious talent, as well as an expatriate who left his native Ireland but discovered that Ireland never left his imagination, even when he lived away from it.

Joyce not only marks the turn of a new century for us, but he also marks a decided turn towards symbolism and what would come to be called Modernism. He was a writer, like Henry James, who was completely and totally dedicated to his art; he was a consummate writer and literary artist. He was a writer of realistic stories, but he also conferred a poetic sensibility onto his short fiction, as well as his novels. He gave us the great novel *Ulysses*, as well as other major works of fiction, and gave us one of the 20th century's finest collections of short fiction, called *Dubliners*.

To some degree, James Joyce and Henry James were contemporaries, but yet when we go from Henry James to James Joyce, as we're doing, we see a kind of quantum jump, in many ways, from one kind of storytelling to another—both great storytellers, both capable of producing masterpieces. Next on our list, another short fiction masterpiece, a great one from the canon of the great James Joyce, and from *Dubliners*, "Araby."

Lecture Seven

Epiphany and the Modern in Joyce's "Araby"

Scope:

James Joyce, one of the 20th century's most respected writers, is most well known for his inventive use of language, his incorporation of archetype and myth in this work, and his concept of the epiphany, which plays a central role in his story "Araby." Also central to the story are the Catholic Church and some of the major concerns of Modernism. This lecture explicates the archetypal journey of the young protagonist in "Araby" and the initiation into an inner world of profound darkness for both the boy and the reader. We also discuss the important role of symbolism in the story and Joyce's influence on other writers in this arena. The lecture concludes with an assessment of why the story continues to have enduring power.

Outline

I. "Araby" is from a collection of stories by James Joyce called *Dubliners*, first published in 1914. The collection as a whole gives us a kaleidoscopic picture of constricted, repressed, and impoverished lives.

   A. North Richmond Street, where "Araby" begins, is a dilapidated though decent neighborhood. From the outset, the street is described as "blind," and early in the story, we get a picture of children playing in shadows.

   B. "Araby" is a coming-of-age story, a story of adolescence and a journey of discovery.

   C. It is the quest of a young boy, smitten by what he believes to be love, who commits himself to an excursion to an exotic-sounding destination, the bazaar called Araby, only ultimately to be disillusioned.

   D. The story is an awakening but also a loss of romantic idealism, similar to the movement in literature of the time away from Romanticism to a harsher Realism and Modernism.

II. "Araby" is built, like all the stories in *Dubliners*, around the notion of an epiphany—a Joycean term that refers to an ephemeral moment of spiritual-like revelation. Such a moment occurs suddenly and may manifest itself in vulgar (common) speech, an everyday gesture, or a memorable expression of the mind. We as readers experience the protagonist's epiphany through his enlightenment at the story's conclusion.

III. Irish Catholicism is at the heart of the story and infuses its meaning. We note, for example, the juxtaposition of fantasy and the romance of the imagination with the religious world of Irish Catholic practice and the tawdry surroundings in which the boy lives.

- **A.** The Christian Brothers' School, we are told, "set the boys free," suggesting early on the metaphor of institutional imprisonment for their lives.
- **B.** A former tenant of the family, a priest, left behind in his room the romantic works of Sir Walter Scott and the yellow-leafed *Memoirs of Vidocq*, both of which offer an escape from the isolated and musty life associated with another work left behind: *The Devout Communicant*.
- **C.** Nothing frivolous, worldly, lustful, or romantic can emerge from the nearly ubiquitous power of the Church or the drabness of the Dublin world.
  - **1.** The countenance of the boy's teacher turns to sternness at the perception of his becoming idle and, thereby, inviting the mind to become the devil's playground.
  - **2.** The boy's aunt wants to make sure Araby is not "some Freemason affair."
  - **3.** Mrs. Mercer, we are told, collects stamps for some pious purpose.

IV. The story immerses us in Modernism.

- **A.** The Modernist movement was steeped in criticism of the church and other powerful institutions and the portrayal of what T. S. Eliot and others would later show as urban decay tied to the industrialism of the age.
- **B.** The Modernist view was also tied to disillusionment with Romanticism and to themes of waste and spiritual desolation—themes that run strong in Joyce's story.
- **C.** The point of view in the story is of a man looking back on his moment of disillusion. The point of view in Modernism

is often complex, somehow simultaneously in the present and the past.

D. The story is replete with symbolism, which would become one of the hallmarks of the Modernist movement in literature, connecting back to Flaubert and Baudelaire. Moreover, Modernist symbolism has multivalent associations and meanings.

V. Creeping past "ruinous houses" and "a twinkling river," the boy travels on his romantic errand in a third-class carriage of a deserted train.

A. The bazaar called Araby turns out to be an ordinary shop of dim lights and shop girls—from no father east than England—who are really concerned only with money.

B. The epiphany occurs at the end of the story, when the boy is crushed by anguish and anger and derided by vanity—feelings tied directly to the Catholic teachings he has neglected in his pursuit of love.

C. The ambiguity in the story's meaning can be seen in the attitude of the adult narrator describing his epiphanic moment as a boy surrounded by darkness.

1. This perspective may be reminiscent of Joyce's Stephen Dedalus in *Stephen Hero* or *A Portrait of the Artist as a Young Man*, a character who has grown from his youthful feelings of vanity and derision.

2. At the same time, the narrator may still see himself as a boy having been appropriately derided by vanity for his foolish romanticism.

VI. It is no accident that "Araby" is so often read, taught, and anthologized.

A. The epiphany has a profound impact on the reader—the story takes us from the romantic idealization of youth, a kind of Blakean innocence, to the crushing sense of the real and of experience. We move through an initiation into the darkness of modernity.

B. The point of view and the voice are both remarkably intricate and evocative.

C. The language is richly poetic and captures the distinct voice and inner life of the unnamed boy protagonist.

Suggested Readings:

Ellmann, *James Joyce.*

Joyce, "Araby."

———, *Dubliners.*

———, *A Portrait of the Artist as a Young Man.*

———, *Stephen Hero.*

———, *Ulysses.*

Questions to Consider:

1. How do we separate the feelings that the boy in "Araby" experiences from those of the man who is telling us the story?
2. Can this story be separated from its Irish setting or Catholic religious frame? Should it be?
3. Is the epiphany at the conclusion of "Araby" more for the boy or the reader? Or both?

Lecture Seven—Transcript
Epiphany and the Modern in Joyce's "Araby"

The realism and the careful plotting we found in 19th-century short fiction—notwithstanding Chekhov's more open plot in "The Lady with the Dog"—take a decided turn as we make our way into the 20th century and Modernism. The story "Araby" is from a collection of stories by James Joyce called *Dubliners*, first published in 1914. It's the third story in the collection and one of the best-known ones in the volume, which presents a collection of portraits of a desolate and grimy Dublin with lives of ordinary Dubliners and also a view of the religious entrenchment of the Catholic Church.

Born in 1882 in Dublin, Joyce—one of the 20th century's most respected and venerated writers—became an expatriate and lived in Zurich, Trieste, Pula, Rome, and ultimately, in Paris. He was a cosmopolitan in his living quarters but returned inevitably to his roots and to the regional world of Dublin. He was educated in Jesuit schools and at University College Dublin but left both nation and the Catholic Church to—like Henry James—devote his life to literary art. He wrote famous novels—perhaps the century's most famous, *Ulysses*—as well as the semi-autobiographical *A Portrait of the Artist as a Young Man* and *Finnegan's Wake*.

He's best known for his inventive and original use of language, his mastery of the stream-of-consciousness technique that was also used by writers like Virginia Woolf and William Faulkner, and his use of archetypes, myth, and what he called the epiphany, a word that he made famous. What this represents is a moment of a revelation of truth for a character in a story. Myth, archetype, and epiphany are all prominently used by Joyce in his classic masterpiece story "Araby," which is a tale of Irish poverty, the constriction of the Catholic Church, and a young boy's disillusionment with romantic idealism, the kinds of things that we came to associate with the work of James Joyce.

The opening paragraph of Joyce, just to get a feel for him and of the story "Araby," [reads]:

> North Richmond Street, being blind, was a quiet street except at the hour when the Christian Brothers' School set the boys free. An uninhabited house of two storeys stood at the blind end, detached from its neighbours in a square

> ground. The other houses of the street, conscious of decent lives within them, gazed at one another with brown imperturbable faces.

Here Joyce is setting us up for not only the street where the action takes place initially in the story, but he's telling us that the street is "blind" and giving us a whole sense of its people simply not seeing what they should be seeing. [He is also] making the houses personified as living with decent lives or being somehow even cognizant of even having decent lives within them: "brown imperturbable faces," he tells us, "conscious of decent lives," gazing with "imperturbable faces."

What does this all suggest to us? It suggests, certainly, a setting of a street, but then you have the Christian brothers setting the boys free. There's that feeling right away of a kind of blindness, imprisonment, and living a decent life—or trying to live a decent life—but what might be behind that attempt to live a decent life or what might be forcing or compelling these particular Dubliners on North Richmond Street to live a decent life. This is all part of the Dublin setting, and the *Dubliners*—the whole collection—is important in providing a kaleidoscopic picture of impoverished lives and lives that are repressed. We never even discover the name of the narrator, nor do we discover the name of the young woman he adores. By the way, a lot of modern literature puts us into this world of namelessness—James's story "The Real Thing" even has a nameless narrator—but particularly, we find that identity becomes tenuous, vulnerable, and fragile as we move into the 20th century. People don't necessarily have names in stories, or at least main characters don't have names.

North Richmond Street, where "Araby" initially takes place, is a decent neighborhood, though it's dilapidated and described as "blind." Early on in the story, we get the picture of children playing in shadows. Within this picture begins a young boy's quest. Magnan's sister—that's all she's known as; she's never given a name—his romantic icon, simply tells him that she can't go to the bazaar called Araby. When she tells him this, he commits himself to going to Araby and bringing her back some worthy treasure from this exotic-sounding destination.

Melded into his quest are associations with knights who go off for damsels, and the mention of his "chalice" in the story evokes the Holy Grail. But what begins with the rush of feelings of romantic love turns into an initiation into a kind of darkness. It's not like Hawthorne's Goodman Brown, who is initiated into the dark woods of Calvinist horror, but it's a literal darkness, overshadowed by poverty, Catholicism, and the boy's feelings of vanity.

With his uncle's late arrival home, his journey to Araby began much later than he wanted or hoped for, and his epiphany at the bazaar is one of disillusionment as he faces a mercantile-minded salesgirl flirting with two gentlemen with English accents. "Araby" is a coming-of-age story. It's a story of adolescence; it's a journey of discovery—or a quest—of a young boy smitten by what he believes is love, only ultimately to be disappointed and really transfigured by disillusionment.

I want to tell a story that's instructive here of my own adolescent falling in love with love. I think of myself as Romeo before he met Juliet, with fair Rosaline, because Romeo—if you remember the famous play by Shakespeare—was in love with love. So is this boy: He's taken with the romantic image of love; he's taken with an adoration of Magnan's sister, which has all of the earmarks of being romantic and is inflated with all that romanticism can do. I think many people could certainly relate to this from their own adolescence; I can.

There's a young woman whom I knew for a number of years who I felt—well, Goethe has a character named Young Werther who suffers the sorrows of unrequited love; it's kind of painful but, at the same time, strangely pleasurable. I thought I was in love with this young woman. I remember being at her home, because we were friends, and she saw me more as a friend than as a potential romantic figure. Maybe that was part of the appeal of the unrequited love. I tell this story because it really dovetails nicely with Joyce's figure in the story "Araby." I remember being at her home, and she suddenly took a piece of spiral notebook paper out of her notebook and very casually just pressed her lips—she had that kind of thin lipstick that girls wore in that era—onto the page, blotted her lipstick, in other words, and casually threw it into the wastebasket receptacle. She went out of the room a little bit after that and I dove—at least that's how I remember it—very quickly in to grasp this piece of paper, to take it as some kind of a remembrance, as something that I could cleave to from her.

This is exactly what goes on with the young boy in the story. That is, when she tells him about wanting to go to Araby, he cleaves to that whole idea of going to Araby for her, of making it is his mission and his *raison d'être*, his reason for existence. He finds stumbling blocks along the way. As I said, his uncle comes home late. He lives with his uncle, and there isn't really necessarily a lot of money in this family. He's given a very little, paltry sum of money, and he goes out and meets with disappointment and a realization—or epiphany—of what his life is really like, of what the hard straits that he lives under and the circumstances of his life really, truly represent.

The story is an awakening, but it also represents a loss of a kind of romantic idealism similar to the trajectory of what was occurring in the literature of the time as it moved away from Romanticism to really a more harsh Realism and to Modernism. "Araby" is built, like all of the stories in *Dubliners*, around the idea of the epiphany; each of these stories has a different kind of epiphany. Let me get a little more into this term and what it means, because it's an important one. People speak very casually about having an epiphany—"I had an epiphany," like the proverbial light bulb going over the head in a cartoon, or "I had an idea that came to me"—but it means something deeper than that.

Epiphany usually means a realization that has a real illumination to it. In fact, it comes out of theology; it comes out of an ephemeral moment of spiritual-like revelation that's sudden and abrupt and can manifest itself in vulgarity of speech. By "vulgarity" I mean the speech of the vulgate—a common person's speech—just in a gesture and a memorable expression of the mind. We experience it through the boy's enlightenment at the conclusion of the story; that is, we as readers experience it. But one of the things that makes "Araby" such a rich story is that the boy is experiencing an epiphany, as well. The epiphany has to do with a sense of what his life has been and what his life really is; call it "the real thing," if you like.

Irish Catholicism is at the heart of the story. It infuses its meaning, as does the concomitant binary theme of fantasy and the romantic world of the imagination set against the religious world of Irish Catholic practice and the actual tawdry world in which the boy lives. These are all pretty much juxtaposed for us. That is, on the one hand, you have the serious religiosity of the Christian brothers and the school; on the other hand, you have the boy's wild, feral, romantic imagination, which wants to set him free, as the first paragraph suggests.

The Christian brothers set them free because they are imprisoned in that world of repression, of religion. In fact, Magnan's sister is also very much devoted to religion. She wants to go to the bazaar, but it turns out that she can't go because there's a religious convent meeting that she has to attend.

Early on, what we sense, then, in this story, is all of this institutional imprisonment. It's really a metaphor for their lives; it's as if the Church casts a very big shadow. You can see why Joyce was viewed as a heretic in his time, why he was viewed with a great deal of scorn and contempt, in fact, for taking such a strong irreligious and what was seen as a very impious view of the power of the Church over individual lives and over the romantic imagination of an adolescent.

There is a former tenant in this story that we discover, the family's former tenant. It wasn't uncommon, in fact, for families to sublet or to have boarders, as they were called in the United States. He left behind the romantic works of Sir Walter Scott [and] a yellow-leafed *Memoirs of Vidocq*, [which is] an escape from the isolated and musty life associated with another work which was left in his room with no one to inherit, the narrator tells us: a work called *The Devout Communicant*. Even in that back room—which is just mentioned almost seemingly as not even being all that relevant to the love that the narrator feels for Magnan's sister—we come to realize the blending of Sir Walter Scott, who was a Romantic writer, in a priest's room with *The Devout Communicant*, with in other words, the way to live a devout life and the rules and scriptures that one should follow if one is indeed worthy of being called a good and devout Catholic.

We have Mangan's sister and her brown-clad figure—remember that the imperturbable faces of the street are also brown—casting this boy's imagination, summoning what he calls, at the end of the story when he has his epiphany, his "foolish blood." Nothing frivolous, worldly, or tied to a lustful, romantic, or love-seeking spirit can emerge from what is the nearly ubiquitous power of the Church, the drabness of the world of Dublin that Joyce gives us, the decent homes, or even the streets, which appear to be hostile to romance. We begin to realize that, in Joyce, a whole world opens up to you. It's Dublin: It's provincial, Irish, and Catholic, but what he is allowing us to immerse ourselves in—what he is indeed immersing us in—is a boy's world, on the one hand, but also the world of all these conflicting emotions of the inner life and the outer life, of course, but deeper than that, of human longing and yearning. We're looking at a time when writers like Joyce were indeed becoming more aware of the nature of repression and the nature of not only repression by institutions like the Catholic Church but repression that came from attempts to follow or abide by what seemed like devout or harsh morality.

At one point, the boy's teacher's countenance, we're told, turns to sternness at the perception of his becoming idle, thereby presumably inviting the mind to be the devil's playground, which of course, is precisely the point again of this polarization, of this dichotomy. Because, on the one hand, he's longing for—yearning for—some kind of romantic love with Magnan's sister, a connection with her, a way to really receive her attention, idolizing her, and it's taking his mind away from being devout. It's taking his mind away from his studies; it's un-repressing him; it's, maybe you could say, liberating him.

There is so much of the presence of the Church in this story. The boy's aunt, for example, wants to make sure Araby is not "some Freemason affair." Mrs. Mercer, a character who is mentioned in the story, collects stamps for some pious purpose. But here's the story that immerses us in Modernism, and one can't separate the Modernist movement from criticism of the Church and other powerful institutions, even in a poem like *The Waste Land*, written by the very serious Anglican T. S. Eliot. [Joyce] talks, for example, about the "unreal city," as Eliot does. There are writers who are bringing us into an awareness of the force of religion, taking more of a stance toward secularism, but also showing the kind of urban decay, the mechanization tied to the industrialism of the age, and the "unreal city," as Eliot calls really all the major cities of the world in *The Waste Land*. The Modernist view is also tied profoundly to disillusionment—disillusionment with Romanticism—and tied to the themes of waste and spiritual desolation that also run really quite strong in Joyce's story. That's despite the fact that so much of the Modernist view appeared soon after the First World War, and "Araby" and *Dubliners* appeared before it.

The point of view in the story is rather complicated, because it's that of a man looking back on his moment of adolescent disillusionment, and thus, "Araby" has the kind of Modernist complexity of a point of view [that] is simultaneously both in the present and in the past. That's true of Montresor in Poe's "Cask of Amontillado." He's also looking back, but he does so to brag and to justify, even as he inadvertently exposes other parts of himself unwillingly. This is different in Joyce; in Joyce, you have the epiphany. In Poe, there's no moment of self-realization or illumination for Montresor, but in Joyce, there is. Is that moment of realization coming to the young man when he is an adolescent, or is it coming from the perspective of an adult when he's remembering his adolescence, or is it both? You could certainly make the case that it is indeed both, that he is experiencing this adolescent epiphany, which he's also allowing us to experience as an epiphany, but that also embedded in the story is the realization that this is an epiphany that comes with understanding at a later age, as well.

We have one of those moments in fiction where the past and the present coalesce; where they almost become fused, one with the other; where there's a simultaneity of the past and the present being experienced through the narrative voice, memory, and a re-evocation of what occurred. This is a story that's replete with symbolism that would become one of the hallmarks of the Modernist movement—it goes back to figures like Flaubert and Baudelaire—with multivalent associations and meanings, and symbolism with a greater depth of meaning and association than the symbolism that we found in earlier work. Notice, for example, the priest: He lives in a musty room; he has a rusty bicycle pump, which is found underneath a bush. You start thinking to yourself, what is Joyce emblemizing here? What is he symbolizing? Who's the priest who hid this bicycle pump as if to give air under a bush or abandon it there? It's not clear, but nevertheless, it's rusty. And those books, certainly, as I suggested, give us a whole sense of his dichotomized or binary world, the romance of Sir Walter Scott and *The Devout Communicant*.

In the backyard, where the priest is, there's what we call a prelapsarian symbol. It's right out of Genesis—right out of the Bible—a wild garden with a central apple tree. You can't get any more Genesis-like than that, although there's also that bush, and underneath that bush is that rusty bicycle pump. We have a tableau which is rich in symbolism and which really strikes a chord as being more Modernist than the kind of symbolism that we associate with earlier stories. There's a tendency, in fact, among many adolescents—I'm thinking high school students, but even among university students—to think a symbol means [only the] one thing it stands for. Faith's pink ribbons in Hawthorne's story, for example: her innocence. Pink takes on a much greater and deeper meaning as we move into the 20th century, though, which is precisely the point. But symbolism and Modernism, as they kind of coalesce, suggest meaning that goes out like a ripple in a stream when you toss a pebble in it. It radiates out in different directions and suggests many meetings and goes back intertextually to things like the Bible.

This story, after all, is a journey—or a quest—that takes us back in time to so many stories. It takes us back to knighthood quests, as I suggested, quests for the Grail. The boy in the story wants to follow his blood. He wants to move away from this repressive Catholic world of Dublin to bring back something from the East—Araby—for Mangan's sister, the girl he believes he's in love with. Araby—the bazaar he wishes to journey to—is associated with this kind of exoticism, Eastern enchantment, and magic. Even at the mention of the word Araby, the boy's uncle is ready to recite "The Arab's Farewell to His Steed."

There's imagination in Dublin, but it's imagination that has been overshadowed by—and continues to be overshadowed by—this need to keep emotion in check, to keep yearning and longing under guard, under sentry. Waiting and anticipating the journey, he keeps this image of Mangan's sister in front of him. It accompanies him; it obsesses him. He imagines bearing a chalice through a throng of foes as he moves through the noisy, flurrying Dublin streets of bargaining women, drunken men, cursing laborers, and the nascent, violent politics reflected in the street singers' songs of the violent hero of the fight for Irish independence Dynamite Rossa (whose real name was Jeremiah O'Donovan).

What's the meaning of this journey and where it takes the boy, to his epiphany? He creeps past "ruinous houses," though he also passes "a twinkling river," and he travels on this romantic errand in a third-class carriage of a deserted train with very little money in his pocket. The romantic aura that he would like to have fixed upon his journey begins to be diminished just in the journey itself, before he even gets to the bazaar. The bazaar turns out to be an ordinary shop of dimming lights and shop girls from no farther east than England, who are—I said mercantile before—really concerned only with money. They have purchases and items to sell, and that's their job as they see it. They couldn't care less about this boy; his errand, even his presence, doesn't really affect them at all. They're gossiping and talking, and the boy is crushed at the end: crushed by anguish, anger, and by feeling derided by vanity. The importance of vanity here is extraordinary. It's the real key to his feelings of defeat, since they tie so directly to the Catholic teachings, which he has not been tending to because of the summoning of his blood—as he calls it—to his pursuit of this romantic ideal or this romantic dream.

The ambiguity in the story's meaning comes from the fact that the [attitude of the] man who is telling the story toward his epiphanous moment is that of him[self] as a boy surrounded by darkness. Is this the portrait of an artist as a young man, reminiscent of Joyce's Stephen Hero or Stephen Dedalus in *A Portrait of the Artist as a Young Man*, a man who has grown from his youthful feelings of vanity and derision? Or is he still seeing himself as having been appropriately derided by vanity for his foolish romanticism? As I said, I think you can bring the two together. But you have to ask the question: How much of this young man's past intersects with his present as an adult? There's really every reason to believe, from all that we know of Joyce's early life, that the story has many autobiographical roots to it. Certainly, it embodies Joyce's disillusion with the Church and organized religion and the personal crisis he experienced of loss of faith, as well as his youthful disillusionment with romantic love.

One can see, in much of the dark short fiction that emerges, a kind of reaction against the Romanticism that came to be tied to poets like Wordsworth, Keats, and Shelley. Many of our short fiction writers implicitly championed the small and seemingly inconsequential ordinary people. There's a definite sense of the lack of the kind of belief that many Romantic writers had in the transformative powers of the individual. The story has an enduring power to it; there's no accident in the fact that the story is so often read, taught, and anthologized. A lot of this has to do with its brevity, but it's also the epiphany and the impact on the reader, as well as the identification with loss that's tied to feelings of youthful folly and romanticism. [These feelings] are really based in a story which takes us from the romantic idealization of youth to the crushing sense of the real and experience. We move through an initiation into the darkness of modernity. There's a famous play by Eugene O'Neill called *Long Day's Journey into Night*—no accident that he's an Irish, though American, playwright. In fact, O'Neill said, "You can understand me more through my Irishness than anything else." As he moves us from the light into the darkness, it's that kind of movement that we begin to see in the Modernism that's reflected in Joyce's story.

Goodman Brown finds darkness as well in the forest and the heart of humankind, but it's linked to sin and loss of faith. In James Joyce, the specter of the morality of the Church and the dingy and dark urban world of Dublin are what oppresses, while the heart of a young boy deeply and—we discover through him—foolishly craves the nourishing food of love and becomes in his own heart, even if briefly, a knave rather than a knight. We move more directly into the boy's inner life, as one might surmise occurs in Hawthorne with "Young Goodman Brown" but for the fact that Hawthorne is there to tell us what Goodman Brown is experiencing, whereas Joyce's young, tortured Irish kid tells us in his own voice, and he makes us experience what he experiences. Less plot-bound than Poe, Hawthorne, Gogol, Maupassant, or Henry James, Joyce provides us with a much richer inner-life terrain, even as he takes us back, in "Araby," to a kind of transfiguring and powerful sketch.

Joyce's influence on the modern short story is inestimable, and he, along with the poet William Butler Yeats—whom many regard as the greatest poet of the 20th century—and playwrights like Lady Gregory and Sean O'Casey, were all singular in hastening an Irish literary revival and renaissance. But Joyce, in many ways, is really the central, key, and preeminent figure. This renaissance or Irish revival, which involved a lot of Celtic revival, would see a spate of short fiction and literary talent in writers like Liam O'Flaherty, Sean O'Faolain, Frank O'Connor, [and] later on, Samuel Beckett, Edna O'Brien, and Mary Lavin. This story is emblematic of Joyce's use of epiphany, but it really carries a major emotional impact, as well. The point of view and voice are both intricate and evocative. The language is richly poetic, and yet it somehow manages to capture the inflation that youth can bring, as when the narrator says of this angel of his "confused adoration"—and think of the poetry in this—"My body was [like] a harp, and her words and gestures were like fingers running upon the wires."

"Araby" combines two archetypal forms prevalent in fiction: initiation and the journey, or mythic quest. Our next story is also an initiation story, written by another one of the 20th century's great storytellers, the Russian Isaac Babel. [He] takes us into the world of war and violence, which unfortunately—sadly—is often seen as one of the hallmarks of Modernism and much of the reason short fiction is so often downbeat, because the short fiction that burgeoned in the first part of the 20th century really followed—in terms of Modernism—the First and, ultimately, the Second World Wars and then Vietnam, as well. Next we're going to go to Russia once again and read the great initiation and Modernist story of violence and identity: Isaac Babel's "My First Goose."

Lecture Eight

Babel's "My First Goose"—Violent Concision

Scope:

This lecture begins with an overview of the vision, style, and worldview of Isaac Babel's "My First Goose." We then move on to Babel's influences and the story's autobiographical roots—the author's military experiences, his Jewishness, and his association with the Cossacks. We briefly discuss Maupassant's influence on Babel and analyze Babel's style and the major action that occurs in the story: the killing of the goose by the narrator. The lecture probes the moral ambiguity in a story, which like the work of Chekhov, is notable for its harsh Realism and lack of moralizing. We also discuss Babel's connections to his narrator, Liutov, and the larger collection of stories, *Red Cavalry*, of which "My First Goose" is a part. We note the author's ambivalence toward the experience of war and his attraction and repulsion to the Cossacks and their violence. The lecture concludes with a broader discussion of the story's power and the literary debt owed to Babel by other Russian writers.

Outline

I. "My First Goose" is a compressed tale of violence and initiation, both pervasive themes in 20th-century short fiction.

- **A.** The story offers an unrelenting and unapologetic vision of brutality without moralizing or editorializing—a type of Realism reminiscent of Chekhov.
- **B.** Babel's concise style and violent worldview anticipate Hemingway, whose first major collection of stories, *In Our Time*, was also published in 1925.

II. Babel's influences and experiences had a profound effect on his development as a writer.

- **A.** Maxim Gorky, Babel's mentor, told him to experience life, which he did via the brutality and violence of war.
- **B.** Babel fought in World War I on the Russian front and was in both the czar's army and the Soviet cavalry.
- **C.** Although Babel was a Jew, he nevertheless rode with the notoriously anti-Semitic Cossacks, infamous among Jews for

their involvement in pogroms. Babel witnessed a pogrom as a boy, an experience he wrote about in a short work called "The Story of My Dovecote."

D. Like the narrator of "My First Goose," who will join in supping with the Cossacks, Babel was educated—an intellectual and bookish man who wore spectacles and felt like an outsider among military men.

E. Babel emulated Maupassant's firmly etched tales and, like Henry James, sought to achieve an unadorned and powerful Realism in a style both terse and lyrical—a style characterized by the educator and biographer Ann Charters as "sensual and grotesque."

III. The story presents an essential conflict or question: Can an effete intellectual with "spectacles on [his] nose" get on with or be accepted by a rough group of peasant Cossacks?

A. The quartermaster, who carries the "little trunk" that one of the younger Cossacks throws over the gate, gives the narrator (Liutov) the misogynistic key to approbation and acceptance by the Cossacks: "… ruin a lady, yes, the most cleanest lady."

B. After Liutov is humiliated and shamed by the contemptuous, young, flaxen-haired Cossack, he saves face and wins approval by brutally killing the landlady's goose and ordering her to cook it for him.

C. The narrator temporarily overcomes his feelings of loneliness, but his killing of the "inoffensively preening" goose is symbolically identified with rape and crucifixion.

D. At dinner, the narrator reads Lenin's speech from *Pravda* aloud to the Cossacks. He sees within it what the platoon leader Surovkov doesn't see—the secret motive behind the speech, which can be likened to the narrator's secret motive to gain acceptance by killing the goose.

IV. Without moralizing, Babel succeeds in communicating an unrelenting, bleak vision, albeit an ambiguous one in terms of attraction and repulsion toward violence and war.

A. The story reveals a palpable sexuality connected to war and violence.

B. Babel, in contrast to Gogol, portrays the Cossacks as barbaric rather than noble—though also attractive and admirable in their strength as warriors.

V. Essential elements of the story contribute to its great power.

A. Though much is lost in translation, the language is supple, rhythmic, remarkably precise, evocative, and unvarnished.

B. There is immense clarity in the story, despite its astonishing brevity, which creates a powerful, unified emotional impact similar to the epiphany in Joyce's "Araby."

C. The characterization of the narrator and the military men is strong and pungent, as is that of the landlady, with her simple repetition of the words "Comrade, this makes me want to hang myself"—deft, incisive, and trenchant.

VI. Babel had an immense influence on other Russian writers, including the Russian Jewish journalist and novelist Vasily Grossman, along with Boris Pasternak, Aleksandr Solzhenitsyn, Yevgeny Yevtushenko, and Andrei Voznesensky.

Suggested Readings:

Babel, "My First Goose," translated by Walter Morrison.

———, *Red Cavalry.*

———, "The Story of My Dovecote."

Grossman, *A Writer at War.*

Prose, "The Bones of Muzhiks: Isaac Babel Gets Lost in Translation," in *Harper's*, November 2001.

Questions to Consider:

1. How does Babel succeed in making us feel empathic toward the story's narrator?
2. Is there a specific didactic message about violence or war that emerges in this story? What is it?
3. Do the narrator's feelings of guilt and remorse override his feelings of being accepted by the Cossacks? Is Babel suggesting that he (the narrator) is really not brutal enough to be going off to the front, or does the killing of the landlady's goose ensure that he is?

Lecture Eight—Transcript

Babel's "My First Goose"—Violent Concision

Isaac Babel's "My First Goose" is a great compressed tale of violence and initiation—both pervasive themes in 20th-century fiction—from the third Russian writer we have [met], as we move from the early and mid-19th century of Gogol, to the end of the 19th century of Chekhov, and now onto the 20th century, World War I, and the Russian Revolution with Isaac Babel. Unrelenting and unapologetic, it's a vision of brutality without moralizing or editorializing, a Realism reminiscent of Chekhov and his views on adultery, which we don't know about because he just pretty much dramatizes and shows rather than tells. That's precisely what Babel does in this concise style of his, and [this] violent worldview, ultimately, mirrors, on Russian soil, much of what Hemingway gave to the world on the heels of the First World War with his first major short fiction collection, *In Our Time*, which was published in 1925.

This story, "My First Goose," exemplifies the kind of masterful use of language that Babel was capable of and the remarkable way he could economically and with sharp poetic imagery bring a story into fruition. "My First Goose" is also a story of identity, another motif which will take on increasing importance as short fiction moves from the Modernist period to the contemporary. Like James Joyce, Babel was able to pull from his own life material that became stories. *Red Calvary* is a collection of 34 stories by Babel that appeared in Soviet periodicals between 1923 and 1925, drawn from Babel's life and his experiences as a war correspondent and propagandist for the Soviets. This story is from that collection, and there are many parallels between Babel and the narrator of most of the *Red Calvary* stories. The narrator's name is Kirill Vasilievich Liutov, but as in Joyce's work, fiction emerges from a synthesis of the real or the autobiographical and the combined unconscious and structuring impulses of the artistic imagination.

It's important to note that Babel, like Liutov, experienced firsthand the brutal Russo-Polish War fought over territorial disputes between Russia and Poland following the Treaty of Versailles and the Bolshevik Revolution. The war, not that well known in Western history, had an immense impact; the Poles, even briefly, captured Kiev, where Babel had earlier attended university. I want to talk about Babel's influences, because one of those influences was the writer Maxim Gorky, who was his mentor and who told him essentially that he should go out and experience life. Like Hemingway, he did via the brutality and the violence of war. He fought in World War I on the Russian front and was in both the czar's army and the Soviet cavalry, the Red Army. He was a Jew who nevertheless rode with the notoriously anti-Semitic Cossacks, infamous—especially among Jews—for their involvement in pogroms, which were the raiding, plundering, raping, and killing of Jews in Jewish *shtetls*, or villages or settlements. Babel witnessed a pogrom as a boy, an experience he wrote about in a short autobiographical work called "The Story of My Dovecote," in which a young boy personally witnesses the brutal murder of his grandfather. "The Story of My Dovecote" brought accusations against Babel of incitement of class hatred and pornography. Again, it's an important autobiographical link, the link to the 1905 pogrom in Odessa in this famous Babel story.

Like the story's narrator—in the story that we're going to be talking about, "My First Goose"—who joined in supping with the Cossacks, Babel was educated, an intellectual, a bookish man who wore spectacles and felt very much like an outsider among military men. That's precisely the situation that's presented for us in "My First Goose." The story is autobiographical; it's based on Babel's experience before he went to the front in 1920 in the Russo-Polish War, and it appeared in English in 1929, when his first collection of stories appeared as *Red Calvary*, again, based on experiences in war, especially the Galician War.

The narrator is assigned to Cossack troops, just like Babel was, and the narrator, Liutov, like Babel, was a law school graduate. Babel was an educated man, physically frail, very much like Liutov, and Liutov is also probably Jewish. His physical stature and intellect, like Babel's, put him into dramatic contrast to the robust, virile, combat veteran/warrior Cossacks. The essence of this story is of the narrator needing to prove himself manly and capable of violence in order to win the acceptance and the comradeship, the goodwill, of the Cossack soldiers. He's sensitive, educated, poetic, and by contrast to the Cossacks, somewhat effeminate and scholarly. Though his Jewishness is never mentioned, it seems abundantly clear that he is, like Babel, a Jew, devoting himself more to learning than to violence or fighting in battles, like the Cossacks. One can decode his attempts to overcome his Jewishness in his swearing by Christ and eating pork.

But the heart of this story is in his actions of going against his own nature, sensibility, background, and temperament by proving to these men that he can be like them. The way that he does this is essentially by acting rough, impulsive, and devoid of any compassion with an old, nearly blind peasant woman. He brutally kills her beloved goose, crushes its skull with his boot, and then orders her to cook the goose for him. What this does is it enables him to become accepted by the Cossacks but leaves him with a heavy heart at the end of the story and with feelings of guilt and remorse. I should mention here that Babel not only rode with the Cossacks in the Rudenny campaign of the Russo-Polish War, but he was, incidentally—and to the surprise of many of the Cossacks—an excellent horseman.

He was also the first major Russian Jewish writer to write in Russian and would become especially famous with stories based on the lives of the Jews of Odessa, though he so admired Maupassant and Flaubert that he wrote his stories initially—his first stories—in French. He wrote his first stories at the age of 15, mostly patterned after the stories of Guy de Maupassant, including a number with plot twists reminiscent of Maupassant's "The Necklace." He published a story, in fact, in 1932 called "Guy de Maupassant." His famous *Tales of Odessa* was a group of stories published the year before the Maupassant story, in 1931, and it included stories and sketches about Jewish gangsters, like Babel's notorious character Benya Krik, as well as of businesspeople, rabbis, prostitutes, and a whole range of ordinary, everyday people who lived in the Odessa ghetto before the Bolshevik Revolution of 1917.

Babel was one of many of the short fiction writers drawn to writing about ordinary people—as his Russian literary predecessors Gogol and Chekhov also were—but Babel was also doubtless influenced by the rising notions of Soviet art and how it needed to be firmly rooted in the world of the proletariat, or working class, and to reflect the dialectic that one finds espoused in Marx's view of history. Leon Trotsky had written a great deal about art and literature and how literature had to reflect, essentially, a propagandistic view. But this story stands pretty much apart from that, although it's about an ordinary scholarly man who rides with the Cossacks.

Babel is very much like that man, Liutov. I'll tell you something about his background: He was born in Odessa in the Ukraine in 1894. At that time, Jews were prohibited from residing in most of the major Russian cities. After he graduated from the University at Kiev, Babel went with a fake passport to Saint Petersburg—the story setting for Gogol's "The Overcoat," you may recall—to study literature, initially. He was a playwright in addition to being a short story writer, and he worked, as well, on a number of films, including work he did with the famed Russian master filmmaker Sergei Eisenstein.

Babel had a close friendship with Gorky, who was a mentor and a supporter of his, and he was employed with the commission of education, as well as with the secret police—ironic, because he was murdered, we now know, on Stalin's orders in 1940 for espionage, which essentially amounted to charges of being a Trotskyite. For years, his fate had been unknown; it was believed for many years that he died in a forced labor camp. He's widely regarded, despite a small oeuvre, as one of the greatest writers of the 20th century, and I should add that all charges against Babel were officially dropped posthumously by the U.S.S.R. in 1954.

Babel emulated Maupassant's firmly etched tale and, like Henry James, was strongly influenced by Maupassant and wanted to achieve an unadorned, powerful Realism in a style both terse and lyrical and also, as Ann Charters has said, "sensual and grotesque."

The story's opening paragraph presents this giant character Savitsky, who never reappears in this story, with legs that look like two girls "wedged to their shoulders"—that's "sheathed to the neck" in another translation—"in shiny riding boots." This type of erotic imagery is juxtaposed to the character's—that is, this character that we never see again—display of violence in his flat statement of a threat to kill a character named Chesnokov, whom we also don't see, and later on in the story, to the bloody killing of the goose by the narrator.

> Savitsky, the commander of the Sixth Division, rose when he saw me, and I was taken aback by the beauty of his gigantic body. He rose—his breeches purple, his crimson cap cocked to the side, his medals pinned to his chest—splitting the hut in two like a banner splitting the sky. He smelled of perfume and the nauseating coolness of soap. His long legs looked

> like two girls wedged to their shoulders in shiny riding boots.

This is a picture that is really quite vivid, sharply etched, and poetic in many ways. But you have to be struck right away by the sense of the beauty that Babel sees from Liutov, his narrator, in the physical strength and imposing nature of this character Savitsky and also the kind of imagery that suggests the feminine, female, or at least some kind of androgyny. We'll get to this a little bit more, but I think it's important to understand initially that the Cossacks are seen also as being like "heathen priests." Then, in what's tantamount to homoerotic imagery, they're shown shaving each other; they're intertwined in their legs with the narrator at the story's end, when he has become accepted by them as being one of them—or, at least, like them—in acting, in effect, like a worthy barbarian. These are not the Cossacks Gogol's family identified with nobility.

There is, from the beginning of the story, a sense of the physical attractiveness of the Cossacks. There is in Babel, in other words—and we'll see this again in Hemingway, curiously enough—a kind of homoeroticism. There has been a lot of emphasis in literature, both short fiction and novels, on what's called "queer studies"—that is, seeing homosexual themes and homosexual motifs—and one can get a little bit far afield with this sort of thing. There's a famous literary critic named Leslie Fiedler, in fact, who wrote that *Huckleberry Finn* obviously shows homoeroticism because there are Huck and Jim out on the raft, stripped to the waist, naked, and at one point, Jim says, "Come back to the raft, Huck honey."

But there is a blend in Babel—as well as in Hemingway—of violence, and the physical, and an attraction to that violence and the physical, at the same time that there's a repulsion. It really works both ways. The story's essential conflict or question is: Can an effete, intellectual, educated type with "spectacles on [his] nose" get on with or be accepted by this rough group of peasant military Cossacks, whom he wants very profoundly to be accepted by? Why he accepted them is, of course, maybe in part their physical attraction.

The quartermaster, who carries the narrator's "little trunk" that one of the younger Cossacks throws over the gate, has given him the misogynistic way to get approval and acceptance by the Cossacks: "Ruin a lady, yes, the most cleanest lady." In other words, if you want to get accepted by the Cossacks—if you want to be one of them, if you want to get camaraderie with them—do something terrible to a woman.

After the narrator is humiliated and shamed by this contemptuous, young, flaxen-haired Cossack who throws his trunk over the gate, he does exactly what was suggested: He does something terrible to this old lady by brutally killing her goose and compelling her—forcing her—to cook it, at which point the young, flaxen-haired Cossack who threw his trunk over the gate makes room for Liutov, the narrator, to sit, because he has their approval at this point. He did what was necessary to be accepted by them; he gets to eat with them, all because he killed the landlady's goose—by the way, [she] is suicidal—and ordered her to cook it for him.

The narrator temporarily overcomes feelings of loneliness, as well as becoming symbolically identified in a sense with the kind of rape in the killing of the landlady's "haughty"—as it's described, though in another translation, it's "inoffensively preening"—goose. He's identified also—curiously enough—with the crucifixion as he yells, "God damn it!" and thrusts the sword he found into the goose. He proves in all this that he would be able to get on at the front, but it makes him feel depressed; it makes him feel like a prostitute. In fact, this is seen in the image we get from him of the moon hanging like a cheap earring, which contrasts symbolically to the story's earlier image of "the dying sun in the sky, round and yellow as a pumpkin, breathed its last rosy breath," and that's as night descends. You really get the sense of the poetic quality of Babel's prose, even in translation. (There's always something lost in translation, and there are different varieties of translations of this story and Babel's other work, of course, as well.)

The narrator reads Lenin's speech from *Pravda*—which he had read earlier on in the story alone by himself—and he reads it aloud to the Cossacks. He exultingly sees within it what the platoon leader, whose name is Surovkov, doesn't see: the secret motive behind the speech to the Comintern on strategies, which can be likened to the narrator's secret motive of gaining acceptance in killing the goose.

The reading of Lenin's speech also gains him approval, as is revealed in Surovkov's (the platoon, or squadron, commander's) favorable remarks about the content of the speech. The Cossacks, who are likely illiterate, can appreciate the narrator's ability to read now that he has formed a bond with them by killing the goose and ordering the old lady to cook it for him. We'll go to the last section of the story here:

> And in a loud voice, like the triumphant deaf man, I read Lenin's speech to the Cossacks.
>
> The evening wrapped me in the soothing dampness of her twilight sheets, the evening placed her motherly palms on my burning brow. [This, of course, is translation, but you can see once more the kind of poetic, enveloping quality of Babel's language.] I read and rejoiced, waiting for the effect, rejoicing in the mysterious curve of Lenin's straight line.

It's important to point out here that Babel and Liutov both are strong supporters of Lenin; they're pretty much toeing the Soviet line. The Cossacks weren't doing that as much—let's put it that way; we'll get into this in a little more detail—but at this point, we see him following that Lenin straight line, and the Cossacks are going along with him or, at least, listening to him. In fact, let me go back to the text:

> "Truth tickles all and sundry in the nose," Surovkov said when I had finished. "It isn't all that easy to wheedle it out of the pile of rubbish, but Lenin picks it up right away, like a hen picks up a grain of corn."

This is the platoon leader saying, in effect, this is okay—just like they said this boy's okay—because he took the suicidal landlady, humiliated her, ordered her around, killed her goose, and made her cook it.

> That is what Surovkov, the squadron commander, said about Lenin, and then we went to sleep in the hayloft. [Here we get back to this image of what can only be described as a homoeroticism]. Six of us slept there warming each other, our legs tangled, under the holes in the roof which let in the stars.

Legs tangled? Make of it what you will; I think it does suggest that he has become one with them, [that] there is a kind of unification in that. There's more than homoeroticism; there's a sense of acceptance that really he was longing for. But what comes across is the pain that goes with this, because he has done something that's—maybe by his standards—immoral but certainly creates a great deal of guilt, contrition feelings, and remorse. The final line is: "I dreamed and saw women in my dreams, and only my heart, crimson with murder, screeched and bled."

There you get unmistakably the sense of how this has affected him—gone right to his heart—how it has provided a sense of agony but agony that comes with the acceptance by the Cossacks. We get a very morally complex vision of not only this man Liutov but, to a great extent, of humanity—that is, the desire that so many human beings have to overcome their sense of isolation, to gain acceptance, and yet to do things that may go against their nature. It's a real binary, or divided, sense; it's a real sense of the heart against itself, which Faulkner once said "is the sign of all great literature" in his Nobel speech.

Though a good deal—as I have intimated—is lost in this story in translation, the language is supple, rhythmic, and really quite remarkably precise. It's evocative, and perhaps most of all, it's unvarnished. Babel was one of these writers who would strip away language, and strip it away, and strip it away, and get to the very kind of nominal essence of language. It's the sort of thing we'll see again in Hemingway, who was a student of Gertrude Stein's. She really trained him to get language down to the bone as much as possible, getting rid of adjectives and of [an] adorned type of language or language which was really unnecessary. As a result, there's an immense clarity and astonishing brevity, and it creates really a quite powerful, unified emotional impact, similar in its power to a story like James Joyce's "Araby."

There is an epiphany for us as readers in this story. The epiphany is, again, that heart against itself, that sensibility that comes out of someone being very attracted, on the one hand, to physical strength and brutality—as people can be—and wanting to be accepted within that kind of fraternity and also being disposed toward feeling, as if one is sacrificing something essential within oneself in order to gain that acceptance.

The characterization of the narrator and the military men is really quite strong and pungent, as is that of the landlady, with her simple repetition of "Comrade, this makes me want to hang myself": deft, incisive, and trenchant. One can see the Realism that Babel is able to bring off in this story. It's a Realism which includes a thorough and uncompromising chipping away of all that unnecessary, extraneous language or detail and a combining with remarkably etched poetic imagery.

The moral ambiguity that I've been talking about in "My First Goose" and the palpable sexuality we get from a story that really inextricably links to violence and war raise it to a high level of craftsmanship. This is certainly what Babel's reputation is as a writer—well deserved, well merited—and it's what he, in many respects, continues to be remembered for, especially as we view his ability to tell a story like this without editorializing or inserting into the story his own views or opinions. This becomes Liutov's story, and even though I've remarked about how autobiographical the story is and how you see so many parallels between Liutov and Babel, he creates that character almost like a ventriloquist creates a voice that's separate from himself for a puppet. The puppet may be part—you could argue—of the ventriloquist but separate, and that's what we get. We get a kind of what we call a persona—a mask—by which Babel is able to sustain this voice, make this character singular, and create the character apart from him so that we're being shown rather than told. It's not Babel's voice who comes in; it's not Babel who's tortured: It's the character he creates. As in Chekhov, there's no moralizing, no sermonizing, just—and, again, here's the important word—the unvarnished tale.

The power of this story is really in its compression and imagery but also in the humanity of the narrator's moral conscience set against his desire to fit in and be accepted as a man worthy of the exacting violent code by which the Cossacks live. We get a swift but full portrayal of a man anguished by his loneliness, wanting and needing not only the acceptance but the respect of men who are very much unlike him and whom he has to be like if he's to win their acceptance and be seen by them as something other than a four-eyed bookish sort with no hatred of women versus being a fighter and a man of action, who is, to his core, a misogynist. Make no mistake about it: There is in Babel's work a lot of misogyny, but he's dramatizing the misogyny. It's not to say—and we, again, have to separate the author from the work—that Babel is a misogynist. That would be all too easy. He's really showing the misogyny and the depth of it, in a story like this, that the Cossacks have.

Red Calvary is regarded as Babel's best work and is also deemed a major contribution to Russian literature. It's bleak in its portrayal of war, and it's unrelenting in the vicious and cruel portrayal that it provides of the Cossacks, including a story in the collection involving a woman on a train who tries to hide the salt that she's holding on her lap from the Cossacks by deluding them into thinking it's a baby. When they discover her deception, they throw her off the moving train, and when they subsequently discover that she's still alive, they shoot and kill her. This is, again, emblematic of the harshness and the kind of brutality that Babel portrays in the Cossacks and in his worldview. It's a view of the Cossacks that certainly contrasts to the more noble view that Babel's fellow Ukrainian writer Gogol gave us in his famous war novel *Taras Bulba*. Babel was pro-Soviet, and the Cossacks were mostly opposed to the Soviets. That has to be seen as tied in with the whole calculus of Babel's work, but for the most part, he was showing their appeal, as well as their cruelty, misogyny, and sadism.

Babel's Liutov—again, like Babel—is also drawn to the heroism and courage of the Cossacks, not only to their physical stature but their strength, the fact that they are warriors, and the fact that they can go into combat and murder, kill, and do what warriors are supposed to do. What rich attraction-repulsion there is in Babel, as if he is himself split between those two poles. That personal ambivalence doesn't interfere with his art, but it is really melded into his art. It's an ambivalence toward brutality and war—attraction and repulsion—and what it does is elevates his art and gives it much of its power, though it's ultimately clear that Babel, like the great Russian novelist and short story writer Tolstoy, the author of *War and Peace*, was able to see the horror and the barbarism of war with utter clarity.

Tolstoy also viewed the Cossacks, as he presented them in his novel, on the Napoleonic War battlefields, as great warriors, as part of that great warrior quality the Cossacks were identified with that appeals to Liutov and as it appealed to Babel. But, again, let us not mistake Babel for Liutov or Liutov for Babel. He really does create a character who stands apart from him, and I should say that he creates—just in this story, as short as it is and as compressed as it is—a great sense of war without really taking us to war. What happens is all preparatory for going to the front, and modern Soviet writers have really learned a great deal from Babel, particularly a war writer like Vasily Grossman but even Boris Pasternak, who wrote *Dr. Zhivago*, or Aleksandr Solzhenitsyn, who wrote *The Gulag Archipelago*. They owe a considerable literary debt to Babel, as do famed Soviet poets like [Yevgeny] Yevtushenko and [Andrei] Voznesensky.

It's strange that someone with such a—I suppose you could say—small oeuvre had as major an impact as he had. We'll see when we talk about Hemingway, that Hemingway's impact was far greater, but there really are parallels between these two great writers. From the great Modernist writing and the harsh Realism that we find in Babel, we're going to go on to Hemingway, another writer of great distinction, who was a contemporary of Babel's and had many stylistic and thematic similarities, despite their being continents and worlds apart in character and in overall sensibility.

Next, we move onto another classic Modernist initiation story by a writer who single-handedly changed the style of short story writing. Both Babel and Hemingway began as journalists, and both learned from their war experiences that the world can be sudden, brutal, and harsh. In many respects, "The Killers" by Hemingway—published less than a decade after World War I, between his two powerful novels *The Sun Also Rises*, which was published in 1926, and *A Farewell to Arms*, published in 1929—signifies the disillusionment of what Gertrude Stein came to call the "lost generation" that followed the First World War, as well as the sensibility of violence that was fostered by that catastrophe. Many parallels exist, of course, between Babel and Hemingway—as we will discover—but Hemingway had a much greater influence and, to this day, continues to have a much greater influence upon the canon and upon traditional literary endeavors and, particularly, upon the short story.

Lecture Nine

Male Initiation—Hemingway's "The Killers"

Scope:

The distinctive style of Hemingway is tied to both the ideas of Formalism and to the Modernist period in which he was writing. Hemingway's work is parallel in many ways to that of Isaac Babel, though his impact on modern literature has been far greater than Babel's or most other writers of short fiction. In this lecture, we look briefly at Hemingway's collection *In Our Time*, a unified volume of stories similar to Joyce's *Dubliners* or Babel's *Red Cavalry* or later works by such writers as Sherwood Anderson, Jean Toomer, William Faulkner, and Ernest Gaines. We then turn to "The Killers," a story of violence and initiation for Hemingway's recurring character Nick Adams. We explore significant elements of Hemingway's own life and delve into his stoicism and notion of grace under pressure. We will focus on the killers, Max and Al, and on Ole Andreson, who might be seen, along with Nick, as the story's protagonist. We conclude with observations on Hemingway's lasting influence and some of the reasons that this story is still seen as a masterpiece of short fiction.

Outline

I. Hemingway's work represents a revolution in literary style.

- **A.** Hemingway is still working in a vein of Realism but with a much harder edge than the likes of Chekhov or James.
  - **1.** His work embodies the Formalist idea of Cleanth Brooks and Robert Penn Warren that style is content.
  - **2.** Hemingway's stripped-down, brutal view of the world informs his style.
- **B.** The Hemingway style and worldview are tied to Modernism and to such literary figures as Gertrude Stein (Hemingway's mentor), James Joyce, T. S. Eliot, and Ezra Pound.
- **C.** Hemingway started out as a war correspondent writing "cable-ese," using language nominally because of cost per word. He developed a signature stimulus-response style, unadorned, and with minimal use of adjectives.

D. British critic Wyndham Lewis called Hemingway's style "dumb ox" because of its simplicity. Hemingway explained that his style was emblematic of what he called "the iceberg effect": One-eighth of the meaning and content of the language are above water while the rest is subtextual, or under the surface.

E. "The Killers" emerged from a kind of hard-boiled, *noir* American fiction style identified with such writers as Raymond Chandler and Dashiell Hammet.

F. Other Nick Adams stories appear in Hemingway's *In Our Time*, published two years before "The Killers." We see the same the unity in this volume of short fiction that we noted in Joyce's *Dubliners* or Babel's *Red Cavalry*.

II. "The Killers" is an initiation story for Nick, though unlike Babel's "My First Goose," it can be seen as the story of two characters: Nick Adams and Ole Andreson.

A. Nick is on the verge of moving into adulthood, and the story reflects his initiation into manhood and loss of innocence to the realm of experience.

B. Nick learns about violence and the murderousness and evil that are in the world, as well as the concepts of Stoicism and grace under pressure.

C. Stoicism is the philosophy of Zeno, which advocated submission to one's fate out of necessity without visible emotion.

D. Grace under pressure is the essence of the Hemingway ethos and can be seen in Ole Andreson's reaction to the killers, Max and Al, as well as in George's reactions.

III. The killers provide the force behind the initiation in the story.

A. The two men are menacing. Early on, they address both George and Nick with the derisive label "bright boy." Later, Max asks George what he's looking at, then orders Nick to join George on the other side of the counter.

B. There is something palpably absurd and even comic about Max and Al, with their derby hats, tight black overcoats, gloves, and silk mufflers. We are told that they look like twins in a vaudeville team.

C. Hemingway then begins to distinguish them for us; for example, according to Al, his partner, Max, "talks too much." Despite their symbiotic relationship, the two killers are different.

D. When both killers tell George that he is "lucky," the implication is that both George and Nick have had their lives spared.

E. The killers feminize and homoeroticize George and Nick, contributing to an even greater sense of the experience as one that impinges on manhood.

F. Other characters play subaltern roles and seem powerless against the forces that intrude upon their lives.

IV. "The Killers" is considered a masterpiece of short fiction for a number of reasons.

A. The brevity and economy of language contribute to the story's strength and impact.

B. The story has a profound emotional impact both on Nick and on the reader.

C. The Hemingway philosophy and ethos are poignantly conveyed in "The Killers."

D. The power of the story is most clearly seen in its embodiment of the archetypical themes of initiation and manhood.

E. It's hard to separate Hemingway from many of the writers who have tried to imitate him, but he was the first to express a Stoic philosophy in terms of the everyday while also conveying the threat of death as a random and capricious occurrence.

Suggested Readings:

Hemingway, *A Farewell to Arms.*

———, *In Our Time.*

———, "The Killers."

———, *The Old Man and the Sea.*

———, *The Sun Also Rises.*

Hotchner, *Papa Hemingway.*

Mailer, *The Naked and the Dead.*

Young, *Ernest Hemingway: A Reconsideration.*

Questions to Consider:

1. What are we to make of Hemingway's intentions when we consider that his original title for this story was "The Matadors"?
2. Is Ole Andreson or even George at the center of this story rather than Nick?
3. What is Hemingway indicating to us about the nature of the violence of the killers and their obvious tendency to homoeroticize Nick and George?

Lecture Nine—Transcript

Male Initiation—Hemingway's "The Killers"

Ernest Hemingway continues to work in a vein of Realism but with a much harder edge than we found in the likes of Chekhov or Henry James. His work embodies the Cleanth Brooks and Robert Penn Warren Formalist notion that style is content; those, by the way, were two of the preeminent figures in what came to be known as New Criticism: the belief that you find the meaning of a work in the text itself. Those two innovators of Formalism or textual literary criticism came in part to this idea by dint of Hemingway's major influence. And Hemingway's influence has been major; his stripped-down, brutal view of the world informs his style, and he's closest in that sense to Isaac Babel than to any other short fiction writers that we have studied.

Hemingway's style and worldview are tied to Modernism and to literary figures like Gertrude Stein—who was Hemingway's mentor—James Joyce, T. S. Eliot, and Ezra Pound. Stein especially had a major effect on his prose style, getting him to pare down and cut until his language was as spare and concrete as possible. Hemingway started out as a war correspondent writing "cable-ese," using language nominally because of the cost per word. He developed a signature and distinctive style that was stimulus-response, unadorned, minimal adjectival usage, cinematic, and objective, as opposed to subjective. His style would become associated with a school of art called Minimalism, which to the later chagrin and disapproval of Raymond Carver—a fiction writer we'll study later on—was also a label that was put on Carver, though Carver, as we shall see, was a definite heir to Hemingway as well as to Chekhov.

Hemingway's style, as well as his ethic about living life to the hilt and facing its briefness and brutality with courage, [was] singularly influential, even to the extent that two other great American short fiction writers and celebrated novelists—William Faulkner, whose style is the very antithesis of Hemingway's, and F. Scott Fitzgerald—were overshadowed by Hemingway, particularly in terms of influence on fiction writing in the 20th century. There's a little instructive story of a supposed exchange between Hemingway and Fitzgerald that appears in "The Snows of Kilimanjaro," where Fitzgerald says, "Ernest, the rich are different than you and me."

Hemingway supposedly answered, "Yeah, they have more money." It's that kind of basic brevity that we associate with Hemingway, but it's also the philosophy and idea of the Hemingway hero. We're going to meet Nick Adams, who is a prototype in many ways of a Hemingway hero or protagonist that you meet later on in the novels, like Frederic Henry in *A Farewell to Arms*, Jake Barnes in *The Sun Also Rises*, or Robert Jordan in *For Whom the Bell Tells*.

Hemingway was often critical of other writers. He spoke admiringly of Babel, however, commenting with approval on Babel's concision and saying that Babel demonstrated stylistically what could be done with prose when the unnecessary or the superfluous is omitted. Though the two writers are alike in sensibility and style, Hemingway's influence is far beyond that of Babel's. He lived longer, and he produced novels, and [those] novels were made into movies, and he became a figure of popular culture. But it's not only the oeuvre and the public role that Hemingway played, it's his philosophy, concerns, the influential ethos that he developed, and that view of heroism in a world—as he saw it—devoid of meaning that he's able to fashion so powerfully in pretty much all of his fiction. In "My First Goose," we focus on the narrator, Liutov, whereas in "The Killers"—the story we're going to talk about—we have a story that seems to revolve around the experience of Nick Adams but could as readily be seen as Ole Andreson's story.

Before we get to that story, I should mention here that a British critic by the name of Wyndham Lewis called Hemingway's style "dumb ox" because of its simplicity. Lewis seemed to feel also that Hemingway's emphasis on what was often described as "booze, belly, and broads" deserved that dumb-ox appellation. But Hemingway explained that his style was emblematic of what he called "the iceberg effect," where an eighth of the meaning and the content of the language is above water, while the rest is subtextual, under the surface. Examples in "The Killers" are in these wonderful lines like: "Nick had never had a towel in his mouth before." We find out that Nick is being tied up by these two menacing figures who come in, and just that line, "Nick had never had a towel in his mouth before," has so much weight to it, has really a kind of poetry to it. Or Ole Andreson, the boxer whom these killers have come to do in: "Ole Andreson looked at the wall and did not say anything." These are lines that have almost become parodied because of their simplicity, but underneath them is the subtext, and beneath the lines is meaning that resonates far beyond the lines themselves.

Here's the opening of "The Killers," one of the most parodied and imitated—for better or worse—openings probably in modern short fiction:

> The door of Henry's lunchroom opened and two men came in. They sat down at the counter.
>
> "What's yours?" George asked them.
>
> "I don't know," one of the men said. "What do you want to eat, Al?"
>
> "I don't know," said Al. "I don't know what I want to eat."
>
> Outside it was getting dark. The streetlight came on outside the window. The two men at the counter read the menu. From the other end of the counter Nick Adams watched them. He had been talking to George when they came in.

This almost seems like one of those primers you read when you're a kid in elementary school: "Run, Skip, run," that sort of thing. It seems simple, flat, with declarative sentences, and yet it sets a tone; it sets a mood. It provides us with feeling for what will unravel in the story or what will really become revealed in the story. Underneath is simplicity, and underneath it, initially—we begin to discover very quickly—is a kind of menace. These two men come in sort of like the movie with Ernest Borgnine: "Marty, what do you want?" "I don't know. What do you want?" But we're getting into a kind of flavor, a tenor, a rhythm that is characteristically and sometimes exquisitely Hemingway.

Hemingway's first collection of short stories and vignettes is a collection called *In Our Time*, a number of them featuring Nick Adams, in fact. It was published in 1925, two years before the publication of "The Killers." There's a story in that earlier collection called "Soldier's Home," which again, illustrates what I'm talking about here. It centers on a returned soldier, whose name is Krebs, and it's instructive of Hemingway's style. Krebs comes back, and he's a little bit shell-shocked from the war, and all these stories are going around about heroic deeds and things that people did in the war that are confabulated and don't even represent reality. Krebs becomes more and more dissociated, and there's a scene at his home in Kansas in which his mother is saying to him, "You've got to get out. And you've got to go to church. And you've got to go to the dances. And you've got to meet girls. And you got to become more active," because clearly, he's becoming almost semi-catatonic from the war and the way the war weighs on him. And Hemingway describes Krebs as simply looking at the breakfast his mother has laid out for him—which includes bacon—looking at the bacon as it curls, as it changes, as bacon that has been fried will do. Just that sentence alone and all of its subtext—all that iceberg underneath it—is classic Hemingway.

It's not only Hemingway's style, [but] it's his stoic philosophy of life, associated with that famous phrase "grace under pressure," and living with the recognition of death being ever in the forefront of human destiny—it's about as influential in fiction as a work like *The Waste Land* by T. S. Eliot is in poetry.

In Our Time was an experimental and innovative work. It was a fusion of poetic prose, which included sketches and stories, and it was indicative of a trend during this period of individual stories being linked together with the unity that one might associate with a novel. Sherwood Anderson's *Winesburg, Ohio* was a major influence and example of that on Hemingway. Other American writers, like Jean Toomer, who wrote *Cane*; or years later, William Faulkner in *Go Down, Moses*; or African American writer Ernest Gaines in *Bloodline*, followed this pattern of interlocked stories, producing similar works. Volumes of interlocked or interconnected short fiction were what Babel put together in *Red Calvary* or what Joyce published with his landmark *Dubliners*.

"The Killers" specifically is out of a kind of hard-boiled or *noir* American fiction style that became identifiable with writers like Raymond Chandler and Dashiell Hammett. "The Killers" is one of the many Nick Adams stories that's an initiation story for Nick. We go through various forms of initiation that Nick goes through. In this story, he's on the verge of moving into adulthood, and the story reflects his initiation into manhood—as well as his loss of innocence—into the realm of experience, as we've seen before and we'll see again in so many stories. He meets a couple of hired killers. They enter into a diner. They're dressed in black, and they expect to find this ex-boxer named Ole Andreson who eats there every evening. After this initial banter, revealing to Nick and the diner manager, George, why they're there, the killers tie up Nick and the black cook, Sam, and put them in the kitchen. When Ole Andreson fails to show up, and they leave, George, the manager, unties Nick and suggests he go and tell Ole Andreson. Nick does as George suggests, but Ole Andreson tells Nick he's tired of running and he wants to run no more. Nick goes back to the diner and he tells George he can't bear thinking about Ole Andreson waiting in his apartment to be killed by two hit men. Nick indicates that he'll be getting out of town, and thus, the story ends.

Nick learns a great deal in this incident about violence and the murderousness and evil that are out there in the world, as well as the corruption and lethal kind of Mafia paybacks that were all too commonplace during the rough Prohibition era in Chicago.

The story is set nearby Chicago in Summit, Illinois. Hemingway, by the way, was born and grew up in Oak Park, a suburb of Chicago; he was born there in 1899. He once derogated Oak Park in a much-quoted remark as a place of "wide lawns and narrow minds." His own exposure to violence came early on, when he went with his country doctor father to an Indian camp—an experience turned into a fictional piece *In Our Time*. He witnessed a cesarean that was performed by his father without anesthetic on an Indian woman that caused her to scream so much that the husband, who was hearing all this, committed suicide. Hemingway and his father would both later also commit suicide, Hemingway taking his life in 1961 with a shotgun in Ketchum, Idaho. But his personal experience with violence—the experience which shaped his vision—began there, and went on, and can be seen reflected in stories like the ones in *In Our Time* or in "The Killers" just in the sense of the world being such a violent place.

Remember that Hemingway was wounded in 1918. He was a volunteer ambulance driver for the Italian army in World War I. He went out to see action; he went out to experience war, much in the way Babel did, and he saw it. What he saw became something that he internalized and absorbed as an artist. Nick—Hemingway's alter ego, his mask, his persona, his voice—learns in "The Killers" not only of the violence in the world, but he learns also from Ole Andreson some different kinds of initiation experience: stoicism and grace under pressure. Unlike Babel's "My First Goose," which is a story that clearly belongs to the protagonist, Liutov, "The Killers" could just as easily be Ole Andreson's story as it is Nick's, even though we don't meet Ole Andreson until later on in the story.

Stoicism, by the way, is a philosophy that goes back to Zeno. We see it in Brutus, who is a Stoic in *Julius Caesar*. Essentially, it posits the belief in the submission out of necessity to one's fate without visible emotion, breaking down, or showing one's emotions. Grace under pressure is the essence of the Hemingway ethos. I think it was Alfred Casson who said that Hemingway's mother, whose name was Grace, put pressure under grace because she used to dress Hemingway and his sister like twins when they were younger in very feminine kinds of clothes. She wanted two girls.

Getting back to the seriousness of the story though, the stoicism can be seen in Ole Andreson's reaction to the killers, Max and Al, and in George's reactions, as well, since he's more aware and initiated than Nick. He tells Nick, in the story's conclusion: "You better not think about it."

> "What's he going to do?" [Nick is asking George.]
>
> "Nothing." [George really being kind of a mentor for Nick here.]
>
> "They'll kill him."
>
> "I guess they will."
>
> "He must have got mixed up in something in Chicago."
>
> "I guess so," said Nick.
>
> "It's a hell of a thing!"
>
> "It's an awful thing," Nick said.
>
> They did not say anything. George reached down for a towel and wiped the counter.

There again you see that subtext: "They did not say anything." He just wiped the counter. There's a lot of seriousness, stoicism, a lot of real heavy weight here, but you don't necessarily get it in the language. The language is sparse.

> "I wonder what he did?" Nick said.
>
> "Double-crossed somebody. That's what they kill them for."
>
> "I'm going to get out of this town," Nick said.

> "Yes," said George. "That's a good thing to do."
>
> "I can't stand to think about him waiting in the room and knowing he's going to get it. It's too damned awful."
>
> "Well," said George, "you better not think about it."

"You better not think about it." One of the famous Hemingway critics, Philip Young, wrote about how Hemingway heroes avoid what Hamlet called the "pale cast of thought," as Nick does not only here but in the famous concluding story of *In Our Time*, "Big Two-Hearted River," after he has returned from the war. In that story, Nick makes camp, fishes, and stays busy in nature to avoid the psychic wounds of the violence that he has encountered and witnessed. Unlike poor, gloomy Goodman Brown, Nick can do this, though thoughts which carry emotion come rushing in on him uninvited, and he ultimately avoids fishing the swamp because the swamp represents something that he simply can't face. It's that avoidance of thought.

At the end of "The Killers," Nick wants to leave town, to move on, to forge ahead without having to think of Ole Andreson sitting in the rooming house waiting to be killed. This is what Philip Young called an instance of "thought preventative." So much of Hemingway's philosophy—his ethos—is based on thought preventative. When you're facing death—whether it's in combat, you're hunting, you're jumping out of an airplane, doing anything that heightens the sense of life because of the precariousness of it, because of the vulnerability you feel, because of the necessity to be in the moment—it stops thought in many instances, particularly when it's violent, now reflecting on what Hemingway conveys to us. Hemingway heroes often try to prevent thought, and they try to prevent thought through action. You see that through much of his work. Action is a thought preventative. Just doing something like Nick does in "Big Two-Hearted River"—making camp, fishing, and so forth—keeps him away from those thoughts, darker thoughts, thoughts about violence. Action of all kinds does the same thing, but particularly in Hemingway, we see actions which make one feel the thin cord—kind of gossamer thread, if you will—that separates life and death. When you feel that cord or when you feel it more intensely, of course, paradoxically, you feel more alive. That's what Hemingway is communicating in so much of his work, and that's where Hemingway becomes important to and such an influence on so many writers.

The killers provide the force in this story behind Nick's initiation, and—as I said—you can see the story as a story about Nick's initiation or you can see the story about Ole Andreson. We don't know what he did—probably double-crossed someone. That's a pretty good surmise, but it's his stoicism that comes across in the story that's conveyed. These two men are menacing from early on. They come in—I read the passage—but from that point, they become derisive. They use "bright boy" in addressing both George and Nick, and they do the same in asking George what he's looking at and then ordering Nick to join George on the other side of the counter. That's Max, the character. Al and Max seem indistinguishable at first, but then they do become distinct from one another. He orders George.

Then there's something really also palpably absurd and even comic about these characters, Max and Al. They have derby hats. They have tight black overcoats, gloves, and silk mufflers. We're told, in fact, that they look like twins in a vaudeville team. According to Al, his partner, Max, "talks too much." This is what begins to distinguish them. Al says this, by the way, from the kitchen, with Sam and Nick tied up and gagged and a sawed-off shotgun nearby. This is one way that Hemingway distinguishes one from the other; despite their kind of symbiotic relationship, they're different, like Rosencrantz and Guildenstern in *Hamlet*, the hired killers Goldberg and McCann in British Nobel laureate Harold Pinter's *The Birthday Party*, or the two hired killers in Pinter's later play *The Dumb Waiter*. You can see the kind of influence of "The Killers" that spreads out even across the Atlantic.

When both killers tell George that he's "lucky," the implication is that both George and Nick have had their lives spared, [have] come close to death. After Max says [that] George was "a regular little gentleman," Al said, "He knew I'd blow his head off." The killers feminize and homoeroticize George and Nick, contributing to an even greater sense of the experience as one impinging on manhood. Babel, you may recall, evoked homoeroticism in "My First Goose," but Hemingway makes it rather explicit. What is of special interest is the link between male violence and homosexual eroticism, as if both Babel and Hemingway see and dramatize that link that exists between the two. For example, Max calls Nick George's "boyfriend." He tells George he would make some girl a nice wife. Al says George and Nick are tied up "like a couple of girl friends in the convent." There's a reference, by the way, to "a kosher convent," highlighting the possibility that the killers are identifiable with a group of mostly Jewish gangsters who were enforcers for the Mob and came to be known as Murder, Incorporated.

Then we have Ole Andreson, heavyweight prize fighter. The killers have come to murder him. He's powerless against the forces that have come to take his life. He just stares at the wall, resigned to his fate, unwilling to run from those who are seeking his death, and admitting to Nick that he "got in wrong." He tells Nick that there is nothing to be done. You may remember that phrase, "nothing to be done," comes up repeatedly in Samuel Beckett's *Waiting for Godot*, and there is a sense in Hemingway of nihilism, of a sense of nothing to be done, particularly for Ole Andreson. He has made his bed, he's going to have to lie in it, and he's going to have to stare at the wall; that's his fate. We learn from the landlady that Ole Andreson—the Swede, as he's also called—is a nice, gentle man. We know, nonetheless—as Nick does—that he's doomed, that his past has caught up with him, and that he's going to have to pay the ultimate price.

There are other characters in the story who play subaltern roles and seem powerless also against these forces that intrude upon and threaten their lives. Sam, the cook, is only referred to as "the nigger." In other works by Hemingway, such as the Nick Adams story "The Battler" in *In Our Time* or in the novel *A Farewell to Arms*—where Frederic Henry inexplicably says, "Othello was a nigger"—there is use of the so-called "n-word," indicative of the times and—I think [it's] safe to say—Hemingway's bigotry. Sometimes it's a difficult line to separate between the two. I think Hemingway, from what we know about him, was clearly bigoted; he was bigoted against blacks and Jews. But nevertheless, you can look at the story and also recognize that the "n-word," which kind of captures you and makes you wince, was something that was commonly used for anybody with black skin. Hemingway's also dramatizing things as they are.

Sam is depicted in the story as a black man who wants above all to avoid trouble, and that's why he urges Nick not to go see Ole Andreson. He evokes that manhood motif again when Nick decides on his own volition to go and see Ole Andreson, and Sam says, "Little boys always know what they want to do."

George runs the eating place, but it's owned by someone named Henry. Mrs. Bell runs the rooming house where Ole Andreson is, but it belongs to someone named Mrs. Hirsch. The reasons behind sort of the masterpiece status of "The Killers" are many: the brevity and economy of language, the emotional impact of the story on Nick and on us as readers, and also the philosophy we begin to see, the Hemingway ethos that [is] conveyed in the story. [This] includes not only the notion that inherent violence in life is endemic and pervasive but the increased sense of life's intensity and polarities of either stoicism or a call to action when death is faced. Ole Andreson, the ex-pugilist—tired of running—is stoic. He accepts his death and refuses to act. But Nick—the observer, the younger man who has attained this knowledge of Ole Andreson's inevitable fate—goes on the run, leaves, gets out of town.

The power of this story is really in its embodiment of the archetypical themes of initiation and manhood. "The Killers" is, in so many ways, classic, vintage Hemingway. We see it in all the hallmarks of Hemingway's distinctive and profoundly influential style, which was shaped to a great extent by his experiences with Gertrude Stein and Ezra Pound, his mentors, while he was living as an expatriate in Paris, but also has origins in his earlier journalistic work for both the *Kansas City Star* and the *Toronto Star.*

Hemingway wrote his first literary work at the age of 17 and went on to distinguish himself as one of the leading figures of the 20th century. A lot of this had to do not only with his output but the fact that he lived a life that was larger than life and even took on the sobriquet "Papa," which we learn all about in a personal memoir about Hemingway called *Papa Hemingway* by A. E. Hotchner.

In 1953, Hemingway was awarded the Pulitzer Prize for his novel *The Old Man in the Sea*, again, a novel of stoicism and courage, [about] an old man simply sticking with "stick-to-it-ness" and showing great resilience. In 1954, he was named a recipient of the Nobel Prize for Literature. His influence on a host of writers has been singular, especially a bevy of significant American writers, including F. Scott Fitzgerald—they were friends, and they read each other's work—but also John Steinbeck, the African American writer Richard Wright, and Norman Mailer, who compared himself to

Hemingway. He talked about Hemingway as the heavyweight champ and said that—there's that boxing metaphor again; both writers were very drawn to boxing—he, Mailer, wanted essentially to step into his shoes and get the heavyweight title. Joan Didion, contemporary author of novels like *Play It As It Lays*, writes a very sparse, lean prose with a lot of this iceberg effect and subtext. And, as we'll see, Raymond Carver, called America's Chekhov, was certainly not only influenced by Chekhov but influenced to a great extent by Hemingway, as well. It's difficult really not to see the influence of Hemingway as being global because, although he's an American writer and although the writers I've mentioned are American writers, nevertheless, Hemingway was celebrated and much admired throughout Western Europe and Eastern Europe. He was admired, in fact, in the Soviet Union, where Babel's life was snuffed at such an early stage. He was admired to a great extent in the Soviet Union because he was seen as a writer who championed the proletariat, the ordinary people. By the time he came to write *For Whom the Bell Tolls*, he was antifascist, and this, of course, also endeared him to a great extent to the Soviets.

When I compared Hemingway's influence in the modern short story to T. S. Eliot's influence in poetry with *The Waste Land*, it's because of a story like "The Killers." "The Killers" is not only a story that's taught in universities throughout the world, but it's a story that's imitated. It's a story that, to some extent, we see the influence of in so much popular culture: hired killers and guys who almost seem like they are stock out of vaudeville. And all of the kinds of things that are really new in Hemingway have become a part of American and world culture.

It's hard to separate Hemingway from many of the writers who have tried to imitate him, but he was really the first. We've talked about a lot of parallels to Babel—and they are certainly there—but he was the first to really express this stoic philosophy in terms of the everyday, in terms of the ordinary. He's the first to really give us this sense of an inordinate menace that seems to be out there. Suddenly, guys are sitting in an establishment, going about their business, and then from out of nowhere, this threat, this menace, comes into their lives. Why? Because they happen to be there; they happen to be in the wrong place at the wrong time, and they could easily have been killed. They were fortunate, indeed, to get away. That sense of threat—that sense of menace that's simply out there—is something that comes across very strongly in "The Killers" and in Hemingway's work. What Hemingway seems to be saying is that there are killers that are out there, and they're out there to get you. I don't mean to be mordant about this, but I think it's the power of Hemingway's work. He once said that life is like a baseball game, and you know you're going to be thrown out; you just don't know how it's going to happen or why it's going to happen.

There's a scene in *A Farewell to Arms* where Frederic Henry is sitting, and there are a bunch of ants on a log. The ants are crawling along the log, he's looking at them, and he says to Catherine Barkley, his lover, "I could just kick that log over, and all those ants would be dead." It's like a microcosm of how Hemingway viewed the world. What does he decide to do instead? He decides to take his coffee and pour it on the ants so that they steam to death in a much more horrible, brutal death, and he says, "God is a fascist." A horrible kind of conclusion to make, but that sense of the ubiquitousness of death, and the threat and menace of it happening randomly and capriciously, is something we see in "The Killers" and in so much of Hemingway's work.

From this great Modernist writing and from the harsh Realism we find in Babel and Hemingway, we're going to move on to another writer of great distinction who was also a contemporary of theirs and is another of the great Modernist short story writers. [This is] a European Jewish author who, like Babel, experienced the fall of an empire, yet who is far different than Babel and Hemingway in his sensibility and the nature of his storytelling. We have words that are common to our lexicon because of the distinctive style of the individual writers: words like Chekhovian, Joycean, and of course, Hemingwayesque. We go next to the Austro-Hungarian Empire and the work of another inimitable, masterful short fiction storyteller who immerses us into a surreal and cockeyed world we have come to associate with a word of now common usage: Kafkaesque. In the next story, we meet a man—an artist—willing to die for the sake of his art. Next up for discussion: Franz Kafka and his great story "A Hunger Artist."

Lecture Ten

Kafka's Parable—"A Hunger Artist"

Scope:

This lecture begins with a discussion of tormented Kafka's life and the contributions to the conception of "A Hunger Artist" made by his obsession with his father, his Jewishness, his work as a civil servant, and his tuberculosis and depression. We then focus on Kafka's dark humor and satire before moving to the notion of the *donnée* and how it works in "A Hunger Artist." We also discuss the established tradition of the German novella that influenced Kafka, who lived in Prague in the Austro-Hungarian Empire but wrote in German. As we will see, the hunger artist in the story is a symbol of art, of body and soul, and of faith and asceticism. Allegorically, the story suggests the move from the world of the past to the world of Modernism and its ties to conceptions about ontology and Existentialism, as well as the relationship among art, commerce, and life's insatiable hungers. Finally, we discuss the protagonist and his role at the circus and the revelatory final scene with the overseer, concluding with reflections on the story's power and the continuing impact of Kafka's writings.

Outline

I. Shards or elements of Kafka's sad and tormented life are embedded in his short story "A Hunger Artist."

- **A.** Kafka's life, in many ways, was driven by an insatiable and unrealizable desire to please his father, a desire revealed in his "Letter to My Father."
- **B.** Kafka was a strongly self-identifying Prague Jew who gives us, in "A Hunger Artist," a story about the quest for spiritual and artistic fulfillment and the nature of suffering.
- **C.** One also sees in the story Kafka's experience with the tedious, repetitive work of a bureaucratic civil servant.
- **D.** Kafka suffered from advancing tuberculosis while writing this story. His illness rendered him unable to eat, and he was literally starving to death while writing "A Hunger Artist."

II. One of Kafka's most famous aphorisms about literature was that it can serve as an axe for the frozen sea within us. Max Brod, Kafka's close friend and biographer, said that the writer often laughed when reading stories, and there is indeed dark humor and satire in “A Hunger Artist.”

A. A good example of Kafka’s dark humor is the fact that the “permanent watchers” selected by the public to monitor the hunger artist are mostly butchers.

B. The story also satirizes the cliché of the starving artist. Like Kafka, the hunger artist would ultimately give up almost everything for his art but is neither appreciated nor understood by the public.

III. The story’s *donnée* (its premise) gives us a history of a phenomenon that we must accept as real—hunger artistry—much as we accept the idea that Gregor Samsa wakes up as a cockroach in “The Metamorphosis.”

A. The existence of hunger artistry is made utterly real through Kafka’s descriptions of its decline in popularity.

B. Kafka was influenced by the German novella (rooted in work by Goethe), a genre in which everything in the fiction changes with a central turning point. The turning point in “A Hunger Artist” comes when the art of fasting suddenly loses its currency and popularity.

C. The hunger artist signs on as a circus display and becomes largely a figure of nostalgia for those who recall his earlier popularity.

D. Kafka gives us imagined details about hunger artistry, including the ritual and showmanship of the performance, the 40-day period of fasting, the accompanying band and hoopla, and the escorting ladies who seem friendly to the hunger artist but who are, in reality, cruel.

E. The split between the world of the past and the world of the present is highly suggestive of an allegory of the move to modernity and Modernism. Kafka reveals to us the shift in public interest as time moves forward.

IV. The hunger artist functions as a religions, ascetic, and artistic symbol.

A. The hunger artist is portrayed as a troubled spirit who is isolated and hungry for recognition as the greatest performer of his art but feels dissatisfied and cheated because of the manner in which his performance is turned into commerce.

B. Art is shown as a perversion of truth. At the end of 40 days, the impresario presents the artist as needing to stop the performance, but in truth, the artist wants desperately to continue starving himself.

C. The artist is famished for starvation—highly suggestive of the need and pathology of mortifying the flesh in order to elevate the spirit or soul.

D. Kafka contrasts the hunger artist with the hunger for life of the panther—emblematic of our animality—opposing our ontology (being) to what we might imagine our souls to be.

V. The hunger artist nourishes his faith in his life performances through abstention from nourishment—a profound paradox and parable of faith and asceticism.

A. The hunger artist is a suffering martyr, but what his martyrdom signifies remains a mystery.

B. The hunger artist is alienated from everything other than the desire to prove his greatness and remain true to his art. At the story's end, however, we discover that the artist couldn't find any food that he liked, that his asceticism may be linked to being a picky eater!

C. Among all who observe the hunger artist at the peak of his popularity he is the only one dissatisfied with the proceedings. He stands alone, literally, against the world, in his alienation.

VI. One associates the hunger artist finally with the "bread and circuses" from Juvenal's satire of the decadent Roman Empire and its popular debasement of entertainment for the masses.

A. Placed next to the menagerie of animals, it is, ironically, the geography of his cage that draws crowds to the hunger artist—he becomes a relic of the past, overlooked or ignored by the crowds.

B. In the last scene with the overseer, the hunger artist reveals the essential paradox of his life and all that had driven him: He wanted to be admired but felt he shouldn't be because he was unable *not* to fast and couldn't find food he liked. Now that he has apparently been able to eclipse all records in hunger artistry, no one knows or cares.

Suggested Readings:

Brod, *Franz Kafka: A Biography.*

Juvenal, *The Satires.*

Kafka, *The Castle.*

———, "A Hunger Artist," translated by Willa Muir and Edwin Muir.

———, "In the Penal Colony."

———, "Letter to My Father."

———, "The Metamorphosis."

———, *The Trial.*

Pawel, *Nightmare of Reason: A Life of Franz Kafka.*

Questions to Consider:

1. What are we to make of the fact that the hunger artist reveals that he cannot *not* fast?
2. How believable is this story? Does it matter that Kafka invents his own version of hunger artists?
3. What exactly is Kafka suggesting about life and death by the replacement of the hunger artist in his cage with the large, hungry cat?

Lecture Ten—Transcript

Kafka's Parable—"A Hunger Artist"

"A Hunger Artist" is regarded by many—along with "The Metamorphosis"—as one of Kafka's great short fiction masterpieces. Clearly one of the last century's most influential writers of fiction, Kafka was born in 1883 into a middle-class Jewish family in Prague, then part of the Austro-Hungarian Empire. Only a few of his stories and none of his fragmentary novels were published during his lifetime. Though he gave every outward indication that he did not want them ever to be published, this was not the case [with] "A Hunger Artist," which was written and published in a collection of that title near the end of Kafka's life in 1924, when he was dying of tuberculosis. He actually died of starvation from a throat condition caused by the tuberculosis, which made eating too painful; intravenous feeding did not exist then.

Kafka's sad and tormented life and shards or elements of it are embedded in this tale. His life, in many ways, was a life of trying to please his father, which for him, was insatiable, unrealizable—it was like trying to get recognition from God—and is reflected in this story in the insatiability that drives the hunger artist. The tortured relationship between Kafka and his father—Hermann Kafka, a shopkeeper—is revealed in what we know of Kafka's life from his biographers. It is also reflected in the singularly autobiographic work of Kafka's "Letter to My Father," as well as in his highly regarded and widely read and taught story about Gregor Samsa, that young man who wakes up as a cockroach in "The Metamorphosis," which was written in 1915. Kafka's most famous novels, *The Trial* and *The Castle*, also dramatize fruitless and futile quests to understand higher authorities. [These quests] can be seen as tied to trying to find links to distant patriarchic authority or even to a more distant God.

A strongly self-identifying Jew, Kafka gives us "A Hunger Artist," a story about seeking spiritual and artistic fulfillment and also a story about the nature of suffering. One can see in the story the tedious, repetitive work of a bureaucratic, civil-servant claims investigator, which is what Kafka was for many years, though he was a law graduate and the inventor of the first civilian hardhat. Kafka worked for a year for an Italian insurance company and then for a number of years for a Bohemian workers' accident insurance claim company. The work, though by any standards boring, was nevertheless work that Kafka performed—from all that we know—with dedication and excellence.

Kafka was also an artist—a literary artist—and there are stories about Kafka that appear in his biographies and that are told about how he said that he could spend the rest of his life or eternity alone with his work. That feeling of isolation—despite the fact that there were friends and a number of women in his life—that feeling of needing to be isolated, of being committed to his art, of being in some ways consumed by his art—with an emphasis on consumption both in its tubercular as well as its eating meanings—was really what Kafka's life as an artist was about. When he wrote this story, his tuberculosis was advancing. He was suffering depression after a four-week vacation from Prague that had been prescribed by his doctor. He was unable to eat. Though dying of tuberculosis, he was writing away while literally starving to death. According to his biographers, he actually sobbed after writing this story, "A Hunger Artist."

One of Kafka's most famous aphorisms about literature was that it can be "an axe for the frozen sea within us," though Max Brod—who was his close friend and biographer—said that Kafka often laughed when reading stories. There is also, despite all of its painful motifs, dark humor and satire in "A Hunger Artist." A good example of that dark humor comes early on. By the way, when I speak of dark humor, I'm speaking of a kind of humor that's associated with a lot of American writers, like Nathanael West and, later on, Thomas Pynchon or Kurt Vonnegut. It's early on in "A Hunger Artist" that there are "permanent watchers" who watch this man who is literally starving himself as performance art. They're selected by the public, and they're mostly butchers.

The ending, with the overseer, is another example. The hunger artist is saying "forgive me" and importuning the overseer to forgive him, and the overseer thinks, this guy is nuts; he's out of his mind. The hunger artist then says, "Don't admire me"; he admits he couldn't find any food that he really liked. There's really a lot of levity or humor in this, even though it's dark humor, even though it's macabre. There's also satire of artists. I mean, "starving artist" is a cliché, [but] think of all those artists like Kafka who would ultimately give up just about everything for their art. This is a guy who gives up everything for his art, but his art happens to be starving. It's also a satire in the fact that the poor hunger artist feels that nobody really understands the nature of his art, understands what drives him. They think, in fact, that he's not really starving himself. They think he's cheating, sneaking food, or taking food on the sly—all of those kinds of things—and it bothers him, and it bothers him that the world hasn't given him the recognition that he feels that he deserves, that he can't break the records. We'll talk about all that, because he wants to establish himself as the greatest hunger artist. We get a parody, in some ways, or a satire, of all those artists who feel that they're not understood by the world, that the world doesn't appreciate their art, that they aren't given or accorded the kind of respect that they feel their commitment to their art—and all that they give to their art—should result in.

There's a *donnée* in this story. That's the given of the story. We speak of a *donnée* as like: "A man wakes up, and he's a cockroach." Here, it's not quite so supernatural or beyond belief; it's within an alternate history. I'll read the opening in just a moment. We accept the fact that there were hunger artists. This establishes reality for us, just like Gregor Samsa waking up as a cockroach. It's not nearly as fantastical, but nevertheless, we're told by the omniscient narrator that hunger artists existed, that they went through a cycle of being highly popular, and then suffered a loss or a decline of public interest and loss of popularity:

> During these last decades the interest in professional fasting has markedly diminished. It used to pay very well to stage such great performances under one's own management, but today that is quite impossible. We live in a different world now.

Kafka could be saying that with a great deal of weight in so many ways, but he's saying it here about professional fasting, which never really existed.

> At one time the whole town took a lively interest in the hunger artist; from day to day of his fast the excitement mounted; everybody wanted to see him at least once a day; there were people who bought season tickets for the last few days and sat from morning till night in front of his small barred cage …

Kafka is setting a scene here by making it seem utterly real that this kind of performance art—starvation, hunger artistry—existed and making it utterly real that the world has changed because it doesn't exist any more. It's not as popular as it once was; it went from being very popular to being unpopular and probably not existing at all anymore.

Beginning at the end of the 18th century with Johann von Goethe and flowering throughout the 19th century, the German novella was all over the German-speaking world: realistic stories that were based on single events or what has been described as an unheard-of event that has occurred. That was a preeminent fictional form in German literature, and Kafka was certainly influenced by it. Though "The Hunger Artist" deviates from the usual German-novella standard of action being confined to a single central event, the realism of the genre and its emphasis on everything in the fiction changing with a turning point can be seen in the fortunes of the hunger artist. His fortunes change irrevocably. The art of fasting suddenly loses its currency and popularity, and that's the turning point in the story.

During the time of its popularity in the story, there is an elaborate ritual for the hunger artist. He fasts for 40 days, and this is set up by the impresario, his manager. Actually, he would love to go on fasting longer than 40 days, but the irony is that the impresario believes that you're going to have to have 40 days of fasting, because people won't believe otherwise that he's actually done the fasting. There's all of that strange kind of movement between appearance and reality. The impresario wants it to appear to people that the hunger artist is not cheating, and what a great irony, because the hunger artist has this honor code where he will not cheat and will not let any morsel or water even pass his lips. With the butcher monitors I alluded to and the impresario, there's an engineering of a kind of illusion that in 40 days, we'll have a checking of the hunger artist—we'll have the hunger artist looked at by a doctor to make sure that he's okay—and all of these kinds of things, all of these rituals embedded, strictly out of Kafka's imagination. There's even a fanfare conclusion at the end of the 40-day fast, complete with a military band, and that's when the doctors measure the results of the fast. There's a pair of young ladies to accompany the hunger artist out of the cage. We learn that this particular hunger artist is constantly suspected of cheating but, ironically, feels he's being cheated out of his desire to keep on fasting beyond the 40-day limit, whereupon he's forced to eat in a public display.

After hunger artistry falls out of favor, he signs on to be part of a circus, and his cage is placed at the end, where throngs go to see various animals. They don't go to see him; in fact, they often go right past him, or they stop there mainly out of nostalgia: a father telling his son or daughter, "This was something that I saw as a kid, a hunger artist. It used to be popular."

He goes on fasting alone, utterly isolated, until one day, one of the circus overseers sees what looks like a perfectly good empty cage, only to be informed that the hunger artist is in it. He pokes around in the straw, and the hunger artist is found. That's when he asks for forgiveness, admitting that he couldn't help fasting because he was unable to find any food that he liked. They take him away—his corpse—and in his cage, they put a panther (translated sometimes as a number of big cats—a leopard or jaguar—it doesn't really matter, but in the Willa and Edwin Muir translation, the most famous translation, it's a panther). The story concludes with:

> The panther was all right. The food he liked was brought to him without hesitation by the attendants; he seemed not even to miss his freedom; his noble body, furnished almost to the bursting point with all that it needed, seemed to carry freedom around with it too; somewhere in his jaws it seemed to lurk; and the joy of life streamed with such ardent passion from his throat that for the onlookers it was not easy to stand the shock of it. But they braced themselves, crowded around the cage, and did not want ever to move away.

That last imagery of this large cat—full of life, full of *joie de vivre*, full of the joy of life, eager to eat—of course, is the antithesis of the suffering artist, of the hunger artist committed to his art, committed to starving himself, depriving himself, giving up life itself for his art, which in so many ways, tells us so much about Franz Kafka.

There are details in the story of a profession that did not exist. It's made out of whole cloth by Kafka, and yet it reflects so much of Kafka's inner life. We even have the ritual, the showmanship, the 40-day periodicity reminiscent of Noah, the black leotard that the hunger artist wears. There's a lavish breakfast after the 40 days that the hunger artist pays for; there's a band; there's hoopla; and there are these escorting ladies whom I alluded to, who seem friendly to the hunger artist, but we are told in reality are cruel; and the hunger artist has an honor code. All of this is fictional; all of this is what you would call an alternate history of a man's life but also an alternate history of what seems to be generalized for us as hunger artistry. There's the individual artist—a hunger artist, as the title suggests—and there's also hunger artistry suggested [as] once a popular form of entertainment.

There's a real split in this story between the world that was and the different one that we now have; it was in that opening paragraph that I read: "The world is different now." It's highly suggestive to us of an allegorical level in the story, of a move from the world that Kafka lived in and the breaking up of the Austro-Hungarian Empire to modernity and Modernism. Kafka is really right on the cusp of that Modernism, and he's revealing to us the shift in public interest as time marches. There's a sense, perhaps, of almost a kind of indictment of that fickleness—perhaps "indictment" is too strong a word, as Kafka in this story is not necessarily moralizing—[but it is] a recognition that the public interest can change overnight, just as it does for hunger artistry. Hunger artists lose their popularity; the public reveals its fickleness as revulsion to professional fasting sets in, and there's not even any accounting for it. Why is it that one form of literary art—one form of the short story—can be popular, one writer can be popular, and then suddenly that popularity wanes or disappears, and it can disappear for no reason at all? The hunger artist becomes a circus display, which also reveals something about the loss of public interest. He becomes largely a figure of nostalgia for those who recall him during his prominent, famous, showcased days.

This story has so many levels to it that one is hard-pressed to really get into it without a feeling of looking at a feast. The hunger artist, after all, becomes a symbol: religious, ascetic, as well as artistic. Let's talk about the artistic [symbolism] a little bit more first. Remember, again, that this is one of a variety—it's *a* hunger artist, as opposed to being *the* artist—but he's pictured for us, this particular hunger artist, as a troubled spirit: isolated, hungry for recognition, wants to be the greatest, best record–holding, supreme artist at what he does, but he feels dissatisfied and as if the world is cheating him because of his set rituals as a performance artist and the manner in which his performances are turned into commerce.

We have a whole implicit commentary here about how art does turn into show business or performance. We see in Kafka—as we did in Henry James—a concern about the nature of art and the role of the artist with respect to commerce and to the aspirations beyond the commercial of creating true art or what seems to the artist to be true art. The art that we see in this story becomes a kind of perversion of truth. The impresario presents the artist at the end of 40 days as needing to stop performing when the truth is [that] the artist wants desperately to continue to go on starving himself.

It's also, in this story, a kind of division between body and soul: The artist is famished for starvation. What a wonderful paradox. Think about that. He's famished, hungry, and at his wits' end to starve himself. It's highly suggestive of the need and pathology of keeping the flesh down in order to lift or elevate the spirit or soul. It's what ascetics, monks, and men of religion—both East and West—have always thought: the necessity of bringing up their spirit or soul through essentially keeping the flesh and the needs and desires of the flesh—like the flesh that the big cat eats at the end—under control, fasting. Fasting has always been associated, in fact, with the monastic or religious life, the ascetic life. You've got the aesthetic and the ascetic. The artist is contrasted by Kafka to the hunger for life that pulsates in that panther—this particular artist, or hunger artist, starving artist. It's emblematic when we see that panther—or leopard, in some translations—of our animality, of our ontology—that is, our being—as opposed to what we imagine, perhaps, our soul to be. This binary of body and soul is really quite impressed upon us in this short, brilliant story.

It's also a story about faith and asceticism. The hunger artist nourishes his faith in his life performances through abstention from nourishment. What a profound paradox that is and what a parable of faith and asceticism. The hunger artist is a suffering martyr, but what his martyrdom stands for or signifies remains a mystery. We have, in effect, a martyr to a cause, or to a higher power, or to a higher artistic aspiration that we don't necessarily understand and don't know in any specific way, just like we don't know why the hunger artist is so driven. What's the cause behind this man's artistic compulsion to starve himself and to perform as the best performer of starving himself of all performers? What drives art? It's a story that Kafka really brings into a laser focus, and it remains, in many respects, of course, mysterious.

One of Kafka's biographers, Ernest Pawel, called the story "a parable of alienation." Indeed, we see in the hunger artist an alienation from his grounded being—an alienation from his soul—in his aspiring toward being the supreme, consummate artist. What drives him, other than glory and greatness, is remaining true to his art, though, paradoxically, we discover at story's end—and this is, again, something that in some ways is unmistakably humorous, in a dark way, to be sure—that he couldn't find any food that he liked. His asceticism may be more connected to being a picky eater, though that's an easy assumption. But that seems to be at least a big part of it; at least, that's what he says. He gives his reasons: "couldn't find the food I liked."

Among all those who observe the hunger artist at the peak of his popularity, he is the only one dissatisfied with the proceedings. He stands alone—literally, against the world—in this alienation. Where does he wind up? He winds up in the circus. He's driven to perform even as his art has fallen into decline, even as it doesn't have public recognition. He still has to go on performing. This, I think, really reflects for us Kafka the man, but it's also Kafka creating an alter ego for himself, fusing it into fiction, bringing his imagination to bear, and creating this whole alternate world of the hunger artist.

No longer with the impresario—his manager—he signs on with the circus, and in order to spare his own feelings, he avoids reading the conditions of his contract. Clearly, they're getting him for a paltry sum. Clearly, he has fallen from his high place of fame and adulation. Clearly, he's a has-been, but he still goes on with his art. He still continues to starve himself. In fact, [he can continue] now that he's alone in a cage with just straw and a cage that's not really attended to; everybody doesn't look at him because they're more interested in the animals, or if they look at him, they really don't look at him with much interest. In fact, as the story progresses—they used to put the days up, the number of days that the man fasted—the number of days stays the same, and nobody bothers to change it anymore, just like nobody bothers to change the cage. When they find him, he's underneath all that straw, and he's obviously skin and bones, literally emaciated.

One associates the hunger artist, when he's in the circus in the end, with "bread and circuses," the phrase right out of Juvenal's satire of that decadent Roman Empire and the popular debasement of entertainment for the masses. He's there in the circus because the circus can include all kinds of different entertainment; the circus has all kinds of variety. But people forget about him; he's alone. Yet he's able to go on fasting and fasting, and he even loses track of the number of days. He doesn't even know how long he has fasted.

Placed next to the menagerie of animals, it's ironically the geography of his cage that draws crowds, because that's where he is, near the animals. People are interested in seeing the animals, so they go right by him. He's a relic of the past. It reminds me, in some ways, of the great Joe Louis, the world heavyweight boxing champion, who, at the end of his career, was a greeter and doorman at Caesars Palace in Las Vegas. I know that's a difficult analogy in some ways, but in some ways, it really works. There's a kind of circus feeling to Caesars Palace, and if you walked in, saw Joe Louis, and you were a young person and didn't know how great he was—how marvelous he was in the ring—he meant very little to you, if anything at all. You just saw him as another doorman, just like people would go by and just see this as another cage.

In the last scene, with the overseer, the hunger artist is in his circus cage, and he reveals with his last lines the essential paradox of his life and of all that had driven him: how he wanted to be admired, but felt he shouldn't be because he was unable not to fast and couldn't find the food he liked. There again is not only the revelation that he couldn't find the food he liked, but he couldn't *not* fast. There is built into that something really quite significant in Kafka's saying about what drives an artist to create. Nobody's guaranteeing an artist that they're going to get the recognition, glory, adulation, or even the monetary commercial success that perhaps they feel might be deserved if they are completely devoted to their art. There's no correlation between those two. But the point is that real artists—and the hunger artist is a real artist—are driven by forces that they don't even understand. He couldn't *not* fast, and he apparently is able briefly to eclipse all records when he's in the circus. This is the sadness of his story in so many ways: He can keep on fasting, and fasting, and fasting, but no one knows, and no one cares. To a great extent, he even loses track of the number of days he has fasted; he even can't keep track any more.

This story works on so many levels. It's one of those stories that's a testament to Kafka's genius. I should mention that it has an extraordinary power to it that you can find even more in the original German. It's perfect in many ways or as close to perfect as you can find as far as craft and profound ambiguity. It's allegorical. It has strengths, dreamlike or surreal effects, and multi-villain portrayals of the human condition that really expand and ripple out in so many directions. I hesitate to use the word "perfect" because, to some extent, of course, the hunger artist is striving for perfection.

I'm reminded of an interview I once did with the actor—you could say "actress," some of you—Isabella Rossellini, who talked about working with Martin Scorsese. Martin Scorsese had made a piece of a film that he was working on with her that he felt was perfect, and therefore, he had to do away with it. You can't create perfect art—art has to have some flaws to it—is the lesson in that little story.

Kafka is giving us a number of lessons here, as well—built into this story—about art and commerce, about aspiring to great art, [and] about what motivates that aspiration. Maybe there can't be true art any more than there can be this true sense of spirituality through the flagellation and deprivation of the flesh or anything true and absolute. But if one is driven by the absolute or toward the absolute and one has desires or hungers in life—particularly in self-expression or in the hunger for receiving recognition—can [one] ever really be satisfied? I'm not saying that Kafka's giving us a sermon; I'm saying that Kafka's raising these kinds of questions in the story because I believe he is. Kafka, perhaps more than any single writer during the 20th century, understood deeply profoundly, and keenly the isolation and angst, not only of the artist, but—it seems to me, and it's one of the reasons for his greatness—of the human condition, of what I alluded to before as that ontological alienation, and also of the nature of asceticism or of a quest for a higher and more transcendent reality, a spiritual quest, a quest for recognition from one's father when one's father is not willing to give one recognition. That father can be the Father who is divine in heaven, as well.

Kafka was—in so many ways—a prophet, not only of the atrocities of the Second World War but also of Existential thinking that would follow soon after that. Had Kafka lived, he—like his three sisters and their families—would have perished in a Nazi concentration camp. Jorge Luis Borges, Paul Auster, Joyce Carol Oates, and Philip Roth are all writers in whose fiction we see Kafka as a major influence. In fact, one of Roth's stories has Kafka as a character living in

America, teaching Hebrew school, and Kafka actually wrote a novel called *Amerika*, with a "k." Some of you remember in the 1960s that there were radicals who thought it fashionable to talk about Amerika with a "k." They were thinking about Kafka. There was also, by the way, a little button that was popular in the 1960s that said, "Kafka was a *kvetch*." *Kvetch* is a Yiddish word for someone who complains too much. There was also one that said, "Proust is a *yenta*"—which is essentially a gossiper—about the great Marcel Proust.

Kafka was more than a complainer; Kafka was a consummate artist. His life was dedicated to art. He was a man who suffered for his art; suffered, of course, with tuberculosis; and he suffered because of his relationship with his father. His life is not a life filled with joy. But nevertheless, I don't want you to mistake the sense of the humor that's there in the work, as well. It's dark humor—it's what would be called later black humor, or gallows humor—but nevertheless, it's there. Think about this guy in his leotard with his ribs sticking out, starving himself to death because that's his art. It's funny; it's crazy; it's what people do. It reflects the drives and the impetus behind a lot human action, and it's, again, a portal into the human condition through a story that is shorter than a lot of the stories we're going to be reading and discussing but, nevertheless, has that kind of punch and power to it.

Speaking of punch and power, we next go back to England. We're going to concentrate our attention next on a magical, haunting story by another one of the 20th century's preeminent and most important literary figures—novelist, poet, and short fiction writer D. H. Lawrence—and another fantasy called "The Rocking-Horse Winner." [Here,] Lawrence moves us even further away from Realism but, nevertheless, captures some of the more important Modernist themes. Onward next to "The Rocking-Horse Winner" by D. H. Lawrence.

Lecture Eleven

Lawrence's Blue-eyed "Rocking-Horse Winner"

Scope:

"The Rocking-Horse Winner," by D. H. Lawrence, seems, in some ways, like a dark fairy tale. In this lecture, we look at how the story works in terms of its *donnée* and how Lawrence moves us along by craft and pacing. We reflect on Lawrence's biography and philosophy and explore the major contributions he made to modern literature and painting. We then focus on what critic Janice Harris identifies as the social, psychological, and familial levels of meaning in "The Rocking-Horse Winner" and on the story's religious dimension. We conclude with an appreciation of the rich, multilayered meanings suggested by the story (including those germane to imperialism), its inherent mysticism, and its emphasis on human values over materialistic ones.

Outline

I. "The Rocking-Horse Winner" is a fairy-tale story based on the *donnée* of a boy, Paul, looking for "luck" (money) by riding his rocking-horse.

- **A.** The story begins with a description of Paul's mother, Hester, who harbors a secret: She cannot love her children.
- **B.** Paul, too, harbors a secret. We learn as the story progresses that Paul is betting on horses, but only toward the end do we discover the secret of how Paul gets his luck.
- **C.** Lawrence masterfully controls the reader as he builds up the emotional and supernatural effects of the story. Even the house in which the characters live is haunted by the need for money. Paul's family, the rocking-horse, the doll, and the puppy all seem to hear the haunting phrase repeated by the house itself: "There must be more money!"

II. Critic Janice Harris aptly describes the story as social, psychological, and familial.

- **A.** The story is rooted in social hierarchy and the need for a particular family to live in style and to move up into the superior strata of the British class system.

B. The supplanting of life and love by money or materialism is Hester's legacy to her son. (Her name is ironically associated with the heroine of Hawthorne's *The Scarlet Letter*, about which Lawrence wrote a well-known essay.)

C. Money is demonic and connected to a kind of shame and humiliation at one's inability to keep up social position and outward appearances.

D. The oedipal relationship is key in the story and in the life of D. H. Lawrence.

1. The poet and critic W. D. Snodgrass likens Paul's behavior on the horse to masturbation and links it to Paul's oedipal drive to replace his father.
2. Masturbation for Lawrence was a form of solipsism, the belief that the only reality is subjective reality.

III. The story has a significant religious dimension.

A. When Basset, the gardener, discusses Paul, he is "as serious as a church" and speaks of the young master "in a secret religious voice."

B. Luck, the mother tells Paul, comes from God, and with his talent, Paul is (at least, according to Basset) receiving messages from heaven.

C. We sense, however, that Paul is actually more in touch with demonic forces. Uncle Oscar twice calls him "poor devil" at the story's end, and there appears to be a kind of Faustian bargain between Paul and whatever supernatural force is supplying him with the names of the winning horses.

D. The pursuit of money hardens Hester's heart and turns Paul's eyes into a petrified demonic blue with "an uncanny cold fire in them." What appears heavenly to Basset is indeed hellish.

IV. The names Singhalese and Malabar call to mind British colonialism and the idea of the Sun never setting on the British Empire in this rich, multilayered, and remarkable story. "The Rocking-Horse Winner" remains anomalous in Lawrence's canon but a masterpiece of compelling storytelling with an embedded morality.

Suggested Readings:

Harris, "Levels of Meaning in Lawrence's 'The Rocking-Horse Winner,'" from *The Short Fiction of D. H. Lawrence.*

Lawrence, "The Horse Dealer's Daughter."

———, *Kangaroo.*

———, *Lady Chatterley's Lover.*

———, *The Plumed Serpent.*

———, "The Rocking-Horse Winner."

———, *Sons and Lovers.*

Snodgrass, "The Rocking-Horse—The Symbol, the Pattern, the Way of Life," in *The Hudson Review*, vol. xi, no. 2, Summer 1958.

Questions to Consider:

1. What do we conclude from Oscar Creswell's final remarks?
2. What does this story reveal to us ultimately about the nature of luck? Of luck and money?
3. What forces beyond our own does Paul appear to be able to ride to in order to find out the winners of the horse races that he, Basset, and Uncle Oscar bet on?

Lecture Eleven—Transcript

Lawrence's Blue-eyed "Rocking-Horse Winner"

D. H. Lawrence's "The Rocking-Horse Winner" is really a dark fairy tale in many ways. I'd like to begin with the text so you can get a feeling for just to what extent it really is just that:

> There was a woman who was beautiful, who started with all the advantages, yet she had no luck. She married for love, and the love turned to dust. She had bonny children, yet she felt they had been thrust upon her, and she could not love them. They looked at her coldly, as if they were finding fault with her. And hurriedly she felt she must cover up some fault in herself. Yet what it was that she must cover up she never knew. Nevertheless, when her children were present, she always felt the center of her heart go hard. This troubled her, and in her manner she was all the more gentle and anxious for her children, as if she loved them very much. Only she herself knew that at the center of her heart was a hard little place that could not feel love, no, not for anybody. Everybody else said of her: "She is such a good mother. She adores her children." Only she herself, and her children themselves, knew it was not so. They read it in each other's eyes.

That begins really pretty much like "once upon a time" and, in a very sort of expansive way, gives us a sense of this woman's character, of her inner life as well as her outer life. It moves on to what we call a *donnée* (again, the given in a story), and it steadfastly builds up to this—of a boy searching for luck. The mother's name is Hester, and she identifies luck with money. She tells her son, Paul, that they're unlucky because they don't have any money, and he goes on a search for luck.

We learn that the boy—in fact, this is a secret within a secret, much like the mother's secret about her heart being hard where her children are concerned—is riding his rocking-horse, and riding it feverishly and relentlessly, until he's able to somehow find out who the winner is going to be in horse races. That's the given in the story: A boy can actually somehow divine the winners of horse races by riding a rocking-horse, if "divine" is actually the right word here, since it appears in the story more like a demonic process, being in touch with demonic forces.

There's also this supernatural fact in the story that the house Paul and his family reside in continues somehow repeatedly to utter the sentence "There must be more money. There must be more money." Paul, it turns out, is in a partnership with the gardener—whose name is Bassett—who informs Paul's Uncle Oscar that there's an ongoing arrangement that the two have of betting on horses and winning; Uncle Oscar gets in on the action, while Paul continues to pick winners by riding his rocking-horse. He can't always be assured of who the winner is going to be, but when he's sure, he's really sure. Paul and his uncle essentially join forces to give Paul's mother an anonymous gift on her birthday of £5,000, broken down to £1,000 per year for five years. But the voices in the house only become louder, more insistent, and worse than ever: "There must be more money! There must be more money!" Paul starts to actually fail in getting the correct winning horse until he pushes himself for the big one—the Derby—eventually shouting out "Malabar," which is the name of the horse that indeed will win. Then, soon after proclaiming Malabar the winner of the Derby, he falls into a fever and ultimately dies.

That's the story in essence, but it's told masterfully and in a detached tone that yields a whole sense of Lawrence's didactic purpose, because what he's after here is condemning materialism and the pursuit of money. It's not only the old cliché that money is the root of all evil, but the idea that somehow the pursuit of money, the need for more and more money, and an acquisitiveness which seems to be insatiable are the forces that reap tragedy: that to try to fill up the inner emptiness with this need for money—or something outside of the self—can decimate the whole power of love, that money itself can overshadow and take over where love is concerned.

In this case, we're talking, of course, about maternal love: the maternal love that a mother should naturally feel for her only begotten son. What's amazing, in many ways, about this story is that the voices in the house are made credible early on. The reader actually feels that these voices are real, that they're literal. This has a good deal to do with Lawrence's control. He controls us as readers, because he builds up this emotional and supernatural effect in the story, beginning with the house being haunted by this need for money and these voices resounding through the house.

He even tells us that the rocking-horse itself hears these voices, and the doll that's in the nursery and the puppy also appear to hear them. Speaking of the nursery, by the way, what happens in the course of the story is that Paul moves out of the nursery, but the haunting noise—"There must be more money!"—has become absorbed by him in such a way that he feels he needs to prove to his mother that he's lucky, that he can make money. We're in a kind of Rod Serling world—*Twilight Zone*—in this allegorical story.

We find out (just to show you how well Lawrence paces things), initially from Paul to Uncle Oscar and then from Bassett, the gardener, to Uncle Oscar, that Paul is getting winning horses, but it's really only toward the story's conclusion that we actually discover this secret of how Paul gets his luck.

Critic Janice Harris aptly describes the story as social, psychological, and familial. The story is really deeply rooted in British social class and the need for this particular middle-class family to live in style: to be superior by sending their son to Eton, wanting to move up into the higher British class hierarchy that money allows. They have all the appearances, of course, of living that life, but they are terribly in debt, and the debt, to some extent, is what is setting this voice off that says, "There must be more money!"

What we have behind this is the Lawrencian ethos of money or materialism somehow supplanting life and love, and that's the legacy that Hester seems to bequeath to her son. Her name, by the way, some of you may have associated already with the heroine of Hawthorne's *The Scarlet Letter*, which Lawrence wrote a well-known essay on. As in *The Scarlet Letter*—as in Hawthorne—we have a demonic force in this story. It's connected to a kind of shame and humiliation at not being able to keep up social position and acceptable outward appearances. Can that in itself be demonic? Can that somehow be linked to what the great psychologist Rollo May would have called the demonic? Apparently so, as far as Lawrence was concerned. The emphasis on the outer in contrast to the inner ties—really had to do with—Hester's being outwardly a loving mother, but her heart becoming stonier [and] colder, and it intertextually links back to Hawthorne. It also goes back to Chekhov; you may recall Gurov's observation about people leading double lives, split between their outer and inner selves in the "Lady with the Dog" or, again, in "Young Goodman Brown," with the sad and gloomy realization in that story about how people appear versus how they really are underneath their appearances. As with so many themes and motifs in literature, things tend to move along intertextual lines.

There's also, in this story, the Freudian notion of the oedipal relationship, often seen as a very central part of Lawrence's view, as well, largely because there are autobiographical elements in the story. Paul's attachment to Hester and her inadvertently trying to shape him into being unlike her unlucky husband really resonates with Lawrence's own life. His mother was a former schoolteacher, much more high bred and better educated than her husband, who was a coal miner, and she was exceedingly ambitious in her hopes for her quite gifted son, David Herbert Lawrence. Lawrence's autobiographical novel, *Sons and Lovers*, first published back in 1913, shows the profound effect on the protagonist—who's also named Paul—by his mother. Lawrence was especially close to his mother, who died in 1910. In fact, Lawrence has written that for just about a year after his mother's death, he was so badly emotionally struck that he really became, to some extent, almost paralytic emotionally.

Getting back to "The Rocking-Horse Winner," there's a poet and critic named W. D. Snodgrass who wrote a famous Freudian-based interpretative essay of "The Rocking-Horse Winner" that had a good deal of impact on the reading of the story. It appeared in 1958 in *The Hudson Review*. It likens Paul's behavior on the horse—his rocking back and forth, his movements—to masturbation, and it links it to Paul's oedipal drive to prove himself luckier than his "unhappy" father and to replace his father in his relationship with his mother. When you study Lawrence, you learn that masturbation was a form of solipsism—the belief that the only reality is somehow subjective reality—for him. We even see in common usage that people talk about "Well, that's masturbatory." In other words, it's just self-indulgent in some way; it doesn't really reach a level of connection with another human being. It's also a secretive act. It's done usually, of course, in private, and in this case, it's oedipal—according to W. D. Snodgrass and others who have read this story—because it's done to try to win the mother's love.

Remember back to the first paragraph I read: Hester had her children—the narrator tells us—"thrust upon her," which is really striking language. It seems, in many ways, apparent that it's indicative of perhaps a kind of sexual dissatisfaction (sexual dysfunction, you would call it nowadays, with Dr. Phil and the like). It helps account in [large] part for her inner emptiness and tangled sense of her maternality. It's certainly natural for a woman to be maternal, as far as Lawrence is concerned, but something has become twisted in her early on. We learn a little bit about her personal history throughout the course of the story in reflection with her brother, Uncle Oscar, and in things she tells her son.

Before we get to that, I think it's important to understand that Paul's mother, Hester, also has a kind of secret of her own, not only [the secret of] her heart, where her children are concerned, but an artistic sensibility; she does dress sketching. We can see how Paul inherits her habits, as well as her obsessions, but unlike his mother, he succeeds in winning—winning at great cost, winning for her—but only to lose his life and cause her to lose her son. By the way, I should mention that when she goes out and does some dressmaking and things of that sort, she finds that others are making more money than [she is]. There, again, is that dissatisfaction where money is concerned, centrally linked to money.

We also discover, in the course of this story, that Paul's mother is from "a gambling family." Her brother Oscar was lucky because he gave Paul the 10 shillings that led to Paul's winning his first bet; Paul had taken money first from Bassett, the gardener, and had been unlucky with that money. But Uncle Oscar, he feels, gave him luck.

Here's this whole question of what is luck in the story? What is luck, and what does it have to do with money and happiness? Oscar is a gambler. We're told that gambling in the family "caused great damage"; Hester tells Paul that. It's almost as if Lawrence is intimating that gambling is an ongoing family or hereditary disease of some sort, something that really had a good deal of speculation attached to it many years later. Here's a story that gets us deeply into family and lineage or heredity, [as well as] traditions that are passed down that are linked to gambling—not good traditions, but traditions that are, in fact, said to do a great deal of damage. What that damage is, we don't know. Nevertheless, it seems to be something that Paul has inherited; it seems to be part of his legacy.

The story also has a whole religious dimension to it, a religious significance. Bassett is taking money and putting it into horse bets, taking money and holding it for Paul—his money, as well—which started with Uncle Oscar's fronting [Paul] some money. When Bassett, the gardener, speaks to Paul, he is "as serious as a church." He speaks of the young master, as he's called, "in a secret religious voice." All of this suggests something really quite religious—in Bassett's mind, at least—about where Paul is getting this information about who's going to win the horse race.

Luck, Paul's mother had told him, comes from God, and it's as if Paul is—at least according to Bassett—receiving messages from heaven. Of course, the paradox in the story is that Paul perhaps is probably much more in touch with demonic forces. A couple of times, Uncle Oscar calls him "poor devil" at the story's end, and there appears to be a kind of Faustian bargain between Paul and whatever supernatural force is supplying him with the winners in the story.

At the end of the story, even as the boy lay dead, we're told that his mother heard her brother's voice saying to her:

> My God, Hester, you're eighty-odd thousand to the good [that's what he won in the final Derby race], and a poor devil of a son to the bad. But, poor devil, poor devil, he's best gone out of a life where he rides his rocking-horse to find a winner.

Notice the mention of God first but then "poor devil" repeated. That's just a phrase, in many ways—a common phrase, at that—but nevertheless, it does give us a sense of something demonic that has gone on. His eyes are blue and frozen; his mother's heart is frozen. There's something about all of this pursuit of money—mad pursuit, pursuit that causes brain fever, finally, that causes the boy to lose a hold on life—that is linked to the demonic. The pursuit of money and the avarice that is tied to that really petrify Hester's heart. They turn Paul's eyes into a petrified blue with "an uncanny cold fire in them." What appears heavenly to Bassett is more likely hellish.

We've got names of horses like Singhalese and Malabar, so even British colonialism and the whole ideal of the Sun never setting on the British Empire enters this story. It's intimated in this rich, multilayered, and remarkable story that Lawrence gives us, which nevertheless remains somewhat anomalous in Lawrence's canon but really is a singular masterpiece of compelling storytelling. It begins with that first paragraph, takes us in, and keeps us, and has also an embedded morality. Many consider the story Lawrence's most accomplished work of short fiction, even though he wrote many truly fine and exceptional stories, as well as novels, essays, poetry, literary criticism, and travel books. What's important to remember, in many respects, about this story is just the way it brings us in, almost like a fairy tale.

There's a great psychoanalyst named Bruno Bettelheim who writes about fairy tales and says that what they do is take us into the forest, maybe scare the whatever out of us, and then they restore things. It's like Hansel and Gretel going off into the forest, and after they meet with the witch and everything, they come out, and things are okay—like bedtime stories you tell kids, but everything is restored at the end. There's order once again after going into the woods, forest, or wherever that dark place might be.

Lawrence takes us into a fairy tale which is a dark fairy tale from which there really seems to be no escape. Remember that Lawrence was a realistic writer until he came to "The Rocking-Horse Winner" and decided to move in a different direction. If anything, I think it reflects on his versatility, because in addition to being a novelist, travel writer, and poet, he could write stories like "The Rocking-Horse Winner"; he's capable of writing a dark fairy tale. He was also, by the way, an accomplished painter, and he gained some posthumous fame for his Expressionistic paintings from 1920. He was certainly one of the 20th century's greatest writers and one of the truly great Modernists. The poet and literary critic Allen Tate, among others, called "The Rocking-Horse Winner" a nearly technically perfect short story.

It was first published in 1926 in *Harper's Bazaar* and made into a film in 1950 directed by Anthony Pelissier. Lawrence is one of those writers who developed an entire philosophy that was both embodied and embedded in much of his work. He was a son of the working class and of a lower-class, impoverished background; his father was a miner. He was born back in 1885 in Eastwood, Nottinghamshire, [in] central England. Nevertheless, he became educated, like his mother, and married a German woman named Frieda von Richthofen, who was the wife of a German professor and who, when Lawrence married her, had three children of her own by that German professor.

Lawrence had a pretty colorful and remarkable life. He was accused of spying for the Germans in World War I, and then he was arrested and accused by the Germans of being a British spy. Despite a kind of ephemeral fascination with fascism that can be seen in the later novel of his, *Kangaroo*, which was published in 1923, Lawrence pretty much remained, throughout his lifetime, removed from politics and dedicated to art. He had a credo predicated on the efficacy of sexuality and spontaneity, living on the basis of one's impulses and virility, talking with one's blood, talking intuitively to one's self, realizing what those intuitions were leading to, and acting on them, as well as a kind of philosophy tied to androgyny. Lawrence believed that there was a hidden lady within him, and he believed, to some extent, that his own artistic impulses came out of a sense of cross-fertilization between masculine and feminine.

He was mostly a writer of realistic stories, and certainly his major novels all fall under that rubric, but it's instructive to compare a well-known story of his—one of the best known stories—"The Horse Dealer's Daughter," which was published in 1922, with "The Rocking-Horse Winner," which appeared four years later. "The Horse Dealer's Daughter" is a lot like so much of Lawrence's fiction before "The Rocking-Horse Winner," not only anchored in Realism but with Lawrence's ethos of sexuality. For example, you have a doctor in the story and a young woman who is on the verge of suicide. The doctor rescues her, there is some exposure of flesh, and as a result, there is a sense of something within their blood—chemistry, electricity, whatever you want to call it—that draws them to each other. Suddenly, there's a marriage proposal, and it seems like they're destined to be together.

Compare that to "The Rocking-Horse Winner," which opens up with an entirely different vein of fantasy and the supernatural. This was written at the time a mystical novel of Lawrence's appeared, in 1926, originally titled *Quetzalcoatl*. It was a novel about Mexico called *The Plumed Serpent*, and it had a pre-Christian cult in it and all kinds of things that really bore more perhaps on the supernatural.

Lawrence was vilified particularly because of the publication of his last novel, *Lady Chatterley's Lover*, which again, gets us back to so many of the major themes that we call Lawrencian. This is the story of Mellors, who is essentially a workman—who speaks like a workman and is of the working class—and becomes a lover of Lady

Chatterley, whose husband is pretty much an invalid. It was published first in 1928 in Florence, but afterward, confronting a number of court battles, Lawrence was able to overcome the fact that it had been banned. It's, again, a realistic story; it's not supernatural like "The Rocking-Horse Winner," which in so many respects, stands alone.

To the present day, Lawrence is considered one of the world's greatest writers, and "The Rocking-Horse Winner," one of his—and, certainly, one of the world's—finest stories. It's one of those stories—despite W. D. Snodgrass's criticism that really had a great deal of influence on the way people have continued to interpret this story in this Freudian way—that has set critics and scholars debating a wide range of interpretations. It has a lot to do with the fact that there are so many different levels of meaning in the story and that it can be read in all of these different contexts: social, psychological, familial, or religious, just to name a few. It's also a story very much rooted in class divisions.

Lawrence had, for his entire life, an interest and disposition toward the mystical—what we call intuitive—as opposed to rational thinking, and I believe this, too, is reflected in the metaphysical tapestry of "The Rocking-Horse Winner." It's really a story, however, that particularly conveys to us the consequence of the absence of love. The French poststructuralist [Jacques] Derrida would call this the "presence of absence": the presence of that absence, especially of maternal love, and the need for human beings to live within their humanity rather than something outside of themselves—acquisition, money, colonialism—to be able to release themselves from solipsism and the sense of the self that takes a vaunted and preeminent role, as opposed to being able to extend the self.

These are really important themes here and are themes that we come back to in Lawrence's work and also in stories like "The Necklace" by Maupassant. But we're not anchored to Realism or the natural world in "The Rocking-Horse Winner." It takes us really into an alternative reality, not only a supernatural world but into the whole sense of allegory, the sense of the heart being cold and stony, and of a boy who can somehow commune with what Yeats would have called *spiritus mundi*, or the world of spirits. It takes us into, in other words, a different dimension; it takes us into what we perhaps could call the *Twilight Zone*, as I said earlier.

One of the particularly engrossing and enrapturing elements—dimensions—in this story is that it has a movement to it that follows linearly and right up until the rather stark and tragic conclusion. In other words, think back to Poe for a moment: Think back to the linear relentlessness of moving us along a line and making us engaged in a story the way Poe can do, and you realize what Lawrence is able to do, as well. From the beginning of that story, with its fairy tale–like beginning, we're moved along a trajectory that makes us want to know more and is revealing to us more as we move along. [Lawrence is] revealing to us that something is going on here with this house speaking, something that is not necessarily revealing itself but taking place and transpiring, that we want to know about, that we're curious about, that arouses not only our curiosity but also, to some extent, our suspicion, with hints that something deeper and more profound indeed is transpiring. [We're in a state of] wanting to find out what's going on, and then finding out a secret from the beginning that's in Hester's heart, and then a secret within a secret of Paul's—if you agree with Snodgrass—masturbatory, secret activity of riding his rocking-horse and finding out the winners. It is all moved with a kind of craft and an omniscient point of view that really is quite astonishingly good.

I want particularly to emphasize the fact that emotions are aroused in us in this story, as well, that we're made to feel for this young boy. He has moved out of the nursery; he's becoming, perhaps, a young man, and he's in that strange phase between boyhood—moving out of childhood and moving into, perhaps, adolescence. We begin to feel a kind of empathy with him because his mother has gone cold, and as a result, he feels that he has to prove something to his mother; he becomes fiendishly, demonically possessed by the need to show his mother. This is all presented, again, in supernatural ways, but it's presented in such a way that readers can easily identify with it. It's universal in the way it speaks to us and, I think, the way we respond to it.

We want to move next to a friend and, actually, a literary associate of D. H. Lawrence, another great figure in Modernist fiction, Katherine Mansfield, whose origins were in New Zealand, but who spent a good deal of her life in London after her family moved to England.

Mansfield, along with her husband—a literary critic, John Middleton Murry—was a prototype for a couple in Lawrence's famous novel *Women in Love*. Lawrence and his wife, Frieda, actually shared a home with Katherine Mansfield and John Middleton Murry in England from 1914 to 1915.

What we're going to discuss is a story by Mansfield—much praised and much deserving of the masterpiece mantle—called "The Garden Party." It reflects a return to Realism. It's a very Chekhovian story; in many ways, it's really influenced preeminently by Chekhov. What we're going to also see in Mansfield's work are the beginnings of the spectacular rise which would come a few decades later—but I think is certainly, in some ways, emblematic of the importance of writers like Katherine Mansfield getting the kind of recognition that she was able to get in her lifetime—of the role women will play in short fiction; it's [an] essential role, particularly as the years go by and as waves of feminism begin to have their impact. Next, it's onward and—certainly, we hope—upward to another very much rooted Chekhov-type story by Katherine Mansfield: "The Garden Party."

Lecture Twelve

Female Initiation—Mansfield's "Party"

Scope:

This lecture begins with a look at Mansfield's life and her association with the Bloomsbury Group of artists, including Virginia Woolf, and other influential writers, such as D. H. Lawrence. We then probe the character of Laura in "The Garden Party" and the initiation and growth she experiences at the psychological center of the story. We also discuss Mansfield's position as a woman writing at a time before the acceptance of the feminist perspective that we find in the work of Betty Friedan, Simone de Beauvoir, Grace Paley, and others. We follow with a discussion of the story in the context of class division, the ways in which the story emotionally affects readers, and its revelations about Laura's perspective on death. We end the lecture with a comparison of this story to another one by Mansfield in the same collection, "Her First Ball," and tie it as well to Luigi Pirandello's "War."

Outline

I. "The Garden Party" is based on an incident in Mansfield's life: her mother giving a garden party at their home in Wellington, New Zealand, after an accident had killed a neighbor living in a nearby poor quarter.

- **A.** Mansfield's experiences living in London gave her grist for a deeper understanding of class differences, which she put at the center of this story.
- **B.** Like Kafka, Mansfield suffered from tuberculosis, and the loss of her brother brought her closer to earlier material in her life as a girl in New Zealand.
- **C.** She was a friend of D. H. Lawrence but influenced most by Chekhov and Joyce and the idea of a story's emotional impact being central to its experience.
- **D.** Mansfield was part of the famed Bloomsbury group of artists and writers.

II. The plot of "The Garden Party" is what Willa Cather characterized as "a trivial incident" turned into a psychological drama. It is an initiation story centering on Laura's character.

Mansfield's personal history is relevant here, as is the evolving role of women writers.

A. Laura's ambivalent encounter with death—seeing it in the face of the workman—brings bewilderment, aesthetic elevation, and a visceral sense of contentment. After seeing the dead man, Laura's already abstract feelings about death become abstract in a different sense.

B. In keeping with her adolescent nature, Laura's character shifts throughout the story.

1. When she asks the workmen about the marquee, she tries to sound like her mother but then stammers "like a little girl."

2. She insists that the party be stopped after the workman's death but is then caught up with how charming she looks in the mirror wearing the hat her mother gave her.

C. Laura is presented as artistic (versus her practical sister Jose), self-conscious, and sensitive about the workers, in contrast to Jose, who feels perfectly comfortable ordering servants around.

III. "The Garden Party" is a story of class division.

A. Mansfield employs an omniscient point of view that comes across as both Laura's and her family's. The cottages in the impoverished section of town, for example, are "far too near," "an eyesore," and "had no right to be in the neighborhood at all."

B. As children, the Sheridans were forbidden to go into the impoverished quarter, but they did so with the ethic that one must see and experience everything.

C. Mansfield's status as an expatriate enables her to portray class differences from the vantage point of an outsider, a perspective she shared with James, Joyce, Hemingway, Márquez, and James Baldwin.

D. Mansfield's work begins to bring short fiction written by women into prominence, though many years would elapse before women writers received appropriate recognition.

IV. The story is created by atmosphere and setting, but the focus on Laura and her growth are the heart of the story's unity and its emotional effect on the reader.

A. Laura's experience of the garden party as "a perfect afternoon … slowly faded, … its petals closed" leads, as the story progresses, to the encounter with the poor. It is a movement from innocence to experience, dawn to dusk, light to dark, life to death.

B. Her attitude toward her hat shifts from vanity to self-consciousness and embarrassment. Her experience of the afternoon changes from the gaiety of the party to the woman on a crutch, the widow's sister, and her oily voice and smile—from cream puffs to death.

C. Laura's response to the dead workman is both contentment and tears, which she sheds in "a childish sob." Her sister Jose's song contrasts her attitude toward death, but Laura's response is ultimately an ineffable one. In both, we see the ineluctable link between life and death.

D. Feminist critics have interpreted the story as revealing a young woman's coming into the recognition of her own identity, though ultimately, Laura looks to her brother, Laurie, for affirmation.

V. The story is a masterpiece, yet it has had somewhat of a mixed critical reception.

A. Critic Warren Walker wrote of Mansfield's "near perfection" as a short story writer, and Virginia Woolf said that Mansfield's was the only writing she was jealous of.

B. There remains critical dispute over the efficacy of the ending, but few would take issue with the overall deftness of craft and the Chekhovian mastery with character, subtlety of language, and the wonderful attention to detail, such as "the sunbeam playing on an inkwell."

Suggested Readings:

Beauvoir, *The Second Sex.*

Gilbert and Gubar, *The Madwoman in the Attic.*

Mansfield, "The Garden Party."

———, "Her First Ball" and other stories in *The Garden Party.*

Pirandello, "War."

Smith, *Katherine Mansfield and Virginia Woolf: A Public of Two.*

Walker, “The Unresolved Conflict in ‘The Garden Party,’” in *Modern Fiction Studies* (Winter 1957–1958).

Questions to Consider:

1. To what extent does the story appear to embody feminist values?
2. How tied to her artistic sensibility is Laura’s concern about class differences or her feelings about the workman’s death?
3. What does the ending tell us about what Laura learns from her encounter with the dead man?

Lecture Twelve—Transcript

Female Initiation—Mansfield's "Party"

The story "The Garden Party" by Katherine Mansfield is based on an incident in Mansfield's life when her mother gave a garden party at their home in Wellington, New Zealand, in March 1907 [after] an accident [had] killed a neighbor living in a nearby poor quarter. In that sense, this is a story that shows how memory—and recreating memory from the distance of time—along with imagination and structuring it all into a story can be distilled into great fiction. Mansfield's experiences living in London also gave her grist for a deeper understanding of class differences, which she put at the center of this story.

Like Kafka, she suffered from tuberculosis, and the loss during the First World War of her brother—"Chummie," as he was called—which was devastating to her, brought her closer to this earlier material in her life as a girl in New Zealand. In fact, the main character, Laura, has a very close relationship—we find out—with her brother, Laurie, as he's called in the story.

Katherine Mansfield was a friend of D. H. Lawrence and Virginia Woolf and a member of the renowned and influential Bloomsbury Group of artists and writers that also included the economist John Maynard Keynes. She and her second husband, literary critic and editor John Middleton Murry, were close friends of Lawrence and his wife, Frieda. But as a writer, Mansfield was most significantly influenced by Chekhov, Joyce, and the idea of a story's emotional impact being central to it as an experience.

The story "The Garden Party" is what Willa Cather, an American writer of short and long fiction, characterized as a "trivial incident" turned into a psychological drama. It's an initiation story centering on Laura Sheridan's character. The plot is actually quite simple and straightforward: A young girl in Wellington is excited about a garden party about to take place at her family home. Let's get a sense of the mood and atmosphere of the story from the first paragraph:

> And after all the weather was ideal. They could not have had a more perfect day for a garden-party if they had ordered it. Windless, warm, the sky without a cloud. Only the blue was veiled with a haze of light gold, as it is sometimes in early summer. The gardener had been up since dawn, mowing the

> lawns and sweeping them, until the grass and the dark flat rosettes where the daisy plants had been seemed to shine. As for the roses, you could not help feeling they understood that roses are the only flowers that impress people at garden-parties; the only flowers that everybody is certain of knowing. Hundreds, yes, literally hundreds, had come out in a single night; the green bushes bowed down as though they had been visited by archangels.

What do you get in this first paragraph? Something of almost perfection: It's simplicity, but it's also a lovely day for a party, and a day when all of the atmosphere and the sense of what's conveyed in this opening paragraph is of loveliness. Superficial, you might call it. Certainly, we associate a party with superficiality; we find out that there's a band, and concern about flags on the sandwiches, and cream puffs, and all kinds of things that are frivolous. But nevertheless, this plants us firmly in the excitement of a party in this upper-class home: people out there working on the garden, having roses in it, lots and lots of roses appearing overnight, money to do that sort of thing; quite a perfect, unbridled sense that the day will be a beautiful one.

Laura talks with some of the workmen—"four men in short sleeves"—about the marquee. It's the first indication in the story of class differences, which will turn out to play a preeminent role in the story. We find out soon enough that a man in the working-class section nearby—a laborer who lives below the Sheridan family—has died and left a wife and five children. This causes Laura to want to put a stop to the garden party. Laura's mother suggests taking a basket with sandwiches, and Laura goes to the home of the widow and sees the dead man lying within.

Just trying to give you a brief summary of the story here; this takes us to the end of the story, where Em, the widow's sister, says:

> "You'd like a look at 'im, wouldn't you?" said Em's sister, and she brushed past Laura over to the bed. "Don't be afraid, my lass,"—and now her voice sounded fond and sly, and fondly she drew down the sheet—"'e looks a picture. There's nothing to show. Come along, my dear."
>
> [Laura came.] There lay a young man, fast asleep—sleeping so soundly, so deeply, that he was far, far away from them

both. Oh, so remote, so peaceful. He was dreaming. Never wake him up again. His head was sunk in the pillow, his eyes were closed; they were blind under the closed eyelids. He was given up to his dream. What did garden-parties and baskets and lace frocks matter to him? He was far from all those things. He was wonderful, beautiful. While they were laughing and while the band was playing, this marvel had come to the lane. Happy … happy … All is well, said that sleeping face. This is just as it should be. I am content.

But all the same you had to cry, and she couldn't go out of the room without saying something to him. Laura gave a loud childish sob.

"Forgive my hat," she said.

And this time she didn't wait for Em's sister. She found her way out of the door, down the path, past all those dark people. At the corner of the lane she met Laurie.

[Her brother]. He stepped out of the shadow. "Is that you, Laura?"

"Yes."

"Mother was getting anxious. Was it all right?"

"Yes, quite. Oh, Laurie!" She took his arm, she pressed up against him.

"I say, you're not crying, are you?" asked her brother.

Laura shook her head. She was.

Laurie put his arm round her shoulder. "Don't cry," he said in his warm, loving voice. "Was it awful?"

"No," sobbed Laura. "It was simply marvelous. But Laurie—" She stopped, she looked at her brother. "Isn't life," she stammered, "isn't life—" But what life was she couldn't explain. No matter. He quite understood.

"Isn't it, darling?" said Laurie.

Not a lot has taken place here in the story. When Laura first hears of this worker dying, she takes pity, empathizes, and wants the party to stop. Of course, the party doesn't stop; the party goes on. The mother suggests taking a basket down, and that's when we are below—in this lower-class home—when Laura has this transfiguring experience, this epiphany looking death in the face, looking at this young workman lying there as a corpse. She wants to apologize to him directly for her hat. Her hat plays a role in the story, as we see when she puts on a hat after first hearing that the workman has died, and she looks in the mirror and looks kind of attractive. In fact, she looks very attractive, and her brother, Laurie, tells her she looks stunning just as she's about to tell him about the workman's death. This is really a story of a young girl's initiation into seeing death. It's considered Katherine Mansfield's best piece of short fiction, and Mansfield is regarded as one of the best short story writers of the Modernist period.

Before we get into the story more, let's talk about Katherine Mansfield. That wasn't her original name; she was born Kathleen Beauchamp in 1888 to a prominent, well-established New Zealand family. By high school, she was publishing short fiction, though her first love was the cello. She changed her last name to Mansfield in 1911 after her first collection of short stories, *In a German Pension*, was published. She had been sent by her mother to Bavaria after becoming pregnant, though she ultimately suffered a miscarriage. She had been living a bisexual and bohemian life—by those days' standards, quite daring—in London that included a marriage that lasted only a few days and also included contracting a very serious case of gonorrhea (though she wound up dying, like Chekhov and Kafka, of tuberculosis).

In 1923, she died at the Institute of the Russian mystic George Gurdjieff in Fontainebleau, France. There were a number of writers who were taken up with Gurdjieff, who was a mystic who believed that one could spiritualize one's existence though bringing the body and the mind together. There were all kinds of dance steps, exercises, and various sorts of physical motion that led to this higher level of spiritual consciousness in Gurdjieff's teachings. Hart Crane, the American poet, was a student of Gurdjieff's; so was Jean Toomer, author of *Cane*. Katherine Mansfield's last words at the institute at Fontainebleau were "I love the rain, I want the feeling of it on my face."

Her total output as a short story writer included 62 finished stories and 26 unfinished. I found myself reflecting on why we don't have a word like Mansfieldian or, for that matter, any other woman short fiction's writer name that can compare to the adjectival equivalents of Chekhovian, Joycean, Kafkaesque, Hemingwayesque, or Lawrencian. Is it simply the exclusionary nature of what the feminist Germaine Greer would have called sexual politics? Perhaps. But we deserve to have Mansfieldian in our language. She really has given us some extraordinary stories.

When she came along, there were already many established women fiction writers in both the novel and the short story. Virginia Woolf in England, of course, but [also] Sarah Orne Jewett, Kate Chopin, Charlotte Perkins Gilman, and Ellen Glasgow in the United States—significant figures in the evolution of short fiction. After emancipation and the vote, figures like Katherine Anne Porter and Edith Wharton emerged. However, women writers remained second class, and it wasn't until Simone de Beauvoir and Betty Friedan and the wave feminism that followed that women began to receive and garner the kind of recognition that was their due and that we're now more accustomed to seeing for women short fiction writers.

Though Mansfield and other short fiction writers concentrate on women characters, it isn't until Grace Paley that we begin to see a spate of first-person narratives in women's voices in short fiction that bears on feminist issues. Mansfield was a good enough writer, though, that she got a good deal of recognition in her own time—unusual for women writers except those figures like Virginia Woolf. She was also the kind of writer who could bear in on a young girl's life and show her initiation—as she does in this story—and have readers come away from the story thinking that there are elements of feminism in this story, even though one could make the argument (and I would make it) that it's a story about a girl growing up and facing death and the confusion that she has about death. But it's also really—as so many initiation stories are—a story of a young [person] coming into awareness, who happens to be a girl and who happens also to be artistic, more artistic, by contrast, than any of her siblings, to be sure. I think if you want to make a feminist case for this story, you would have some difficulties simply by dint of the fact that she looks to her brother, Laurie, for advice, just as she does to her father. We're still in that kind of patriarchal world.

In Mansfield's case, however, leaving home seemed to have a direct and lasting effect on her independence, autonomy, and imagination, as we see in this story, which takes her back to her native New

Zealand, just as James Joyce, away from Ireland as an expatriate, seemed to me to open up more to his past as grist for the fiction that he produced. The same can be said of Hemingway, who was an expatriate, and to a lesser extent, of Henry James, who was also an expatriate, as well as other writers that we'll be discussing, like Gabriel Garcia Márquez and James Baldwin.

Laura goes through a metamorphosis in "The Garden Party"—I suppose you could say from party girl to this ambivalent encounter with death—which brings bewilderment, aesthetic elevation, and a visceral inner sense of contentment from literally looking at death in the face. After being rather abstract and removed about death, she becomes abstract about it in a different sense after seeing the dead man. She shifts as an adolescent would, and this is consistent with her character throughout the story. She also feels the palpable, real sense of death and a sense of the life of the working class. [As] she has entered into the home, she has not only entered into an encounter with death in meeting it face on, [but] she has also seen what these people live like, and it's not very pretty: They're down and out, have-nots, and strugglers.

There are shifts that go on early in the story. She shifts, for example, when we first see her asking the workmen about the marquee. She tries to sound like her mother and then "stammers like a little girl." She also feels she has to sound businesslike with the workmen, and yet she's drawn to them and their affability. This all prepares us in part for the effect of the story's final scene, when she looks at the face of the dead workman. She also shifts when she goes from insisting that the party be stopped to getting caught up in it after seeing how charming she looks in the mirror with the hat her mother gave her and told by her brother, Laurie, that she looks stunning in it. It's the same hat, of course, that she apologizes for in the story, when she goes into this world of the working class more intimately and sees the dead man.

Laura is also presented to us as artistic, and this is important, because this is a story—as many of these great stories are—about a developing consciousness. We see it in James Joyce's boy in "Araby"; we see it in a later story that we'll talk about by Updike called "A & P": an imaginative young boy—or, in this case, girl—who is developing that imagination and moving it forward so that we can understand the birth of an artist. Laura is described as artistic;

her sister Jose is described as practical by contrast. She is self-conscious and sensitive about the workers, as opposed to Jose, who feels perfectly comfortable ordering servants around, and as opposed to her mother and Jose, who feel that it's extravagant and not very realistic of her to feel that she needs to stop the party, the band, and all the frivolity because this man has died, a man she doesn't even know. From a practical standpoint, they feel what if he had actually died—you wouldn't stop the party if he had died not by this tragic accident but if he had died—let's say—from a disease that was long-lingering or something like this. She can't argue with the logic along those lines.

When Laura goes out to talk about the marquee with the workmen, she takes bread and butter out with her. She feels self-conscious about the bread and butter at first, but then she takes a big bite out of it to make herself feel like a working girl. There are all these shifting emotions in Laura. We feel the sense of all these emotions coming together, coming apart, shifting ground, and so forth, but what they really show us is a picture of a young girl of an artistic sensibility. An artistic sensibility presumably would also involve, as a kind of priority, understanding life and death and how they are connected and understanding the thin membrane that can separate the two of them.

Before Laura actually sees with a kind of Chekhovian realism what this dead man and his dwelling look like, she has abstracted death. She feels she's doing the right thing in response to her sensitivity by saying let's stop the party, but it really isn't until she looks at his face that she sees life in a deeper sense, that she sees humanity in a deeper sense. She thinks of it as beautiful and aesthetic, but at the same time, it's real to her. When she's with those workers, they're smiling and nice to her. One even takes a pinch of lavender at one point, which makes her wonder, why can't they be friends? Why can't they all get along (like Rodney King said)? Yet she also wonders if it is proper, given her upbringing, when one of them uses the phrase "a bang slap in the eye." (He's talking about how the marquee looks.) She thinks, is this proper? Is this right that he should use a phrase like this, kind of vulgar and inappropriate? She says of class distinctions that they are absurd and that she didn't feel them. With that in mind, she takes a big bite out of the bread and butter that she was at first reluctant to display and tells herself that she feels like a working girl. Her moods are already shifting before she even hears of the workman's death.

Laura's response to the workman's death is at first to want to call a halt to the entire party, not to allow the band to play. Jose and her mother find this extravagant. Her mother even responds coldly about "people like that" not "expecting sacrifices from us" (and notice that "people like that").

The story, when Laura gets into the swing of the party, is reminiscent of another famous Mansfield story that I want to talk about briefly called "Her First Ball," also published in 1922. But before that, let me just say again about the class differences that one of the remarkable things about this story is that we're told how mean, indigent, and impoverished these houses look, how they almost seem like an insult to the houses on the higher level that the Sheridans are a part of. It's almost as if the point of view takes on a collective identity to it that would stand for the mother, Jose, and these others that feel very differently than Laura, who has this kind of different empathy for the workmen and would like to associate and be friends with them but knows that her status in life—her perch in life—doesn't allow for that. What I'm getting at, though, with respect to these class differences is the fact that the point of view is always—to some extent—Laura's in this story, but we shift, and we get into a point of view that sounds as if it could be that of the whole neighborhood that the Sheridans live in. It's really quite adroit on the part of Mansfield to be able to move the way she does and give us an omniscient point of view that is still or could be the point of view of all these people.

"Her First Ball" is a story which is in the 15-story volume with the same title as the story "The Garden Party." It's about a young, 18-year-old ingénue named [Leila] who's very excited about going to her first ball, and then suddenly she becomes disillusioned when an older, fat man asks her to dance. While they're dancing, he tells her about how her youth will fade, her body will turn old, mortality will creep up, and one day she's going to look very different than she does now in the flush of her youth. This upsets her terribly. She thinks to herself, is it true? Could it all really be true? Then she's asked to dance by a young man, and she becomes caught up in the dance and forgets all about this brief, ephemeral feeling of disappointment and facing mortality, and [she] smiles radiantly at the fat man and doesn't even recognize him.

The story highlights for us a lot of what's going on in the "The Garden Party": There's the ephemeral moment when Laura feels that she really has to do something about this man who died and left his children and a widow. She feels empathy, but is it really empathy? She's quickly caught up in the spirit of the party and the way she looks in her hat. She forgets about him, but then her mother takes the initiative. Mansfield is telling us something about youth: about the ephemerality of even sensitive young women and young women who are responsive to life and are filled with a desire to be very involved in life. Laura is like that, and Laura is sympathetic for those reasons. But she's also—like many adolescents—flighty, and yet something takes place that's beautiful, final, and climactic after she sees the dead man.

When Mansfield employs this point of view that I spoke of earlier about the cottages being impoverished, "far too near," and an eyesore—in fact, that they "had no right to be in the neighborhood at all"—that's the point of view of the people who live in the neighborhood and the Sheridans themselves. Her mother says some things that are very revealing of a kind of class distinction that's rather harsh. But Laura doesn't feel that way, and this is an artistic sensibility as well as a sensibility that's tied more to empathy. She thinks, aren't they interesting, these workmen? Aren't they nice? But [she is not] being patronizing, because it's easy to slip over that line as well. There's something about her that's desiring to extend herself to them, and that accounts for extending herself to the workman and his family, and finally, to the workman in his dead state, as a corpse.

The Sheridan children, when they were little, were forbidden to go into that impoverished quarter, but they did so, and they did so with an ethic again that comes from Laurie, the brother, the one who must see and experience everything. Laura is sent by her mother with this basket heaping with food but not with the arum lilies, and this is what I mean by the mother's feeling of class distinctions. The mother says, "people of that class are so impressed by" arum lilies, and Jose, her practical sister, points out that the stems will ruin Laura's frock.

This story is created by its atmosphere and setting but really mostly by the focus on Laura, her journey, and her growth that are at the heart of the story's unity and its emotional effect on us as readers.

Laura's experience of the garden party as "a perfect afternoon … slowly faded, … its petals closed" leads, as the story progresses, to the encounter with the poor and with the dead man. It's a movement from innocence to experience, dawn to dusk, light to dark, and from life to death. Her attitude toward her hat goes from vanity to self-consciousness and embarrassment, and when she begins to move into the territory of the poor people, she's actually kind of frightened. She feels she shouldn't do this, all empathy not withstanding. She even calls upon God to help her when she goes in—and she doesn't want to go in—and it's only the sister of the man whose wife is there, beside herself with grief, who leads her in, takes charge of everything, and sees to it that she actually goes and sees the corpse of the workman.

She goes from all of this party gaiety to seeing a woman on a crutch and to seeing the widow's sister and what's described as her oily voice and smile—from the frivolousness of the cream puffs to death. Even when she looks at death in the face of the young workman, she goes from abstracting it to feeling its reality, as if both are somehow bound together.

I'm reminded of a very short story by a man who's usually thought of as a playwright: Luigi Pirandello. It's called "War," and it's all of maybe two pages long. A man meets another man on a train. (And, by the way, you have a lot of stories that take place on trains, where someone can tell a story to a total stranger; it's almost a convention in storytelling. That it's easier to tell a story to a stranger, of course, is the whole point.) This man talks about his son's death; his son died in the war. He says, "But I feel my son died for a noble cause. I feel he died in the spirit of patriotism, and therefore, I know he died for his country, and I can feel good about his death. I can feel blessed about his death." After this rhetoric, the other man who hears this narration looks at the Pirandello character—a rather portly man—and says, "But is your son really dead?" All of a sudden, it hits the man with full force. He has tried to dress it up as best he can—he has tried to think about death in entirely different ways—but he starts sobbing uncontrollably because the reality of death hits him.

There's some of that in "The Garden Party" with Laura's response. Her response to the dead man is contentment, but it's also tears, and she feels the need to shed those tears in what's described as "a childish sob." Her sister Jose has a song about life's weariness and

“Love that Chan-ges / And then … Good-bye!” In fact, the song appears fairly early on in the story, and they sing it together with Jose playing the piano:

> This Life is Wee-ary,
> A Tear—a Sigh.
> A Love that Chan-ges,
> This Life is Wee-ary,
> A Tear—a Sigh.
> A Love that Chan-ges,
> And then … Good-bye!

Jose winds up being somewhat frivolous in her attitude toward this—makes fun of it, doesn’t take it very realistically—but embedded in that song is a good deal of meaning about the story itself and what happens to Laura in the story. Love does change life, life can change to death, and life can change, and then it’s goodbye.

Laura’s attitude toward death is ultimately what I would describe as an ineffable one. She sees that inevitable link between life and death, but still she can’t even express it to her brother, whom she loves and feels so tenderly toward; it’s beyond language. That’s why I say it’s ineffable; that’s why it has such a strong emotional climax. Because we’re getting at the ineffability of a young, sensitive girl artistically attuned with an artistic sensibility, experiencing, absorbing, and integrating death; trying to understand it; feeling its beauty and liberating force; dreaming; looking at the man and projecting all that onto him: sleeping, at peace at last, the finality of it. All of that comes into play; all of that merges.

A number of feminist critics have interpreted this story as revealing a young woman’s coming into the recognition of her own identity. As I’ve said, she ultimately looks to her brother, Laurie, for affirmation about what she has experienced—as ineffable as it is—at the end of the story. She looks to Laurie for some degree of either approval or disapproval of her feelings about stopping the party earlier on.

But this is a story that really captures a young girl’s thoughts and sensibility, and that’s important, because women writers had not received their due, and Mansfield was receiving a good deal of recognition because of the character and stature of her art. There’s a critic named Warren Walker who wrote of Mansfield’s “near perfection” as a short story writer, and Virginia Woolf—her fellow

Bloomsbury member—said that Mansfield's writing was the only writing she (Woolf) was jealous of. There remains some critical dispute over the efficacy of the ending and how satisfactory it is, but few would take issue with the overall deftness of craft and the Chekhovian mastery of character, the subtlety of the language, and the wonderful attention to detail, such as "the sunbeam playing on an inkwell."

What is abundantly clear in this wise, lyrical story—aside from an acute awareness of class differences that would make some critics eager to see Mansfield as a Socialist critical of the bourgeoisie—is the sharp sense that she provides of loss of innocence that carries with it the coming into greater knowledge. Laura, the more artistic one in the Sheridan family, comes into an epiphany—a recognition—of the thin cord that separates our lives from death, as well as the impermanence that marks our existence and the mortality from which none of us can escape.

Laura manages to buoy her spirits up in spite of the formidable nature of what she observes, and that fact summons up some words of Mansfield's which bring us to a conclusion our study of her memorable masterpiece. She said, "All that I write, all that I am—is on the borders of the sea. It is a kind of playing." There is in this story tragedy—facing death and all that—but there is also a kind of playing as well, particularly in the party part, but even later on, when she sees Laurie and talks about how beautiful everything was, what she had seen and experienced.

We may be talking about playing in "The Garden Party," but we're also talking about death, and the specter of death is really at the forefront of this story. If anything, the war that followed the First World War expanded the specter of death as it did the specter of violence and created an even greater cultural crisis, especially given the horrid and frightful specter of people indiscriminately put to death in ovens and gas chambers in places like Auschwitz, Buchenwald, and Dachau or by blasts from atomic bombs dropped on Hiroshima and Nagasaki. That kind of indiscriminate and random violence leading to death, as well as the seemingly natural propensity people appeared to have to do evil—something we saw as far back in American short story writing as Poe and Hawthorne—is right at the heart of the next story we're going to discuss in this course on short story masterpieces: "The Lottery" by Shirley Jackson.

Timeline

1350–1354 .... Giovanni Boccaccio writes the *Decameron*.

1387–1400 .... Geoffrey Chaucer writes The *Canterbury Tales*.

1678 .... John Bunyan's *The Pilgrim's Progress* published.

1741 .... Jonathan Edwards delivers his sermon entitled "Sinners in the Hands of an Angry God."

1775–1783 .... American Revolution.

1787–1799 .... French Revolution.

1812–1822 .... Appearance of three volumes of *Grimm's Fairy Tales*.

1819–1820 .... Washington Irving's "Rip Van Winkle" and "The Legend of Sleepy Hollow" both appear in *The Sketch Book of Geoffrey Crayon, Gent*.

1835 .... Gogol's "The Overcoat" first published in *St. Petersburg Stories* and Hawthorne's "Young Goodman Brown" in *New England Magazine*.

1842 .... Poe's "The Importance of the Single Effect in a Prose Tale."

1846 .... Poe's "The Cask of Amontillado" published in *Godey's Lady's Book*.

1850 .... *Harper's New Monthly Magazine* (later known as *Harper's Magazine*) founded.

1857 .... *Atlantic* magazine (later known as *Atlantic Monthly*) founded.

1884 .... Maupassant's "The Necklace" published in a Paris newspaper and included in the anthology *Tales of Days and Nights*.

1890 ....James Frazer's *The Golden Bough* published.

1892 ....Henry James's "The Real Thing" published in *Black and White* magazine.

1899 ....Chekhov publishes "The Lady with the Dog."

1911 ....Katherine Mansfield's *In a German Pension* published.

1913 ....D. H. Lawrence's *Sons and Lovers* published.

1914 ....Joyce's *Dubliners* published, including "Araby."

1914–1918.................................World War I.

1915 ....Kafka's "The Metamorphosis" published.

1916–1921.................................Easter Rising and Irish War of Independence.

1916–1922.................................Constance Garnett translates Chekhov's stories.

1917 ....Bolshevik Revolution.

1918 ....Breakup of the Austro-Hungarian Empire.

1919 ....Sherwood Anderson's *Winesburg, Ohio* published.

1922 ....Katherine Mansfield's "The Garden Party" first published in a collection called *The Garden Party and Other Stories*.

1923 ....Jean Toomer's *Cane* published.

1923–1925 .... Stories from *Red Cavalry* by Babel appear in Soviet publications.

1924 .... Kafka's "A Hunger Artist" published in a collection of four stories titled *A Hunger Artist*.

1925 .... Ernest Hemingway's *In Our Time* published.

1925 .... *The New Yorker* founded.

1926 .... Lawrence's "The Rocking-Horse Winner" published in *Harper's Bazaar*.

1927 .... Hemingway's "The Killers" published in *Scribner's Magazine*.

1929 .... Babel's *Red Cavalry* published, including "My First Goose."

1939 .... *Scribner's Magazine* ceases publication.

1939–1945 .... World War II.

1948 .... Jackson's "The Lottery" published in *The New Yorker*.

1955 .... Flannery O'Connor's "A Good Man Is Hard to Find" published.

1955 .... Gabriel García Márquez's "A Very Old Man with Enormous Wings" published in *Leaf Storm and Other Stories*.

1957 .... Baldwin's "Sonny's Blues" published.

1959 .... Grace Paley's "An Interest in Life" published in *The Little Disturbances of Man*.

1961 .... Updike's "A & P" published in *The New Yorker*.

1963 ....Malamud's "The Jewbird" published in *Idiots First*; Betty Friedan's *The Feminine Mystique* is also published.

1976 ....Kingston's *The Woman Warrior* published, including "No Name Woman."

1983 ....Atwood's "Happy Endings" published as part of *Murder in the Dark*.

1984 ....Carver's *Cathedral* published.

1988 ....Gordimer's "The Moment Before the Gun Went Off" published.

Glossary

allegory: Representation through symbolic figures that convey a deeper, often moral meaning.

anecdote: Reports, observations, or short, significant or humorous encapsulated narratives.

apartheid: The system of segregation of the non-white population that existed in South Africa.

arabesque: An ornamental style of intricate patterns in fiction.

archetype: An original or prototypical model, pattern, or character in literature tied to myth.

Ashkenazi: Jewish person of Central or Eastern European origins who used Yiddish as opposed to Ladino, the language of the Sephardic Jews.

bildungsroman: A novel of the growth from innocence to experience that emerged from German literature of the 19th century.

Calvinism: The theology of John Calvin based on the belief in predestination.

carnivalesque: Having the festive and merrymaking costumes and rituals associated with carnivals.

catharsis: A purging or releasing of the emotions.

Comintern: The Communist Third International, dedicated to international communist revolution.

Czarist Russia: The line of rulers in Russia before the Bolshevik Revolution.

denouement: The final resolution of a plot.

dialectic: A form of logical process going back to Hegel and Marx that sees forces in opposition ultimately synthesizing—as was posited by Marx about feudalism and capitalism synthesizing into socialism.

dicty: A pejorative term used among some African Americans during the first part of the 20th century to describe African Americans who were snobbish and had lighter skin tones.

didactic: Intentionally designed to teach or to be instructive.

donnée: The given in a story that the reader accepts; it may be implausible but once accepted becomes the fulcrum or departing point of the story.

epic theater: Bertolt Brecht's notion that staged drama could keep an audience removed in order for them to learn and be politicized.

epiphany: In literature, a term from James Joyce tied to an illumination or revelation.

Existentialism: A philosophy based on the individual's responsibility for choice.

Fabulism: A kind of fiction writing particularly linked to myth and fable.

Formalism: A school of literary criticism connected to Cleanth Brooks and Robert Penn Warren that sees the meaning and interpretation of literary works as essentially being tied to the text.

gevalt: A Yiddish exclamatory word of surprise or disbelief.

hubris: The Greek notion of pride commonly connected to arrogance.

Immorality Act: Under apartheid, the law forbidding sexual relations between whites and non-whites.

intentional fallacy: The notion put forward in literary criticism by Monroe Beardsley and W. K. Wimsatt that one cannot determine authorial intention in a work of literature.

intertextuality: The belief in literary criticism and analysis of literature that meaning in a text is derived from its relation to other texts.

Magical Realism: A term coined by German art critic Franz Roh in 1925 to refer to a style of painting, but which has come to mean in literature the fusion or blending of the real with the fantastic or supernatural.

metafiction: Fiction that is reflexive of fiction or its conventions.

mimetic: Mimicking or representing reality in literature in whatever the form.

Minimalism: A style in literature based on simplicity, sparseness, and unadorned language.

Modernism: A term applied to the movements in literary style and innovation associated with the 20th century.

Naturalism: A philosophy prevalent in literature throughout the 20th century that views human behavior as deterministic.

pièce-à-thèse: A term used largely in dramatic literature to represent a work that has a clear and apparent thesis embodied in it.

pogrom: An attack or massacre against Jews living in the Russian *shtetls*.

Postmodernism: In literature, a movement away from the Modernism of the early and middle parts of the 20th century. Postmodernism emphasized such elements as self-reflexivity and the fantastical.

prelapsarian: Before mankind's Fall from Eden when Adam and Eve were still in the garden.

proletarian: Of or related to the working class.

Puritanism: The principles and practices of the Puritans tied to the theology of John Calvin and often identified with strictness and austerity.

secular: The view that separates itself from religion or religious policy or policies.

shtetl: A Jewish village in Eastern Europe.

solipsism: The philosophic belief that meaning comes only through the self or subjectivity.

Stoicism: The philosophy from Zeno of unemotional removal of the self and resignation to one's fate.

superstructure: A Marxist idea that posits a relationship to the base or mode of production and the social order that enforces it to the entire remainder of society, culture, and institutions.

Symbolism: In literature, the finding of symbolic meaning in a text. Based on the Symbolist movement that took place largely in France in the 19th century.

third wall: The imaginary barrier that separates a narrator or narrative voice from a text (also referred to as the "fourth wall").

Trotskyite: A follower of Leon Trotsky whose communist ideology differed from that of both Lenin and Stalin and emphasized a dictatorship of the proletariat and an international revolution of socialism.

unreliable narrator: A narrative voice that is lying, self-deceiving, or too biased to be reliable.

verisimilitude: Something in literature that is true to life and gives every appearance of being truthful or true to life.

willing suspension of disbelief: A notion from the poet Samuel Taylor Coleridge that readers will willingly suspend their disbelief if engaged strongly enough in a tale.

Yiddishkeit: The culture of Eastern European Jewry built around the Yiddish language and tales.

Biographical Notes

Margaret Atwood (1939–): Born in Ottawa, Ontario, in 1939, Atwood was the daughter of an entomologist and a dietician and was expected by her parents, especially her father, to become a scientist. Instead, she fell in love with literature and studied at the University of Toronto and at Radcliffe and later taught at a number of universities. Her interest in science continued throughout her life and can be seen particularly in her dystopian novels *The Handmaid's Tale* and *Oryx and Crake*. Known chiefly as a short story writer and a novelist—and the recipient as a novelist of the coveted British Booker Prize, as well as a number of Canadian Governor General's Awards—Atwood has also published poetry, essays, and literary criticism. She is a political and social activist, a writer who once defined being an artist as being a guardian of the moral and ethical sense of the community. An active environmentalist and feminist, she was involved for many years in the Writers' Union of Canada, Amnesty International, and International PEN. Though she once described herself as a Red Tory, she has been a member of the Green Party.

Isaac Babel (1894–1940): Babel was born in 1894 in Odessa in the Ukraine. At that time, Jews were prohibited from residing in most of the major Russian cities and, after graduating from university at Kiev, Babel went with a fake passport to Saint Petersburg to study literature. He was a playwright in addition to being a short story writer, and he worked on a number of films, including with the famed Russian master filmmaker Sergei Eisenstein. His best-known works are the stories in *Red Cavalry* and *Tales of Odessa*. Babel had a close friendship with Maxim Gorky, who was a mentor and supporter of his, and he was employed with the commission of education and the secret police. He was murdered, we now know, on Stalin's orders in 1940 for espionage, which amounted to charges of being a Trotskyite. For years, his fate had been unknown, and it was believed that he had died in a forced labor camp. He is widely regarded, despite a small oeuvre, as one of the greatest writers of the 20th century. All charges against Babel were officially dropped posthumously by the U.S.S.R. in 1954.

James Baldwin (1924–1987): In addition to being a short story writer, Baldwin was a novelist and an essayist. He was born in Harlem, where his stepfather was a clergyman; his grandfather had been a slave. As a boy, Baldwin preached in the Pentecostal church but gave up preaching while he was still in high school and went off to live in Greenwich Village, where he met Richard Wright. In 1953, Baldwin published his groundbreaking autobiographical novel, *Go Tell It on the Mountain*. "Sonny's Blues" appeared in 1957. Baldwin was a novelist in the tradition of Henry James—deeply concerned with both the demands of a higher and noble artistic calling and with his own black identity and racial justice. Baldwin was rooted in Harlem and Greenwich Village and nourished in the great tradition of the spirituals, gospel, the blues, and jazz. The Harlem Renaissance flourished in the 1920s and saw one of the greatest outputs of black identity and artistry that would carry on in Baldwin's own boyhood and youth. He left the United States and lived most of his adult life in France. Baldwin's great theme throughout his writing career was freedom, and as a black homosexual man, he understood forces that oppressed freedom. He died in 1987.

Raymond Carver (1938–1988): Carver was born in 1938 in Clatskanie, Oregon, and grew up in Yakima, Washington. His father was a mill worker, and his mother, a retail clerk and waitress. Both Carver and his father were alcoholics. By the age of 20, Carver was married with two children—a boy and a girl—and he struggled through many menial and service-type jobs to provide for his family. He would later write that providing for and taking care of children was his greatest single obstacle as a writer and a source of deep resentment. Still, he managed to become educated in California colleges, including Chico (where his mentor was the novelist John Gardner) and Humboldt State, and later on, at the Iowa Writers' Workshop. He published his first story in 1960 and continued to publish both short stories and poems, often written out of economic necessity. He also wrote essays and reviews and was a literature teacher at a number of universities, with most of his teaching career spent at Syracuse University in upstate New York. "Cathedral" was published in 1981 in *The Atlantic Monthly* and as a volume under that title in 1984. Carver, a heavy smoker all of his adult life, died of lung cancer in 1988.

Anton Chekhov (1860–1904): Chekhov's grandfather was the grandson of a former serf. Though serfdom was officially abolished in 1861, the year following Chekhov's birth, peasants remained woefully unequal both socially and economically in Russia throughout Chekhov's lifetime. Chekhov had a deep and abiding empathy for this class of people, who were still shackled by poverty, quite possibly at least partially the result of his own lineage. He is one of our greatest and most humane storytellers, as well as a dramatist and a physician. As a doctor, Chekhov treated scores of poor people for free. He once said, "Medicine is my lawful wife and literature is my mistress." He produced hundreds of short stories, four plays, and a novel and was a major influence on a score of fiction writers. Chekhov's source of humanity is often attributed to his soft and kind storytelling mother, as opposed to his tyrannical, abusive, and religiously fanatic father. He married the actress Olga Knipper in 1901. Chekhov died in 1904 of tuberculosis. He was first diagnosed with it in 1897 while in Moscow and spent the years after living in Yalta with his mother and sister and traveling to Moscow where Olga, his wife, resided.

Gabriel García Márquez (1928–): Born in Aracataca in Colombia in 1928, García Márquez is a Nobel laureate in literature (1982) and one of the 20th century's most famous and respected writers—author of the famous novels *One Hundred Years of Solitude*, *The Autumn of the Patriarch*, and *Love in the Time of Cholera*. García Márquez was educated in the law at the Universidad Nacional in Bogotá; has been a journalist and screenwriter, as well as a novelist and short story writer; and has been known throughout his life as a political activist. He was raised by his maternal grandparents and strongly influenced by the supernatural and fantastical stories his grandmother told him throughout his childhood. He wanted to write stories in a fashion similar to the way his grandmother told them—"with a brick face" was how he phrased it—and an early chance encounter with Kafka's "The Metamorphosis" seemed to free him. He was also greatly influenced by Sophocles, the Greek dramatist and author of *Oedipus*, and by American Nobel laureate William Faulkner. He spent time living in Venezuela and under asylum in Mexico because of his radical political activities. He became identified in his literary career with Magical Realism, a form of writing that blends the real and the fantastical and is largely associated with writers of Central and South America.

Nikolai Gogol (1809–1852): Nikolai Gogol was born in the Russian Ukraine in 1809 to a fairly prosperous family. Gogol's father was educated and a writer. The family name was originally Ianovskii, but Gogol's grandfather changed it in order to claim noble Cossack ancestry. Gogol was sent off as a boy to boarding school, and we know that he was physically so unattractive that he was teased by his classmates and called "the mysterious dwarf." Some of those earlier experiences may help to account for Gogol's empathy for a character like the hapless and much-teased Akaky of "The Overcoat." Gogol wanted initially to be a poet. He had a close relationship with the great Russian writer Aleksandr Pushkin and was deeply affected by Pushkin's death, only three years before the publication of "The Overcoat." Gogol settled in Saint Petersburg, Russia's capital city, and there is much in the story "The Overcoat" that is tied to that city and to its mythology, as well as to the experiences Gogol had working there at a number of minor governmental jobs. Gogol went on to work as a teacher and private tutor and published a volume of short stories in 1835 called *St. Petersburg Stories*. "The Overcoat" was part of a collection called *The Overcoat and Other Stories of Good and Evil*, published in 1842. Gogol had an enormous influence on short fiction and produced novels, drama, and satires. He died in 1852.

Nadine Gordimer (1923–): The daughter of Jewish immigrants and anti-apartheid activists, Gordimer was born in the mining town of Springs in 1923. She once said, "Politics is character in South Africa." She settled in Johannesburg after receiving an education (but not graduating) from Witwatersand University. Gordimer published her first story at the age of 15 and has commented that not even winning the Nobel Prize (which was awarded to her in 1991) was as thrilling as seeing a story of hers in print at that age. Her first collection of stories, *Face to Face*, was published in 1949. She once remarked that "the short story is the literary form of our age," but she has also written many novels and essays and has been awarded a host of honors in addition to the Nobel, including the Booker Prize and the Orange Prize, a prestigious British literary prize for the best original novel by a woman of any nationality writing in English. Gordimer refused to accept the Orange Prize in 1988 because it is awarded only to women. She also was awarded a literary prize by the French Legion of Honor. Three of Gordimer's books were banned during the apartheid years. She was a member of the African National Congress (ANC) when that group was officially banned, and she was a long-time friend and supporter of ANC leader Nelson Mandela, who would become head of state in South Africa following the abolition of apartheid. In addition to her leadership and activism in the fight against apartheid, Gordimer has been involved in anti-censorship activism, served as vice president of International PEN, and worked on behalf of causes related to HIV/AIDS.

Nathaniel Hawthorne (1804–1864): Hawthorne was born in the infamous Salem, Massachusetts, and descended from ancestors who participated in the Salem witch trials and believed in a stern form of Puritanism tied to the teachings of John Calvin. His ancestor William Hathorne was a colonial magistrate who persecuted Quakers, and William Hathorne's son John was a Puritan investigator of those accused of witchcraft. Hawthorne was obsessed with Puritanism and his Puritan ancestors. He wrote of them in a work called "The Custom House," which is often considered an introduction to *The Scarlet Letter*, and it seems clear that his guilt about the sins of the fathers and his own need to exorcize that guilt are part of the genius behind "Young Goodman Brown." Hawthorne's father died in 1808, when the author (born in 1804) was only four years old, and his mother became a recluse. Hawthorne would also live an isolated life—which shaped both his character and his vision—though all of that would change and he would wind up a famous and prosperous man. He was an editor and novelist, as well as a short story writer, and he wrote children's stories, travel sketches, Gothic tales, and a children's history of the world that sold more than a million copies but made him all of $100.00—the fee paid to him for the book. A college classmate and close friend of America's 14th president, Franklin Pierce, Hawthorne wrote a presidential campaign biography for Pierce and was appointed by Pierce to Liverpool as U.S. consul. Hawthorne published his first tale in 1830 and, five years later, published "Young Goodman Brown" in an issue of *New England Magazine*. The story later appeared in a short story collection of Hawthorne's called *Mosses from an Old Manse*. Hawthorne died in 1864.

Ernest Hemingway (1899–1961): Hemingway was born in 1899 and grew up in Oak Park, a suburb of Chicago, which he once derogated in a much-quoted remark as a place of wide lawns and narrow minds. His introduction to violence came early when he went with his father (a country doctor) to an Indian camp and was exposed to suicide, an experience turned into a fictional piece in his 1925 volume *In Our Time*. He was a reporter for the *Kansas City Star* before volunteering to serve in an American ambulance unit during World War I. He then served at the front in Italy, where he was wounded before his 19th birthday as a volunteer ambulance driver, an experience that helped to shape much of his vision as an author. Hemingway helped revolutionize prose fiction with his concrete and compact writing style that emphasized action. In addition to short stories, he published many novels and was awarded the Nobel Prize for literature in 1954 after the publication of *The Old Man and the Sea*. Both Hemingway's father and Hemingway committed suicide—Hemingway taking his life in 1961 with a shotgun in Ketchum, Idaho.

Shirley Jackson (1919–1965): Jackson was born in San Francisco in 1919. She attended the University of Rochester and Syracuse University and married the literary critic Stanley Edgar Hyman; the couple settled down in Vermont, where he taught as a professor at Bennington. She was a mother of four and a housewife who managed to produce a good deal of published work. Jackson became famous after the publication of "The Lottery," which created a major sensation after it first appeared in *The New Yorker*, though she regularly insisted, "It was just a story." She was repeatedly asked about the meaning of the story and told the *San Francisco Chronicle*, her hometown paper, that the story is about "pointless violence and general inhumanity." Though known mostly for "The Lottery," Jackson was also the author of a number of novels, children's books, and short stories that were published in many of the most popular women's magazines of the day, such as *McCall's*, *Women's Day*, and *Good Housekeeping*. She won a coveted Edgar mystery award for one of her stories, "The Possibility of Evil," published in 1965 as part of a bushel of unpublished work discovered posthumously, and wrote an influential horror novel, *The Haunting of Hill House*. Jackson, a lifetime agoraphobic, was saddled most of her adult life with neurotic fears that would later turn into psychotic paranoia. She died in 1965.

Henry James (1843–1916): James has earned the title of master because of his body of fiction writing and his contributions to literary theory and criticism. His output was prodigious. One would be hard-pressed to find a more consummate man or woman of letters. James wrote novels, biography and autobiography, journalism, plays, travel accounts, reportage, literary criticism, and 112 stories. He published his first story when he was 21. He was prolific, was deeply and passionately committed to the literary life, and made his living as a writer. James published "The Real Thing" in 1891 when he was 48. Another famous James story, *Daisy Miller*, was published in

1878, and James was still publishing great stories, such as “The Beast in the Jungle” and “The Jolly Corner,” in 1903 when he was 60. He was born in New York City in 1843 and came from a distinguished and prominent New York family—though he spent much of his early life in Europe and wound up an American expatriate in Britain, renouncing his American citizenship and becoming a naturalized British citizen after the United States would initially not join Britain and France in the First World War. James’s father was a religious philosopher and his brother William was a famous psychologist and the father of American pragmatism. Henry James died in 1916.

James Joyce (1882–1941): Born in 1882 in Dublin, Joyce—one of the 20th century’s most respected and revered writers—became an expatriate living in Zurich, Trieste, Pula, Rome, and ultimately, Paris. He was a cosmopolitan in his living quarters but returned ineluctably to his roots and the regional world of Dublin. He was educated in Jesuit schools and at University College Dublin but left both nation and the Catholic Church to devote his life to literary art. Joyce wrote famous novels, perhaps the century’s most famous, *Ulysses*, as well as the semi-autobiographical *A Portrait of the Artist as a Young Man* and *Finnegans Wake*. He is best known for his inventive and original use of language; his mastery of the stream-of-consciousness technique that was also used by such writers as Virginia Woolf and William Faulkner; and his use of archetypes, myth, and what he called the epiphany, a moment of revelation of truth for a character in a story. Joyce’s influence on the modern short story is inestimable. He (along with the poet William Butler Yeats and such playwrights as Lady Gregory and Sean O’Casey) was singular in hastening an Irish literary revival and literary renaissance that would see a spate of short fiction literary talent in such writers as Liam O’Flaherty, Sean O’Faolain, Frank O’Connor, and later on, Samuel Beckett, Edna O’Brien, and Mary Lavin. James Joyce died in 1941.

Franz Kafka (1883–1924): Kafka was born in 1883 into a middle-class Jewish family in Prague—then part of the Austro-Hungarian Empire. He remained single his entire life and lived mostly with his parents, though he was fearful throughout his life of his authoritarian and strict father. Only a few of his stories and none of his fragmentary novels were published during his lifetime and, though he gave every outward indication that he did not want them ever to be published, this was not the case with "A Hunger Artist," written and published in a collection of that title near the end of Kaka's life, when he was dying of tuberculosis. His friend and literary executor Max Brod defied his request to burn his novel manuscripts and saw to it that *The Trial*, *The Castle*, and *Amerika* were published after his death. Kafka became, posthumously, one of the most revered and influential writers of the 20th century. He was a civil-servant claim investigator most of his adult life. Though a law graduate and the inventor of the first civilian hardhat, Kafka worked for a year for an Italian insurance company and for a number of years for the Bohemian workers accident insurance claim company. He died in 1924 of starvation from a throat condition, caused by the tuberculosis, which made eating painful.

Maxine Hong Kingston (1940–): Kingston was born in 1940 in Stockton, California, the eldest of six children. Her father had been trained in China as a scholar but in the United States worked in a laundry and as manager of a gambling house. Her mother had trained in China in medicine and midwifery but worked in the United States in a laundry and as a field hand. Kingston graduated from the University of California at Berkeley and married an actor named Earl Kingston. Her work, especially *The Woman Warrior* from which "No Name Woman" is taken, has had enormous influence on Chinese and Chinese American writing, as well as on ethnic and feminist writers. She is an emeritus professor of English at UC Berkeley and was awarded the National Humanities Medal in 1997 by then President Bill Clinton. For many years, she has been a peace activist and continues to work voluntarily as a writing teacher with veterans of war.

D. H. Lawrence (1885–1930): A son of the working class and of a lower-class, impoverished background, Lawrence was born to a miner father and schoolteacher mother in 1885 in Eastwood, Nottinghamshire, in central England. He became educated, like his mother, and married Frieda von Richthofen, the wife of a German professor who was also the mother of three children. Lawrence was accused of spying for the Germans in World War I and arrested and accused by the Germans of being a British spy. Lawrence remained, throughout his lifetime, generally removed from politics and dedicated to art. He had a credo predicated on the efficacy of sexuality and spontaneity and living on the basis of one's impulses and virility, intuition and blood, as well as on a philosophy tied to androgyny. A prolific writer, he published short stories, novels, poetry, travel writing, and essays throughout his life and was also an Impressionist painter. He was vilified as being obscene and pornographic, particularly after the publication of his last novel, *Lady Chatterley's Lover*—published first in 1928 in Florence after a number of court battles to overcome the fact that it had been banned. To the present day, Lawrence is considered one of the world's greatest writers, and "The Rocking-Horse Winner," one of his and the world's finest stories. He died in 1930.

Bernard Malamud (1914–1986): A novelist as well as a short story writer and the recipient of two National Book Awards, a Pulitzer Prize, and an O. Henry Award, Malamud was born in Brooklyn in 1914 to Russian Jewish immigrant parents. He went to City College and Columbia and taught English at Oregon State and Bennington. "Jewbird" was part of his second collection of short stories, *Idiots First*, which appeared in 1963. The first collection featured one of Malamud's other most famous stories, the title story, evocative of Magical Realism, "The Magic Barrel." Malamud was often identified with Saul Bellow and Philip Roth as part of a triumvirate of Jewish American male writers. Roth, a younger writer than the other two, eulogized Malamud upon his death as a man of stern morality whose conscience "was tortuously exacerbated by the pathos of human need unabated." Malamud worked much stronger and more intensely than the other two with traditional Jewish themes of suffering, victimization, exile, the role of being marginal or an outsider, and the paramount importance of law and morality. One of the most famous statements Malamud made was "All men are Jews though few men know it," by which he meant that life universally involves suffering and the Existential condition of being a potential victim simply because one is human.

Katherine Mansfield (1888–1923): Born Katherine Beauchamp in 1888 to a prominent New Zealand family in Wellington, by high school, Mansfield was publishing short fiction—though her first love was the cello. She changed her last name to Mansfield in 1911 after her first collection of short stories, *In a German Pension*, was published. She had been sent by her mother to Bavaria after becoming pregnant, though she ultimately suffered a miscarriage. For a time, she lived a bisexual and bohemian life in London that included a marriage that lasted only a few days and a serious case of gonorrhea. She died—like Chekhov and Kafka—of tuberculosis in

1923 at the institute of the Russian mystic George Gurdjieff in Fontainebleau, France. Her last words were "I love the rain. I want the feeling of it on my face." Mansfield's total output as a short story writer included more than 60 published stories and 26 unfinished. She was a friend of D. H. Lawrence and Virginia Woolf and a member of the renowned and influential Bloomsbury Group of artists, writers, and thinkers. She and her second husband, literary critic and editor John Middleton Murry, were close friends of Lawrence and his wife, Frieda, though she and Lawrence had a serious falling out. As a writer, Mansfield was most significantly influenced by Chekhov and Joyce and the idea of a story's emotional impact being central to it as an experience. Her work continues to be internationally of great and enduring influence.

Guy de Maupassant (1850–1893): Maupassant was a novelist and editor who also wrote travel books and poetry and was a newspaper reporter. He was the author of hundreds of short stories, some of them horror-type stories inspired and greatly influenced by Poe. Maupassant was born Henri René Albert Guy de Maupassant in 1850 to a noble and old Lorraine family settled in Normandy. Maupassant is often described as one of France's most famous writers, one of the fathers of the short story, and along with such figures as Émile Zola, one of the fathers of Naturalism. He was a protégé of Gustave Flaubert, the author of *Madame Bovary*, who was a childhood friend of Maupassant's mother and Uncle Alfred. Maupassant's maternal grandfather was Flaubert's godfather, and Flaubert was a literary godfather to Maupassant, mentoring him, introducing him to other distinguished literary figures of his day, and helping him establish himself as a career writer. Maupassant's parents separated when he was quite young, and as a young man—before he established himself as a writer of wide fame and fortune—Maupassant was expelled from a seminary. He went to Paris at age 21, where he worked as a civil servant. He died of syphilis before his 43rd birthday in 1893 and left a dark and revelatory epitaph that he wrote for himself: "I have coveted everything and taken pleasure in nothing." Maupassant was influenced by the Naturalists and his work is a guidepost of Naturalism beginning to make its headway into short fiction.

Flannery O'Connor (1925–1964): Born in 1925 in Savannah, Georgia, to Roman Catholic parents, O'Connor held devoutly to that faith throughout her life. In 1938, the family moved to Milledgeville, near Macon, Georgia. She attended Georgia State College for

Women and the Writers' Workshop at the University of Iowa. A novelist as well as an essayist and short story writer, she is internationally recognized as a great fiction writer. O'Connor's work is often viewed as reflective of her Catholic faith and seen as grotesque and mysterious—quintessential southern Gothicism. Her father died of the autoimmune disease lupus, which Flannery was also diagnosed with in 1950. After that, she returned from the east and lived on her family's farm with her mother and raised peacocks. In 1956, she was awarded the National Book Award for fiction. Her reputation as one of the 20th century's greatest storytellers is assured.

Grace Paley (1922–2007): Paley was born Grace Goodside in the Bronx in 1922, one of three children, to a Russian Jewish immigrant family. She was educated at Hunter, New York University, and the New School for Social Research, where she studied with the famed poet W. H. Auden. She wanted to be a poet and published a great deal of poetry over a lifetime, but her real gift was fiction, and she produced many wonderful stories with their own peculiar rhythm and cadence evocative of New York. She said of her stories: "None of it happened and yet every word of it is true. It's truth embedded in a lie." She was also known for her social and political activism and described herself as "a combative pacifist" and "a gentle anarchist." Her life ended with breast cancer when she was 84 and living in Vermont as that state's poet laureate.

Edgar Allan Poe (1809–1849): Poe was born in 1809 to poor thespians. He was adopted at age three, after his mother died, by John Allan of Richmond, Virginia. Poe was educated in Virginia and England and expelled from West Point. He married his 13-year-old cousin Virginia Clemm when he was 27. Clemm died some 11 years later. Poe's life, most of it in Baltimore, was one of poverty, depression, illness, and addiction but also of prolific writing, including more than 70 stories, poetry, essays (especially his famous one on the short story), and a novel, *The Narrative of Arthur Gordon Pym of Nantucket*. He also worked as an editor and achieved international recognition during his lifetime. Poe will be remembered as one of the most important figures in American literature—laying the cornerstones of the genre of the short story as both a writer and a theorist. Edgar Allan Poe died in 1849.

John Updike (1932–): As a child, Updike lived in the small Pennsylvania town of Shillington in a working-class milieu. His father was a junior high teacher. Updike went to Harvard on a full scholarship, edited the Harvard *Lampoon*, and studied at the Ruskin School of Drawing and Fine Art in Oxford, England, before taking a job at *The New Yorker*. In 1957, he and his family moved to Massachusetts. He has published stories, novels, poems, and essays and has become one of American literature's most distinguished 20th-century literary figures—acclaimed as a chronicler of American life and manners and of American civilization. He received the National Book Critics Circle Award in 1983 for his collection of essays and criticism *Hugging the Shore.*

Bibliography

Unless otherwise indicated, all stories and many of the essays cited in this course can be found in *The Story and Its Writer: An Introduction to Short Fiction* by Ann Charters (7th ed., New York: Bedford/St. Martin's Press), abbreviated in the listings that follow simply as "in Charters." The collection is the best and most diverse I have found and includes a splendid array of stories from writers from many different backgrounds, as well as solid introductory material to each story and relevant commentaries by selected authors and critics about individual stories and the genre of short fiction. Included are casebooks on major short fiction writers and a casebook on graphic storytelling; appendices that offer good overviews of the elements of fiction, a brief history of the short story, and sections on writing about short stories, elements of literary theory, and critical perspectives; and a glossary and chronology. The sixth edition of Charters has what I feel is the best translation of Isaac Babel's "My First Goose" and many additional stories that are not included in the seventh edition, as well as different stories and commentaries. It does not include the graphic fiction. Both are excellent volumes, and the sixth edition includes all the stories listed as essential reading that are also in the seventh edition except for the selection by Babel.

The Norton Introduction to Literature (9th ed., New York: Norton, 2006), edited by Alison Booth, J. Paul Hunter, and Kelly J. Mays, also has a fine selection of stories, as well as poetry and plays. The volume includes stories featured in this course by Poe, Hawthorne, Chekhov, Lawrence, García Márquez, Baldwin, and Atwood, with good grounding in the elements of fiction and useful, practical introductory material. This source is hereinafter cited by title.

Suggested Readings:

Aristotle. *Poetics.* Oxford: Clarendon Press, 1981. The classical rendering (written in 335 B.C.) of a theory of tragedy by the great Greek philosopher who, for centuries, helped to define the nature of the elements of tragedy.

Atwood, Margaret. *The Handmaid's Tale*. Toronto: McClelland and Stewart, 1985; New York: Vintage, 2007. Atwood's dystopian novel about the subjugation of women in a theocratic state. A good example of the author's unusual powers of imagination and narration.

———. "Happy Endings." First published in 1983 in *Murder in the Dark: Short Fictions and Prose Poems*. In Charters and in a new edition of *Murder in the Dark*, Dallas, TX: Texas Bookman, 1996. This is the great Canadian author at her best—clever, parodic, wise, and full of fun and mischief but intent on showing the how and the why of storytelling.

———. *Oryx and Crake*. Toronto: McClelland and Stewart, 2003; Garden City, NY: Anchor, 2004. A later dystopian novel featuring the last man on Earth and genetic engineering, as well as other futuristic scientific advances based on the science that was percolating at the time Atwood wrote the novel. Another example of her sure sense of craft as a storyteller and her ability to weave in science and technology.

Babel, Isaac. "My First Goose." Published in *Konarmiia* (*Red Cavalry*) in 1926. Also in *Red Cavalry*, New York: Norton, 2003, translation by Peter Constantine, and Charters (6th ed.), translation by Walter Morrison (the best translation). Morrison's translation is more lyrical and closer to the mark as far as approximating the poetic and connotative power of Babel's prose, though if you can read Babel in the original Russian, you will see how formidable and challenging it is to translate his work.

———. *Red Cavalry*. New York: Norton, 2003. This collection, first published in the 1920s, provides a splendid portal into Babel's world of violence and war.

———. "Story of My Dovecote." Appears in *Red Cavalry and Other Stories*. Penguin Classics, 2006. The story is of a boy in Russia experiencing a pogrom is included in the collection of vivid war stories by the great Russian Jewish author set during the Soviet-Polish war.

Baldwin, James. *Go Tell It on the Mountain*. New York: Dell, 1980; New York: Dial Press Trade Paperbacks, 2000. The passionate and emotionally jarring Harlem-set story of a young African American boy and his family's travails (originally published in 1953). Full of soaring, lyrical writing and trenchant insight into black idioms and culture, as well as racism and black spirituality.

———. *Notes of a Native Son*. Boston: Beacon 1984. This collection of Baldwin's essays, first published in 1955, reveals his narrative powers and his strengths as a polemicist and expository writer. The essays in the collection traverse his life and provide a historic lens into understanding the civil rights movement and Baldwin's personal movement toward expatriating.

———. "Sonny's Blues." First published in 1957 in the *Partisan Review*. In Charters and in *Going to Meet the Man: Stories*, New York: Vintage, 1995. A remarkable story about Harlem, the blues, drug addiction, and literal brotherly love by one of America's finest African American authors.

Blake, William. *Songs of Innocence* and *Songs of Experience*. London: Tate Publishing, 2007. These poems by Blake (first published in 1789 and 1794) contrast the duality he saw of the human soul and its division between the innocence of childhood and the experience of the years following. The two most exemplary poems in the two books are "The Lamb" and "The Tyger," each embodying innocence and experience. The poems are particularly important intertextually, that is, in the way they affect, influence, and tie in with other literary works.

Brod, Max. *Franz Kafka: A Biography*. New York: Da Capo Press, 1995. This is the biography of Kafka written by his close friend and first published in 1938. It gives us a lucid and detailed view into Kafka's life from a unique perspective.

Carver, Raymond. "Cathedral." First published in 1981 in *The Atlantic Monthly*. In Charters and *Cathedral*, New York: Vintage, 1989. The story seen by the majority of critics as the most powerful of those written by this gifted author of short fiction and poetry. Here, sight, wisdom, and transcendence come to an everyman from an encounter with his wife's friend, who is blind.

———. *Cathedral*. New York: Vintage, 1989. This volume of a dozen later published Carver short stories includes some of the author's finest work.

———. *What We Talk About When We Talk About Love: Stories*. New York: Vintage, 1989. Seventeen stories appear in this volume which established Carver's worldwide iconic reputation.

———. *Will You Please Be Quiet, Please?* New York: Vintage, 1992. Twenty-two of Carver's early stories were published in this collection when he was under the strong editorial influence of *Esquire* editor Gordon Lish.

Cash, W. J. *The Mind of the South*. Baton Rouge, LA: Louisiana State University Press, 1992. Cash was a genius at weaving together a psychohistory of the American South and revealing a mentality and sensibility that are distinctly southern. The book is invaluable in providing a deep understanding of southern writers.

Cervantes, *Don Quixote*. New York: Harper Perennial, 2005. The classic episodic Spanish bildingsroman and universally admired novel of the adventurers Don Quixote and his loyal sidekick Sancho Panza.

Cheever, John. *The Stories of John Cheever*. New York: Vintage, 2000. This volume, originally published in 1978, is a collection of stories by one of America's finest and most admired short story writers from the post–World War II era. The stories capture Cheever's versatility as a storyteller and the suburban world that he so handily made his own.

Chekhov, Anton. *Four Plays* (*Seagull*, 1896; *Uncle Vanya*, 1897; *Three Sisters*, 1901; *The Cherry Orchard*, 1904). New York: Norton, 1977; London: Nick Hern Books, 2005. Each of these Chekhov plays provides a wider lens for seeing the extension of the author's genius into drama. The four plays have been widely acclaimed and frequently produced through the years. Each has remarkable power, but *Uncle Vanya* is most often designated as the great masterpiece.

———. "The Lady with the Dog." First published in Russian ("Dama s sobakoi") in 1899. In Charters as "The Lady with the Little Dog," translated by Richard Pevear and Larissa Volokhonsky, and as "The Lady with the Dog" in *The Norton Introduction to Literature*, translated by Constance Garnett (the better translation). The Garnett translation is also in *Anton Chekhov's Short Stories*, edited by Ralph Mattlaw, New York: Norton, 1979. Garnett's work as a translator continues to hold up best despite later translations of this beloved author's story—a powerful and enduring tale of forbidden love between a married man and a married woman.

———. *Stories of Anton Chekhov*. New York: Bantam, 2000. Originally published in Russian during the period 1880 to 1904. In this collection, we see Chekhov the master storyteller through the years of his prolific career as a writer of short fiction; the astonishing range of his narrative powers and his ability to evoke our empathy and insight into the human condition are on display.

Chopin, Kate. "How I Stumbled upon Maupassant." In Charters. A short essay of appreciation for Maupassant by the author of *The Awakening* and other works of fiction.

Cobbs, Price, and William Grier. *Black Rage*. New York: Basic Books, 1968; Eugene, OR: Wipf & Stock Publishers, 2000. An early work by two black psychiatrists focusing on the nature of racial identity in America for blacks. The book continues to have relevance to black identity and experience in the United States.

Conrad, Joseph. *Heart of Darkness*. New York: Dover, 1990. The classic novel of Belgian colonialism in the Congo that continues to evoke controversy over its depiction of Africans but remains one of the great novels of the early 20th century (first published in 1902). Francis Ford Coppola's film *Apocalypse Now* was based on *Heart of Darkness*.

Cooke, Nathalie. *Margaret Atwood.* Toronto: ECW Press, 1998. A good overview of Atwood and her importance not only as a Canadian writer but internationally.

de Beauvoir, Simone. *The Second Sex*. New York: Penguin,2007. An ambitious book for its time (published in 1949) and one that continues to resonate, despite the fact that many of the feminist views espoused in it have become integrated into Western thinking. The important thing to remember in reading this book is that it provided a historic foundation to much of modern feminist thinking and was, in its time, groundbreaking.

Dickey, James. *Deliverance*. New York: Delta, 1994. A novel by an American poet laureate that takes its readers into a heart of darkness in rural Georgia and helps us to understand the Gothic and frightful world that Flannery O'Connor projects in her stories. It was published in 1970 and made into a major motion picture in 1972.

Dreiser, Theodore. *Sister Carrie*. New York: New American Library, 2000. Classic American novel of a small-town girl going to the big city and ultimately finding fame and fortune. A fine example of a large-scope novel with Naturalistic writing. Originally published in 1900.

Du Bois, W. E. B. *The Souls of Black Folk.* New York: Penguin, 1996. This is a seminal work of 14 essays (published in 1903) about race or what Du Bois called the "color line." It continues to provide great insight into racial identity and reveals to us the historical record of race at the beginning of the 20th century.

Eagleton, Terry. *Base and Superstructure.* Baltimore, MD: Johns Hopkins University Press, 2000. The work of a highly regarded Neo-Marxist literary critic who provides a useful theoretical framework for understanding literature through a historical and outside-of-the-text approach rooted in Marxist theory.

Edel, Leon. *Henry James*. New York: Harper Collins, 1987. The definitive critical biography of Henry James, originally published as five volumes in 1953. As thorough and comprehensive a literary biography as one is apt to find.

Ellison, Ralph. *Invisible Man.* New York: Vintage, 1995. One of the great works of African American literature, originally published in 1952. This novel takes us through the entire odyssey of a nameless man's life from the Jim Crow South to Harlem and the North and from a belief in American capitalism to an acceptance of rigid communism and, ultimately, a sense of Existential identity. An American classic and a great read.

Ellman, Richard. *James Joyce*. Oxford: Oxford University Press, 1982. One of the finest critical biographies of the last century on one of its most important writers.

Flaubert, Gustave. *Madame Bovary.* New York: Norton, 2004. The classic novel of a woman's adultery that continues to hold up as one of the masterpiece novels of the 19th century. Written by a master of Realism and novelistic detail and originally published in 1857.

———. *A Simple Heart*. New York: New Directions, 1996. Flaubert's famous story of a simple, good-hearted French housemaid.

Forster, E. M. *Aspects of the Novel.* New York: Harvest Books, 1956. The great British novelist provides a greater understanding of the novel and the craft of novel writing in this cogent and incisive work (originally published in 1927).

Frazer, James. *The Golden Bough.* Oxford: Oxford University Press, 1998. A classic work of anthropology of ancient cultures preceding Christianity and their links to Christianity, with emphasis on rites and rituals, superstitions, and taboos. A truly enlightening journey into the mythical past. Originally published in 1890.

Freud, Sigmund. *Civilization and Its Discontents*. New York: Norton, 2005. Freud's great anthropologic work, originally published in 1930, that probes under the surface of civilization in an attempt to hypothesize what unconscious forces enable humans to act civilized and to build civilizations.

Friedan, Betty. *The Feminine Mystique.* New York: Dell, 1963; New York: Norton, 2001. A primer and historically groundbreaking work of women's identity, focusing on why women, specifically post–World War II American women, are unhappy. The book will continue to resonate for contemporary women but is more applicable to the earlier wave of feminist thinking.

García Márquez, Gabriel. *The Autumn of the Patriarch.* New York: Harper Perennial Modern Classics, 2006. Márquez's compelling portrait of an archetypal Latin dictator and his life and times.

———. *Love in the Time of Cholera.* New York: Vintage, 2007. First published in 1985, this is an extraordinary novel by a great storyteller about the many dimensions of love.

———. *One Hundred Years of Solitude.* New York: Harper Perennial Modern Classics, 2006. An epic novel that takes us through the history of a Colombian town and its inhabitants and pictures vividly their lives and struggles. The novel is a towering achievement.

———. "A Very Old Man with Enormous Wings." First published in Spanish ("Un Señor Muy Viejo Con Unas Alas Enormes") in 1955 in *La Hojarasca* (*Leaf Storm and Other Stories*). In Charters translated by Gregory Rabassa and in *Collected Stories*, New York: Harpers, 1984, translations by Gregory Rabassa and J. S. Bernstein. The Rabassa translation is preferred. It is the one most anthologized and universally recognized. A mythic tale by a Nobel laureate and one of Latin America's greatest fiction writers of what occurs after a flying old man lands in a small Colombian village.

Gilbert, Sandra, and Susan Gubar. *The Madwoman in the Attic*. New Haven, CT: Yale University Press, 2000. A major contribution to literary criticism and feminist approaches to literature by two well-established literary critics who enable their readers to see beneath the surface texts of women writers.

Glaspell, Susan. "A Jury of Her Peers." In *Literature and the Writing Process*, 5th ed. Upper Saddle River, NJ: Prentice, 2004. A short story adapted from a one-act play by Glaspell and originally published in 1917. The story concerns the murder of a husband by his wife, which other women are able to solve and understand at a time before women were allowed on juries or able to vote. A strong and compelling tale based on a real Iowa court case the author was familiar with from her work as a reporter.

Gordimer, Nadine. *Jump and Other Stories*. New York: Penguin, 1992. A volume of African set stories by one of the world's most masterful storytellers.

———. "The Moment Before the Gun Went Off." First published in 1988 in *Harper's Magazine*, then in a collection entitled *Jump*, New York: Penguin, 1992. Also in *The Twentieth Century and Beyond: The Broadview Anthology of British Literature*, Toronto: Broadview Press, 2006 (hereinafter cited as *The Broadview Anthology of British Literature*). A heartbreaking story by a Nobel laureate fiction writer of an accidental death as South Africa begins its break with apartheid.

Gogol, Nikolai. "The Nose." In *The Collected Tales of Nikolai Gogol*. New York: Vintage, 1999. A classic Fabulist tale (originally published in 1831) by a Russian storyteller known for his Realism; the story concerns a man who loses his nose.

———. "The Overcoat." First published in Russian ("Shinel") in 1842 in *The Overcoat and Other Stories of Good and Evil.* In Charters translated by Constance Garnett and in *The Collected Tales of Nikolai Gogol* translated by Richard Pevear and Larissa Volokhovsky, New York: Vintage, 1999. The Garnett is the recommended translation. As is true of her work with Chekhov, one can get a superior sense in her translation of the rhythms and cadences of Gogol's language, as well as the fluidity and overall narrative power of his storytelling in this timeless tale of great compassion for a man who barely seems to exist.

Grossman, Vasily. *A Writer at War*. London: Harvill, 2005. A contemporary Russian Jewish fiction writer and journalist strongly influenced by the work of Isaac Babel takes us into Soviet war. Originally published in Russian in 1941–1945.

Harris, Janice. "Levels of Meaning in Lawrence's 'The Rocking-Horse Winner.'" In *The Short Fiction of D. H. Lawrence*. New Brunswick, NJ: Rutgers University Press, 1984. Also in Charters. An illuminating analysis of interpretative levels of meaning in D. H. Lawrence's much beloved story by a perspicacious and able literary critic.

Hawthorne, Nathaniel. "The Birthmark." In Charters (6th ed.). First published in 1843, "The Birthmark" is considered one of Hawthorne's greatest stories. It tells the tale of a scientist and his

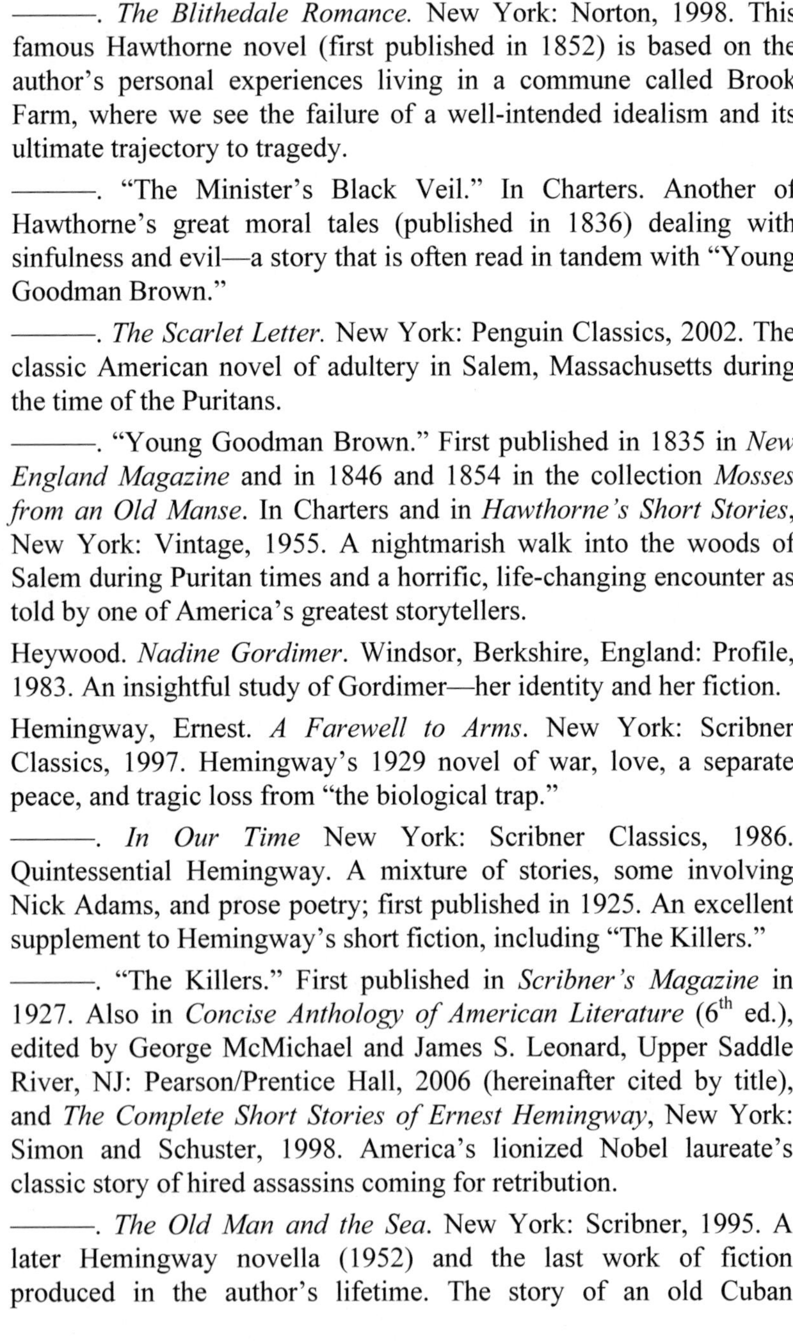

beautiful, nearly perfect wife (but for her birthmark) and how seeking aesthetic perfection can bring doom.

———. *The Blithedale Romance.* New York: Norton, 1998. This famous Hawthorne novel (first published in 1852) is based on the author's personal experiences living in a commune called Brook Farm, where we see the failure of a well-intended idealism and its ultimate trajectory to tragedy.

———. "The Minister's Black Veil." In Charters. Another of Hawthorne's great moral tales (published in 1836) dealing with sinfulness and evil—a story that is often read in tandem with "Young Goodman Brown."

———. *The Scarlet Letter.* New York: Penguin Classics, 2002. The classic American novel of adultery in Salem, Massachusetts during the time of the Puritans.

———. "Young Goodman Brown." First published in 1835 in *New England Magazine* and in 1846 and 1854 in the collection *Mosses from an Old Manse*. In Charters and in *Hawthorne's Short Stories*, New York: Vintage, 1955. A nightmarish walk into the woods of Salem during Puritan times and a horrific, life-changing encounter as told by one of America's greatest storytellers.

Heywood. *Nadine Gordimer*. Windsor, Berkshire, England: Profile, 1983. An insightful study of Gordimer—her identity and her fiction.

Hemingway, Ernest. *A Farewell to Arms*. New York: Scribner Classics, 1997. Hemingway's 1929 novel of war, love, a separate peace, and tragic loss from "the biological trap."

———. *In Our Time* New York: Scribner Classics, 1986. Quintessential Hemingway. A mixture of stories, some involving Nick Adams, and prose poetry; first published in 1925. An excellent supplement to Hemingway's short fiction, including "The Killers."

———. "The Killers." First published in *Scribner's Magazine* in 1927. Also in *Concise Anthology of American Literature* (6th ed.), edited by George McMichael and James S. Leonard, Upper Saddle River, NJ: Pearson/Prentice Hall, 2006 (hereinafter cited by title), and *The Complete Short Stories of Ernest Hemingway*, New York: Simon and Schuster, 1998. America's lionized Nobel laureate's classic story of hired assassins coming for retribution.

———. *The Old Man and the Sea*. New York: Scribner, 1995. A later Hemingway novella (1952) and the last work of fiction produced in the author's lifetime. The story of an old Cuban fisherman and his stoic endurance. The novel helped Hemingway to win the Nobel Prize for literature.

———. *The Sun Also Rises*. New York: Scribner, 2006. The wastelander expatriates in a novel of doomed love and the Hemingway ethos. Based on Hemingway's personal experiences in Europe, this is considered by many to be his seminal and best novel. Originally published in 1926.

Hotchner, A. E. *Papa Hemingway.* New York: Random House, 1966; New York: Carroll & Graf, 1996. A personal and favorably biased memoir of the public Hemingway by a man who was a friend and close associate, offering a good though slanted picture of Hemingway.

Howe, Irving. *The World of Our Fathers.* New York: Galahad Books, 1994. A full and detailed history, by one of America's important literary critics, of the migration of Eastern European or Ashkenazi Jews to the United States and the obstacles and prejudices they faced. A first-rate recreation of the early immigrant experience and a distillation of adaptation to America. First published in 1976.

Jackson, Shirley. *The Haunting of Hill House.* New York: Penguin, 1984. A haunting, scary story of the supernatural and madness that shows Jackson's skill in creating fright and sustaining a narrative that juggles around a number of characters. Originally published in 1959.

———. "The Lottery." First published in *The New Yorker* in 1948. In Charters and in *The Lottery and Other Stories*, New York: Farrar, Straus and Giroux, 1982. In one of the most controversial short stories ever published, Jackson tells the dark tale of the violence that lurks beneath a seemingly tranquil and ordinary, small 20th-century town.

———."The Morning of June 28, 1948, and 'The Lottery.'" In *Come Along with Me*. New York: Viking, 1968. Also in Charters. In this essay, Jackson documents how she came to write the story that made her famous and what aftereffects and aftershocks occurred following its publication.

———."The Possibility of Evil." In *Shirley Jackson: Collected Stories*. Princeton, NJ: Peterson, 2001. The story of a seemingly innocuous woman with the conspicuous name of Strangeworth in a town called Pleasant; it was published in 1965, after the author's death, and won an Edgar Allan Poe mystery story award. It is

American Gothic in the tradition Jackson established with "The Lottery." We enter into a world where anonymous malicious notes are sent out by the woman to her neighbors and fellow townspeople.

James, Henry. *The Beast in the Jungle*. Whitefish, MT: Kessinger, 2003. A later novella (1903) by James that takes us into the relationship of a man and a woman prevented from reaching fruition because of the man's fears. An unsettling but moving tale of love unrealized until too late.

———. *Daisy Miller*. New York: Penguin, 1987. A fine introduction to Henry James as a novelist in a short (especially for James), early (1878) work of an American woman abroad and the kinds of New World versus Old World conflicts that abound.

———."From Guy de Maupassant." In Charters. This is Henry James in appreciation of Guy de Maupassant's style, talent, and craft and serves as a worthwhile introduction to the connection of these two masterful storytellers.

———."The Genesis of 'The Real Thing.'" In Charters. Here is Henry James describing how he came to write "The Real Thing" and the nature of his intentions. A rare look into a short fiction writer's intentionality and the way it evolved.

———. *The Jolly Corner*. Whitefish, MT: Kessinger, 2004. Another much-beloved James ghost story that also involves a romance and the unusual facet of the ghost being the protagonist's alter ego. Originally published in 1908.

———. "The Real Thing." First published in 1892 in *Black and White* magazine. In Charters and in *Henry James: Selected Short Stories*, New York: Penguin, 1963. One of the finest and most accessible stories by the great American master—all about art and life and life and art.

———. *The Turn of the Screw*. New York: Dover, 1991. A novella (published in 1898) that demonstrates the skills James possessed in telling a story that is not just a garden-variety ghost story. Though touching on the paranormal and the supernatural, the story really embodies a Modernist sense of ambiguity and uncertainty. It is, above all, a scary story exceedingly well told.

Joyce, James. "Araby." First published in 1914 in *Dubliners*. In Charters and in *Dubliners*, Clayton, DE: Prestwick House, 2006. The story by the great Irish literary genius of a Dublin boy's quest for romantic love and his suffering.

———. *Dubliners.* New York: Viking, 1967. The collection of 15 epiphany stories, originally published in 1914, in which the setting of Dublin plays a central role and Joyce demonstrates his extraordinary powers as a storyteller who focuses on ordinary lives.

———. *A Portrait of the Artist as a Young Man.* New York: Bantam, 1998. Joyce's 1916 novel that shows his skills in portraying, through a semi-autobiographical character named Stephen Dedalus, the escape from institutions and conventions and the development of an artistic consciousness and an artist's sensibility

———. *Stephen Hero.* New York: New Directions, 1963. The earlier version of *A Portrait of the Artist as a Young Man*, written between 1904 and 1906 and published in 1944. This work shows much of the earlier defiance, rebellion, and aesthetic development of young Stephen Dedalus and his move toward exile.

———. *Ulysses.* New York: Vintage, 1990. The great, mythic, all-in-one-day novel featuring Stephen Dedalus and his search for a father figure in the Jewish character of Leopold Bloom, husband of the irrepressible Molly. A rich harvest of language embedded with great erudition and stunning wit. *Ulysses* is a true novel masterpiece. First published in 1922.

Juvenal. *The Satires.* Cambridge: Cambridge University Press, 1996. Sixteen satiric poems from ancient Rome in five separate books of verse that represent classical satire written between A.D. 100 and A.D. 120.

Kafka, Franz. *The Castle* New York: Schocken, 1998. Kafka's unfinished novel (published in 1926) about the land surveyor K, who is unable to penetrate the mysteries of the castle or the world of those in the village he has presumably been summoned to work in. The novel serves as an initiation into the surreal, impenetrable, and enigmatic view of life that makes up Kafka's vision.

———. "A Hunger Artist." Published in German in a collection by the same name (*Ein Hungerkünstler*) in 1924. In Charters translated by Willa and Edwin Muir (6th ed.) and by Charters (7th ed.). Also in *The Complete Stories*, New York: Schocken, 1995. The Muir translation in the sixth edition of Charters is preferred. I give Charters high marks for grappling with Kafka's language and working through her own translation from the German, but I find I am more moved by the Muir translation and feel that it is closer to the true spirit of Kafka's vision of the artist. This is an astonishing

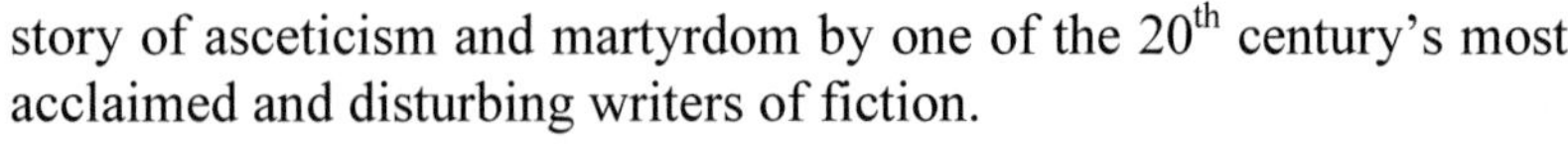

story of asceticism and martyrdom by one of the 20th century's most acclaimed and disturbing writers of fiction.

———. "In the Penal Colony." In *The Metamorphosis, In the Penal Colony, and Other Stories*. New York: Schocken, 1995. A Kafka short story that immerses us in the surreal world of torture and a machine that brands and executes. Well plotted and one of Kafka's best tales; first published in 1916.

———. "Letter to My Father." In *The Sons*. New York: Schocken, 1989. A letter Kafka wrote to his father (in 1919) that provides great insight into the author's abiding fear of his father and how this fear in many ways warped and possessed the son.

———. "The Metamorphosis." In *The Sons*. New York: Schocken, 1989. Kafka's great story of a man, Gregor Samsa, who wakes up to discover that he is a cockroach or dung beetle, an insect; his life gets worse from there. A novella of identity and a searing, grotesque parable of human existence reduced to the creepy and crawly stage. Originally published in 1915.

———. *The Trial.* New York: Random House, 1995. Kafka's dense and labyrinthine novel (also unfinished; published in 1925) about the plight of Joseph K, his arrest for a crime that is never specified, and the consequences that befall him. We as readers grapple with the strange and unsettling occurrences in Joseph K's life. A mystifying and brilliant story of alienation.

Kincaid, Jamaica. "Girl." In *At the Bottom of the River.* New York: Farrar, Straus and Giroux, 1988. Also in Charters. Though it seems more like a monologue than a short story, "Girl" has within it the story of the troubled relationship between a girl and her mother and the values that prevail upon the women of a colonized race. Astonishingly compressed and effective prose narration.

Kingston, Maxine Hong. *The Fifth Book of Peace.* New York: Knopf, 2003. A personal mixed narrative work of remembrance and meditation on war and peace and Kingston's own loss of her fourth book of peace in a fire.

———. "No Name Woman," in *The Woman Warrior*, New York: Vintage, 1975 and 1989. A story of an awakening to ethnic identity and the significance of a long-buried family secret by a distinguished and richly talented Chinese American woman novelist and short story writer.

———. “On Mortality.” In *China Men*. New York: Alfred A. Knopf, 1980. A Taoist parable from Kingston’s collection with strong cosmologic and mythic elements reflecting gender differences.

———. *Tripmaster Monkey*. New York: Vintage, 1990. A novel about a Chinese American, 1960s hippie and would-be playwright. Any Kingston writing is worth reading, including this first foray of hers into a novel that sometimes created confusion.

———. *The Woman Warrior*. New York: Alfred A. Knopf, 1976. The subtitle is *Memoirs of a Girlhood Among Ghosts*, and the ghosts are the supernatural kind in the stories of the young girl’s Chinese past and the California Caucasians of her present life. A powerful, unified collection of autobiography, myth, and what the Chinese call “talk story” brought together in a unique and remarkably written volume about Chinese American and gender identity.

Lawrence, D. H. “The Horse Dealer’s Daughter.” In *The Broadview Anthology of British Literature*. A Lawrence short story about love and its power and spontaneity. One of his best and most powerful stories, embodying many of the Freudian and erotic ideas that were ripening in his thinking and that would become singularly identified with his writing. First published in 1913.

———. *Kangaroo*. Cambridge: Cambridge University Press, 2002. Not Lawrence’s best novel (his eighth, published in 1923), this book nevertheless reveals many of his ideas about love and politics. It also includes vivid accounts of his World War I experiences and his attitudes toward fascism, as well as enduring descriptions of the novel’s setting in New South Wales.

———. *The Plumed Serpent*. New York: Vintage, 1992. Lawrence’s novel of an Irish woman in Mexico and the appeal of ancient and primal pagan spirituality combined with the author’s distinct and revelatory views of sexuality and the battle of the sexes. Much politically incorrect content (it was first published in 1926) but definitely worth the read.

———. “The Rocking-Horse Winner.” First published in 1926 in *Harper’s Bazaar*. In Charters and in *D. H. Lawrence: The Complete Short Stories* (2 vols.), New York: Penguin, 1976. A mystical and Faustian tale of a boy’s love for his mother and the darker regions to which he will travel to acquire it.

———. *Sons and Lovers*. New York: Modern Library, 1999. Lawrence’s first autobiographical novel (published in 1913) is a landmark achievement of a high order that takes us into his own peculiar oedipal and class-divided life, rendered with great skill and melded into a most memorable novel.

Leavis F. R. *Valuation in Criticism and Other Essays*. Cambridge: Cambridge University Press, 1986. A career collection of essays and reviews by one of the 20th century's most distinguished literary critics. Of particular note for the purposes of this course are Leavis's fine essays on D. H. Lawrence and Henry James.

Lubbock, Percy. *The Craft of Fiction*. New York: Penguin, 1955. A primer work of literary criticism that continues to provide much useful illumination.

Lukács, Georg. *History and Class Consciousness.* London: Merlin, 1967. This work by an important literary critic is heavily marinated in Marxist theory and extends Marx into a more contemporary context. A major influence on South Africa's Nadine Gordimer. First published in 1923.

———. *The Meaning of Contemporary Realism.* London: Merlin, 1963. Another work drenched in Marxist theory but useful in understanding Realism and Modernism. It includes some interesting writing on Kafka.

Mailer, Norman. *The Naked and the Dead.* New York: Picador, 2000. Mailer's novel set in the South Pacific in World War II remains a classic and his best work of fiction.

Malamud, Bernard. "Angel Levine." In *The Magic Barrel*. New York: Farrar, Straus and Giroux, 1999. A magical short story by the masterful Malamud about a man experiencing Job-like personal suffering who meets a black angel.

———. *The Assistant.* New York: Farrar, Straus and Giroux, 2003. Suffering and Jewishness fuse in this tale of a poor grocer and his Italian assistant. A testament to Malamud's storytelling powers, it is a story about love and redemption and living by the law.

———. *The Fixer.* New York: Farrar, Straus and Giroux, 2004. Another Malamud novel about Jewishness and suffering set in Russia and based on an actual case that Malamud turned into fiction. Not as riveting or well written as *The Assistant* but well worth the read.

———. *Idiots First*. New York: Dell, 1966. The second volume of Malamud stories; includes "The Jewbird" and a range of the author's fine and enduring short fiction.

———. "The Jewbird." First published in 1963 in *Idiots First*, New York: Farrar, Straus and Giroux. Also in *American Short Stories Since 1945*, edited by John G. Parks, Oxford: Oxford University Press, 2002 (hereinafter cited by title). One of the great and most masterful Jewish American storytellers gives us a mythic tale of the old world of the *shtetl* violently colliding with American assimilation.

———. *The Magic Barrel.* New York: Farrar, Straus and Giroux, 1999. Malamud's first collection of short stories. The title story, concerning a rabbinical student and a matchmaker, is a gem, as are others in this wonderful volume.

Malcolm, Janet. *Reading Chekhov: A Critical Journey*. London: Granta Books, 2003. The talented *New Yorker* essayist goes to Russia in search of a deeper understanding of Chekhov.

Mansfield, Katherine. "The Garden Party." First published in 1922 in *The Garden Party*. Also in *The Broadview Anthology of British Literature*. This story of a young woman's awakening to the intersections of life and death and the chasms of the classes is generally regarded as one of Mansfield's most compelling, well-crafted, and aesthetically pleasing works.

———. *The Garden Party.* New York: Penguin Classics, 1998. Also in *The Broadview Anthology of British Literature*. A terrific sampling of 15 stories by one of the 20th century's finest storytellers.

Maupassant, Guy de. *The Complete Short Stories* [in 3 vols.]. London: Cassell, 1970. The prolific, enduring output of one of the fathers of the short story.

———. "The Necklace." First published in French ("La Parure") in 1884 in the anthology *Tales of Days and Nights*. In Charters translated by Marjorie Laurie and in *Selected Short Stories* translated by Roger Colet, New York: Penguin, 1971. The Marjorie Lurie translation is the better of the two simply because it gets us closest to the subtleties of expression used by Maupassant and the declarative and unvarnished style so closely associated with his brand of storytelling, which is epitomized by the shocking ending of this classic tale.

———. "The Writer's Goal." In Charters. A short essay by Maupassant on how writers need to select from life and create the illusion of what is real.

Melville, Herman. "Bartleby the Scrivener." In *Billy Budd*. New York: Signet Classics, 1998. One of Melville's great works of short fiction. Set in Wall Street in the 19th century, this story is about a man who, quite simply, would prefer not to.

———. "Benito Cereno." In *Billy Budd*. New York: Signet Classics, 1998. A dark, haunting, and powerful tale of slaves taking over a slave vessel, the Spanish captain who is overpowered by them, and the good-natured Yankee captain who boards the ship.

———. "Billy Budd." In *Billy Budd*. New York: Signet Classics, 1998. A novella about an innocent young sailor impressed into service and falsely charged with conspiracy to mutiny by the motiveless, malignant John Claggart. A gripping story with a serious meditation on the nature of the law and how it is executed.

———. "Blackness in Hawthorne's 'Young Goodman Brown.'" In Charters. Melville reviews Hawthorne's *Mosses from an Old Manse* and focuses on blackness in Hawthorne's classic Salem-based tale "Young Goodman Brown."

Meyers, Jeffrey. *Edgar Allan Poe: His Life and Legacy.* New York: Cooper Square Press, 2000. An excellent look into Poe's life and character.

Nabokov, Vladimir. "Gogol's Genius in 'The Overcoat.'" In *Nikolai Gogol*. New York: New Directions, 1961. Also in Charters. The Russian born author of *Lolita* writes an appreciative essay of Gogol and his classic tale that enhances our understanding.

———. "A Reading of Chekhov's 'The Lady with the Dog.'" In *Lectures on Russian Literature*. New York: Harvest/HBJ Books, 2002. The essay is an interpretation and assessment by the great Russian author Vladimir Nabokov of Chekhov's story in a collection of Nabokov's essays on Russian writers.

O'Connor, Flannery. *Complete Stories*. London: Faber, 2000. The complete stories of one of America's greatest short story writers. You might include the adjectives American or southern or woman, but she is one of the greatest with or without them.

———. "A Good Man Is Hard to Find." First published in 1955 in a collection of the same title. In Charters and in *The Complete Stories*, New York: Farrar, Straus and Giroux, 1971. America's great southern Catholic fiction writer's most widely anthologized and published story of evil and grace in Georgia as a family meets up with a mass murderer.

———. *Mystery and Manners.* New York: Farrar, Straus and Giroux, 1969. Prose selections by O'Connor about the craft of writing, the role of spiritual mystery, and southern mores and manners. A valuable work to read before or after reading O'Connor's fiction.

———. *Wise Blood.* New York: Farrar, Straus and Giroux, 1967. O'Connor's novel of religious fanaticism in the South cast in comedic and satiric veins. Not as powerful as many of her stories but indicative, like her short fiction, of her genius and her inimitable prose style.

Paley, Grace. "A Conversation with My Father." In *Enormous Changes at the Last Minute.* New York: Vintage, 1974. A work by another great American woman short story writer from the post–World War II era. This story concerns a fiction writer and her father arguing about fiction at the father's deathbed. It embodies Paley's American philosophy about storytelling versus the older, European view.

———. "An Interest in Life." First published in *The Little Disturbances of Man*, New York: Penguin, 1985. Also in *American Short Stories Since 1945.* One of America's earliest and best feminist writers tells the story of a likable woman's survival by taking a lover after her husband abandons her.

———. *The Little Disturbances of Man.* New York: Penguin, 1985. Paley's first and most celebrated volume of 11 stories about ordinary men and women "at love," written in the distinctive style of storytelling that ensured lasting literary fame for her as a writer of short fiction.

Pawel, Ernst. *Nightmare of Reason: A Life of Franz Kafka.* New York: Farrar, Straus and Giroux, 1984. The best extant biography of Kafka, with rich insight into his life and times and his genius.

Peeples, Scott. *The Afterlife of Edgar Allan Poe.* New York: Camden House, 2007. An English professor and Poe scholar examines the author's life and work and comes to a number of original conclusions.

Pirandello, Luigi. "War." In *The Medals and Other Stories*, New York: E. P. Dutton, 1939. Also in *The Norton Anthology of Short Fiction*, edited by Richard Bausch, New York: Norton, 2005. A remarkably concise, dramatically moving story by a writer more known for his plays than for his short stories. The story takes place aboard a train and dramatizes a conversation between two men, one who has recently lost his son to the war at the front.

Poe, Edgar Allan. "The Cask of Amontillado." First published in 1846 in *Godey's Lady's Book*. In Charters and in *Complete Stories and Poems of Edgar Allan Poe*, New York: Doubleday, 1984. This classic story of horror and revenge by America's great spellbinding storyteller brings us into a world of codes of honor and carefully planned murder.

———. "The Fall of the House of Usher." In *Concise Anthology of American Literature* and in Charters. A frightening Gothic story of an entombed twin sister and a decaying house that exemplifies Poe's ideal of the story being unified by all of its details toward the effect of a single impact.

———. "The Impact of the Single Effect in a Prose Tale." In Charter. The seminal essay on the short story that puts forth Poe's theory of the aesthetics of the genre. A must read for understanding the theoretical basis of the short story.

———. "The Tell-Tale Heart." In *Concise Anthology of American Literature* and in Charters. Another one of Poe's frightening stories and one of his most famous—a pulse-throbbing tale of murder and guilt.

Pritchett, V. S., ed. *The Oxford Book of Short Stories*. Oxford: Oxford University Press, 2001. A first-rate volume of short stories compiled and with an introduction by famed literary critic Pritchett.

Prose, Francine. "The Bones of Muzhiks: Isaac Babel Gets Lost in Translation." *Harper's Magazine*, November 2001. Also in Charters (6th ed.). A gifted critic and fiction writer, Prose muses on how Babel's translators fail to get the full effect of his brilliant style.

Reynolds, David. "The Art of Transformation in Poe's 'The Cask of Amontillado.'" In *New Essays on Poe's Major Tales*, edited by Kenneth Silverman. Cambridge: Cambridge University Press, 1993. Also in Charters. An excellent analysis of the morality and effect of Poe's famous horror story by an astute and insightful literary critic.

Rosten, Leo. *The Joys of Yiddish*. New York: McGraw-Hill, 1968. A classic introduction to the rich multiple and historic meanings of Yiddish words, presented with a good deal of wit and charm.

Runyon, Randolph Paul. *Reading Raymond Carver*. Syracuse, NY: Syracuse University Press, 1994. A critical study of much of

Carver's work that seeks to show connections between different stories in different volumes.

Salinger, J. D. *The Catcher in the Rye*. New York: Penguin, 1994. The classic American novel that tells the story of a disturbed adolescent boy and his journey at this crucial phase of his life. The only novel by Salinger, who published three volumes of short stories and a novella.

Smith, Angela. *Katherine Mansfield and Virginia Woolf: A Public of Two.* Oxford: Clarendon Press, 1999. A thoughtful analysis of how these two important women writers influenced and mirrored each other's work, as well as an exploration of their friendship.

Snodgrass, W. D. "The Rocking Horse: The Symbol, the Pattern, the Way of Life." In *The Hudson Review*, vol. xi, no. 2, Summer 1958. This essay, by a distinguished American poet, had a weighty influence on how Lawrence's "Rocking-Horse Winner" was read. Based on Freud's Oedipus complex, Snodgrass's reading may seem quaint to some in our present era but continues to resonate as a way of seeing deeper meaning in the story.

Spiegelman, Art. *Maus*. New York: Random House, 1986. A graphic novel by an American cartoonist about his father's experiences during the Holocaust and as a Holocaust survivor and of his own life and relationship with his father. All groups are presented as animals: Jews as mice, Nazis as cats, Poles as pigs, and Americans as dogs. A seminal work.

Updike, John. "A & P." First published in *The New Yorker* in 1961. In Charters and in *Pigeon Feathers and Other Stories*, New York: Ballantine, 1996. A charming story of a boy growing up and entering into the real adult world by one of America's most celebrated contemporary writers of fiction.

———. *A & P: Lust in the Aisles*. Minneapolis: Redpath Press, 1986. The first published version of this story from Updike's volume of short stories *Pigeon Feathers*.

———. *Pigeon Feathers and Other Stories*. New York: Knopf, 1962. An early, classic volume by a young, stylistically dazzling, and inventive Updike; includes the story "A & P."

———. *Rabbit Quartet* (*Rabbit Run,* 1960; *Rabbit Redux*, 1971; *Rabbit Is Rich*, 1981; and *Rabbit at Rest*, 1990). New York: Knopf. Four novels about Harry Angstrom, known as Rabbit, as we watch him develop through life and see, through Updike's considerable skills, a detailed rendering of American cultural history.

———. *Trust Me*. New York: Ballantine Books, 1996. A volume of contemporary stories by the contemporary masterful American storyteller.

Walker, Warren. "The Unresolved Conflict in 'The Garden Party.'" In *Modern Fiction Studies*, Winter 1957–1958. An essay by a literary critic who praised Mansfield's story but is troubled by its ending.

Williams, Tennessee. *The Glass Menagerie.* New York: New Directions, 1999. The poignant, tender, semi-autobiographical family play by one of America's finest playwrights. Williams experiments with lighting and music in ways that are reminiscent of Brecht and the epic theater. One of his best plays.

Young, Philip. *Ernest Hemingway: A Reconsideration*. University Park, PA: Penn State University Press, 1986. One of the best critical studies of Hemingway's work by one of the world's leading Hemingway scholars.

Additional Recommended Short Stories (Lecture Twenty-Four):

Anderson, Sherwood. "Death in the Woods." In Charters (6th ed.).

———. "I Want to Know Why." In Charters.

Bambara, Toni Cade. "The Lesson." In *Gorilla, My Love*. New York: Vintage, 1992. Also in Charters.

Barth, John. "Lost in the Funhouse" and "Night-Sea Visitors." In *Lost in the Funhouse*. Garden City, NY: Anchor, 1988. "Lost in the Funhouse" is also in Charters.

Barthelme, Donald. "The School." In *Unspeakable Practices, Unnatural Acts*. New York: Bantam, 1969. Also in B. Minh Nguyen and Porter Shreve, *The Contemporary American Short Story*. New York: Longman, 2003 (hereinafter referred to by title).

———. "Views of My Father Weeping." In *American Short Stories Since 1945*and *The New Yorker* (December 6, 1949).

Borges, Jorge Luis. "The Circular Ruins." In *Ficciones*. New York: Everyman's Library, 1993. Also in Charters.

———. "The End of the Duel." In *A Personal Anthology*. New York: Grove Press, 1994. Also in Charters (6th ed.).

Boyle, T. C. "Greasy Lake." In *Greasy Lake and Other Stories*. New York: Penguin, 1986. Also in Charters.

Caputo, Philip. "In the Forest of the Laughing Elephant." In *Exiles.* New York: Random House, 1998.

Cheever, John. "The Country Husband" and "The Swimmer." Both in *The Stories of John Cheever*. New York: Vintage, 2000. "The Swimmer" is also in Charters.

Cisneros, Sandra. "The House on Mango Street." In *The House on Mango Street*. London: Bloomsbury Pub. Ltd., 2004. Also in Charters.

Coover, Robert. "The Babysitter." In *Pricksongs and Descants*. New York: Grove Press, 2000. Also in *American Short Stories Since 1945*.

Danticat, Edwidge. "Night Women." In *Krick? Krack!* New York: Vintage, 1996. Also in Charters.

Erdrich, Louise. "The Red Convertible." In *Love Medicine*. New York: Perennial Classics, 2001. Also in Charters.

Faulkner, William. "A Rose for Miss Emily" and "That Evening Sun." In *The Collected Stories of William Faulkner*. New York: Vintage, 1995. Both also in Charters.

Flaubert, Gustave. "A Simple Heart." In *Three Tales by Gustave Flaubert*. New York: Limited Editions, 1978. Also in Charters.

Jen, Gish. "In the American Society." In *Who's Irish?* New York: Vintage, 2000. Also in *The Contemporary American Short Story*.

Kincaid, Jamaica. "Girl." In *At the Bottom of the River*. New York: Farrar, Straus and Giroux, 2000. Also in Charters.

Lahiri, Jhumpa. "Interpreter of Maladies" and "The Third and Final Continent." In *Interpreter of Maladies: Stories*. Boston: Houghton Mifflin, 2000.

Le Guin, Ursula. "The Ones Who Walk Away from Omelas." In *The Wind's Twelve Quarters*. New York: Harper Perennial, 2004. Also in Charters.

Lessing, Doris. "Our Friend Judith" and "To Room Nineteen." In *Stories*. New York: Vintage, 1980.

Mason, Bobbie Ann. "Shiloh." In *Shiloh and Other Stories*. New York: Modern Library, 2001. Also in Charters.

Mukherjee, Bharati. "The Management of Grief." In *The Middleman and Other Stories*. New York: Grove Press, 1999. Also in Charters.

Munro, Alice. "Boys and Girls." In *Dance of the Happy Shades*. New York: Vintage, 1998. Also in *The Norton Introduction to Literature*.

———. "The Turkey Season." In *The Moons of Jupiter and Other Stories*. New York: Vintage, 1991. Also in *The Contemporary American Short Story*.

Oates, Joyce Carol. "How I Contemplated the World from the Detroit House of Corrections and Began My Life Over Again" and "Where Are You Going, Where Have You Been?" In *Wheel of Love*. New York: Vanguard, 1970.

O'Brien, Tim. "The Things They Carried." In *The Things They Carried*. New York: Chelsea House Publications, 2004. Also in Charters.

Ozick, Cynthia. "The Shawl." In *The Shawl*. New York: Vintage, 1990. Also in Charters.

Packer, Z. Z. "Drinking Coffee Elsewhere." In *Drinking Coffee Elsewhere*. New York: Riverhead Trade, 2004. Also in Charters.

Porter, Katherine Anne. "Flowering Judas" and "Pale Horse, Pale Rider." In *The Collected Stories of Katherine Anne Porter*. New York: Harvest Books, 1979.

Silko, Leslie Marmon. "Storyteller" and "Yellow Woman." In *Storyteller*. New York: Arcade, 1989. "Storyteller" is also in *American Short Stories Since 1945*. "Yellow Woman" is in Charters.

Stone, Robert. "Helping." In *Bear and His Daughters: Stories*. Boston: Houghton Mifflin, 1997. Also in *American Short Stories Since 1945*.

Tan, Amy. "Half and Half" and "Rules of the Game." In *The Joy Luck Club*. New York: Penguin, 2006.

Viramontes, Helena Maria. "The Moths." In *The Moths and Other Stories*. Houston, TX: Arte Publico Press, 1995. Also in Charters.

Walker, Alice. "Everyday Use." In *In Love and Trouble: Stories of Black Women*. New York: Harvest Books, 2003. Also in Charters.

Wharton, Edith. "Roman Fever." In *Roman Fever and Other Stories*. New York: Scribner, 1997. Also in Charters.

Wolff, Tobias. "Hunters in the Snow." In *In the Garden of the North American Martyrs*. New York: HarperCollins, 1981. Also in *American Short Stories Since 1945*.

———. "The Rich Brother." In *Back in the World*. New York: Vintage, 1996. Also in Charters (6th ed.).

Woolf, Virginia. "Kew Gardens." In *A Haunted House and Other Stories by Virginia Woolf.* New York: Vintage, 2003. Also in Charters.

Internet Resources:

The Literature Network. www.online-literature.com/author_index.php. Site includes biographies and full-text stories by Poe, Hawthorne, Gogol, Maupassant, Chekhov, O. Henry, Lawrence, Kafka, and Joyce.

Narrative Magazine. www.Narrativemagazine.com. Founded in 2003, this site aims "to bring great literature into the digital age, and to provide it for free"; it features short fiction by well-known and fledgling writers, as well as poetry, essays, novel excerpts, articles, and interviews.

Plath, James. *The American Short Story: A Selective Chronology*. titan.iwu.edu/~jplath/sschron.html. A timeline of the development of the American short story from the Romantic through the Postmodern periods and a bibliography.

Zoetrope All-Story. www.all-story.com. Francis Ford Coppola set up this site for stories to appear and for connections between the short story and art, one-act plays, and film.

Credits

Booklet Text Credits:

"A & P," from *The Early Stories, 1953–1975* by John Updike, copyright © 2003 by John Updike. Used by permission of Alfred A. Knopf, a division of Random House, Inc.

Excerpts from "The Killers" are used with the permission of Scribner, an imprint of Simon & Schuster Adult Publishing Group, from *The Short Stories of Ernest Hemingway*. Copyright 1927 by Charles Scribner's Sons. Copyright renewed 1955 by Ernest Hemingway.

Excerpts from "The Lottery" by Shirley Jackson. Copyright © 1948, 1949 by Shirley Jackson, copyright renewed © 1976, 1977 by Laurence Hyman, Barry Hyman, Mrs. Sarah Webster, and Joanne Schnurer. Used by permission of the Estate of Shirley Jackson.

"Happy Endings" reprinted by permission of Margaret Atwood. Copyright © 1983, 1992, 1994 by O. W. Toad Ltd. Currently available in the United States in *Good Bones and Simple Murders*, published by Nan A. Talese, an imprint of Doubleday.

"My First Goose," from *Complete Works of Isaac Babel* by Isaac Babel, edited by Nathalie Babel, translated by Peter Constantine. Copyright © 2002 by Peter Constantine. Used by permission of W. W. Norton & Company, Inc., and The Jennifer Lyons Literary Agency, LLC.

Transcript Text Credits:

"A & P," from *The Early Stories, 1953–1975* by John Updike, copyright © 2003 by John Updike. Used by permission of Alfred A. Knopf, a division of Random House, Inc. For regions outside USA, its dependencies, Canada, and Philippines, reproduced by permission of Penguin Books Ltd.

Excerpts from "The Killers" are reprinted with the permission of Scribner, an imprint of Simon & Schuster Adult Publishing Group, from *The Short Stories of Ernest Hemingway*. Copyright 1927 by Charles Scribner's Sons. Copyright renewed 1955 by Ernest Hemingway. For the UK and Commonwealth, excerpts from "The Killers" from *The First 49 Stories by Ernest Hemingway*, published by Jonathan Cape. Reprinted by permission of The Random House Group Ltd.

Notes